GAMER TROUBLE

Gamer Trouble

Feminist Confrontations in Digital Culture

Amanda Phillips

NEW YORK UNIVERSITY PRESS
New York

NEW YORK UNIVERSITY PRESS
New York
www.nyupress.org

References to internet websites (URLs) were accurate at the time of writing. Neither the author nor New York University Press is responsible for URLs that may have expired or changed since the manuscript was prepared.

ISBN: 9781479870103 (hardback)
ISBN: 9781479834921 (paperback)
For Library of Congress Cataloging-in-Publication data, please contact the Library of Congress.

New York University Press books are printed on acid-free paper, and their binding materials are chosen for strength and durability. We strive to use environmentally responsible suppliers and materials to the greatest extent possible in publishing our books.

Manufactured in the United States of America

10 9 8 7 6 5 4 3 2 1

Also available as an ebook

For all the troublemakers

CONTENTS

FIGURES

Introduction

I continue to be committed to the emergence of a post-postmodern critical framework that emphasizes the more flexible, kaleidoscopic thinking about human experience that computer-based narrative formats could help us achieve.

—Janet Murray, *Hamlet on the Holodeck*

Confessions of a Troublemaker

I'm here to make some trouble for gamers. You'd be right in thinking that they don't really need any help from me on that score; gamers have been in trouble since games have been around. However, while games themselves have experienced a rehabilitation at the hands of many dedicated designers and academics seeking to rescue their formal qualities for the good that they could theoretically do in the world, gamers have been more disposable in our imaginations.

To be fair, the gamer has always been associated with trouble. In English, the term emerged in its earliest form as a name for gamblers and other unsavory characters. Examples from the Oxford English Dictionary are unequivocal, spanning centuries:

From 1450: "That who soevyr suffer eny dise-player, carder, tenys player, or other unliefull gamer, to use unlifull games in their house"

From 1654: "All you scoffers and scorners, & backbiters, and revilers, and extortioners, and whoremongers, & envious ones, & Gamers, and sporters . . . are all shut out from the true faith."

From 1845: "The gamer is farther from restoration even than the drunkard, because what he does he does in the light of sobriety and reason."

This is a long time to spend being the bad guy.

Gamer no longer shares such close association with gambling, but it remains mired in infamy nonetheless. Popular culture is full of representations of screen-addicted teenagers, grown men living in their mothers' basements, and socially awkward outcasts.[1] These benign, if undesirable, losers even enjoyed heroic status at one point as the "gamer boy genius[es]"[2] whose particular talents for wrangling computers could save the world. As the community has become more mainstream, however, we've heard stories of twitchy ten-year-olds squealing hate speech in online multiplayer games, faceless masses sending death and rape threats on Twitter, and pranksters calling in SWAT teams half a continent away.[3] In the wake of the 2016 United States presidential elections, gamers were said to be a core demographic (perhaps even the origin) of what media dubbed the "alt-right," that cesspool of internet hatred that propelled an unqualified, unapologetic bigot to the head of state.[4] The boyish charms on display in *WarGames* (1983) and *TRON* (1982) have been supplanted by the entitled rich kids, militant white supremacists, and abject waffle-dippers of *Gamer* (2009). Worse than losers, we now see gamers as toxic. In the popular imagination, they are actively contributing to the deterioration of society through malice rather than passively through apathy and neglect. And they are still in trouble: with their parents, with their peers, and increasingly, with the law.[5]

As a gamer myself, I wrote this book to grapple with the barrage of contradictions that has plagued my coming of age at the turn of the ludic century. I used to play on my uncles' PC and Nintendo Entertainment System until my brother and I received our first console, a Super Nintendo, when I was ten. Being a gamer informed my childhood, my adolescence and, eventually, my professional career. Being a gamer even informed my sexual and gender identity. Video games allowed me to play around with (toxic, militarized) masculinity and the thrills of falling in love with women before I was ready to be queer in meatspace. They gave me a way to connect to my brother and other boys in the restricted gender landscape of my youth and, in my adulthood, to a vibrant community that uses technology and play to interrogate the very foundations of gender and normalcy.

Somewhere along the way, I also developed a strong sense of political accountability. My training as a graduate student in English and feminist studies capped off a long adolescence of becoming aware of the structures of white supremacist cisheteropatriarchy that had been woven into the fabric of my reality since birth. A true geek, I knew this process as *taking the red pill*, from the transgender Wachowskis' sci-fi epic *The Matrix*—and I'm more than a little pissed that angry misogynists on the internet have perverted the phrase to mean rejecting a fantasized hegemony of feminism. Gaming served as the background, and eventually the foreground, of my political development, which was fraught with contradictions between the utopian conditions that I desired for the world, the fantasies offered to me by mainstream entertainment media, and the actual limitations that I and those around me lived with every day. Eventually, I accepted the reality that one can never arrive, as game designer Porpentine describes it, at "A PERFECT FEMINISM AS SYNTHESIZED BY 1000 YEARS OF SOCIAL JUSTICE ALGORITHMS."[6] I am not the first to discover this, of course, but the gamer in me was shocked to find out that social justice is an endless grind, not a boss battle, and while the stakes are high, if I'm doing it right, I won't be the one reaping most of the rewards—including the psychological self-soothing of a sacrificial hero. One does not become woke; one must stay woke. It's a process without end.

Staying woke is particularly exhausting when you are also committed to pleasure, which is necessary to live a full life and ultimately the purpose of social justice activism: to provide full lives to those who are prevented from living them by cultural and institutional injustices. As a gamer, I recognize the frustration that other gamers feel when someone points out the ways that games contribute to inequality in society. I recognize the rage that comes from it—how it feels to want to avoid taking the red pill and retain as much easy pleasure for oneself as possible—and even the simple desire for simple desires, which deters us from engaging with complicated, difficult, and unpolished media.

Perhaps I'm a bit of a masochist, but my response to this emotional turmoil has been to run toward the trouble rather than away from it. This has informed my scholarly approach to studying games. While important work has been done to draw attention to the innovative games and designers that fall outside of the hegemonic games industry, I am interested, in this project, in meeting gamer trouble on the battlefield of big-budget mainstream games—AAA, as these are known in the industry—where so many controversies rage about the identities of players, of avatars, and of game developers themselves. This approach has its limitations, including the danger that paying more attention to problematic games simply reinforces our status quo. For me, that danger also comes with the promise that understanding the draw and power of the popular will help us cast its energies in more liberating directions, by either directly appealing to creators or indirectly complicating the desires of players.

Fans have been doing this kind of negotiation with popular culture for decades. I approach this work as a fan and a critic of video games but also as an academic who has the privilege of getting a paycheck to use my time to think and write about these problems at length. This means that my responses are less timely than fan and journalist criticism but also that they are well seasoned and, ideally, rooted in a tradition of intellectual work that can add additional flavors to our conversations. Many academics write about AAA games even while harboring a deep fear that they are not worth writing about at all, either because coming to their defense looks very bad and is probably bad for society or because the bad things about them are such low-hanging fruit for critique that it is difficult to sustain a nuanced conversation about them. As a result, we have a lot of theoretical work that avoids engaging with games that most people play, a lot of critical work that glosses over the politics of representation, a lot of descriptive work that looks over but not into the structures of racism and sexism in gaming culture and the industry, and a lot of hit pieces that resonate with our academic and politically minded peers. However, these never quite square with the phenomenological experience many of us have while playing a racist, sexist, homophobic, violent game.

Gamer Trouble seeks out uncomfortable and turbulent places in popular gaming culture and dives into them, excavating the technological and ludic processes that underwrite, reinforce, and contradict what's happening outside of the game console. Sometimes the turbulence isn't visible at first glance. This book puts surface into conversation with depth in an attempt to come to a more productive relationship with the problems that gamers face today. For me, gamer trouble extends beyond an unsavory reputation. It encompasses the constrained dances we perform with our technologies in our struggles for avatar identification and ludic conquest, the truly disgusting behaviors enacted in the name of enjoying a treasured pastime, and the very serious reminders from within the community that its exclusionary practices cannot last for much longer. But *trouble* is also a verb, and this book also works to trouble the ways we think about gamers, the ways we write about them, and the ways we ask them to change. And for those gamers willing to take on the challenge, I hope to trouble the way we think about our own relationships to technology, games, narratives, and each other.

Throughout this journey through gaming, I also search for ways to channel the gamer's love for trouble (a love that I happen to share) into a love for grappling with contemporary political problems. I am a mixed-race, queer, feminist gamer, but I'm not trying to solve the Problem of Representation in gaming. No one can do that. What I am trying to do is explode that problem into lots of new problems, to deepen our engagement with those things we're tempted to reject outright, and even to ruffle the feathers of some influential and beloved colleagues. And I'm doing it in the name of queer (and) women of color feminism and as a social justice warrior seeking change in the world.

Gamer Trouble at the Turn of the Ludic Century

The study of video games as an important cultural form has been on the rise for decades. By now, there are numerous academic journals, major conferences, and published monographs dedicated to the topic. Game studies classes are regular features in universities across the world, even in some of the older and seemingly more traditional places (like my own institution, Georgetown University). Game studies crosses disciplines, from computer science to English to music to psychology. And where academics aren't yet studying games, they're definitely trying to make them.

Most books like this one justify the study of games in terms of numbers: games make a lot of money—more than cinema, depending on who you ask[7]—and a lot of people play them. In 2018, the Entertainment Software Association reported that sales of gaming hardware and software reached $36 billion, an 18 percent increase over the previous year,[8] and, in 2019, that in the United States, 65 percent of homes included "someone who plays video games regularly."[9] Beyond statistics, we can recognize the diffusion of gaming throughout popular culture in other ways—perhaps most strikingly when journalists identified gamers as the origin of the election-hijacking alt-right movement in 2016. The content exchange between the games industry and Hollywood has become bidirectional, with robust film franchises like *Tomb Raider*, *Mortal Kombat*, and *Resident Evil* and one-offs like *Doom* (2005), *Rampage* (2018), and *Silent Hill* (2006) taking inspiration from digital originals.[10] Other films like *TRON* and *Gamer* explore the imaginative possibilities presented by our multimedia, interactive, networked entertainment systems. In mediums from novels to music, video games loom large in the cultural landscape—as they have for decades.

On a more abstract level, there are also those who believe we have entered a cultural moment defined by the affects and actions of gaming. In one of the earliest academic studies on video games, Patricia Marks Greenfield advocated for the use of video games and other electronic media in classrooms to facilitate necessary cognitive training for future generations, including the ability to understand complex systems.[11] For Jane McGonigal, games can fundamentally reshape the way we live and work and unlock our potential for increased productivity and happiness—an epic win for the individual and society.[12] In "Manifesto for a Ludic Century," Eric Zimmerman argues that while games have been a part of human culture for much of history, computers, as well as the information manipulation that they enable, have facilitated their rise to prominence in the latter half of the twentieth century. He also claims the reverse—"computers didn't create games; games created computers"[13]—gesturing toward how analog games and digital media share structural similarities as well as the fact that game development frequently drives computer development. This paradoxical entanglement ultimately leads him to the conclusion that, in a world directed by dynamic technological systems interacting with one another, the way to get ahead is to think in terms of games. These perspectives tap into the structures of gaming rather than their surface representations. They point toward how games uniquely capture and encourage behaviors that are important for life in the twenty-first century, whether it is learning how to intuit the complicated patterns of interlocking systems or how to motivate ourselves into maximum productivity.

If this all sounds too optimistic for your tastes, there are also plenty of folks who are worried about what it means to live in a ludic century. Their concerns go beyond violence and problematic representational practices to interrogate how games prime us for a life of constant competition and work. Janet Murray, for example, declared that games like *Tetris* perfectly capture "the constant bombardment of tasks that demand our attention and that we must somehow fit into our overcrowded schedules and clear off our desks in order to make room for the next onslaught."[14] Christopher Paul argues that the meritocratic structures of gaming reinforce the hierarchies that uphold white supremacy and toxic masculinity.[15] According to Nick Dyer-Witheford and Greig de Peuter, "*Video games are a paradigmatic media of Empire*," crucial for the continuation of the current political order: "a school for labor, an instrument of rulership, and a laboratory for the fantasies of advanced techno-capital."[16] Media theorists have made similar claims about other forms like television and film, and rather than take that as a refutation of any such type of argument, I would like to embrace all the research on the topic as an indication that media does, in fact, both reflect and reinforce the politics of our time in ways that go beyond the representation of certain types of characters and stories. And games, as we have already discussed, occupy a significant portion of our contemporary media landscape. Whether they are central to our understanding of the twenty-first-century condition or merely an ancillary component of a much larger political economy, games are increasingly important to the way we make meaning: as integral parts of the economy, as activities that put us in intimate relationships with machines and others and that force us to reverse-engineer complicated systems for the purpose of mastery; and as influential storytelling platforms that can help us imagine new ways of living.

If the twenty-first century is a game, then it follows that we are its players. The gamer, in addition to being the problem child of contemporary culture, is a useful metaphor for understanding our relationship to media, technology, and politics. I am reaching for the figure of the gamer (separate from games and gaming) for inspiration in understanding the world, though I am not the first to do so. McKenzie Wark constructs another metaphor of the gamer, as the individual navigating our nightmare capitalist simulacrum. In her *Gamer Theory*, ideology is "gamespace," and it "wants us to believe we are all nothing but gamers now, competing not against enemies of class or faith or nation but only against other gamers."[17] This is the space of late capitalism and the military-entertainment complex, in which the individual's desire for potency and advancement is the key operating principle for maintaining a sense of alienation from other workers. I hold Wark's deployment of the term *gamer* very close to the center of this project and wish to explore the ways that games and gamers are key components of our current neoliberal order.

Throughout this book, I invoke the notion of the gamer to think about those who play video games. In doing so, I am in conversation with researchers like Adrienne Shaw, who argues that the continued attempts to reclaim and diversify the term in critical theory and activist writing reify a figure with which many players do not identify and encourage us to engage in a neoliberal politics of diversity that places importance on spending power and marketing for the purposes of recognition.[18] Leigh Alexander makes a similar point when she declares that gamers are "over," gesturing toward the cycle of toxicity that likely generated the exodus in the first place: "'Gamer' isn't just a dated demographic label that most people increasingly prefer not to use. Gamers are over. That's why they're so mad."[19] I do not disagree with these critics, particularly as they seek to deconstruct the identity as one that has been leveraged to consolidate power and influence in the hands of a few while reinforcing a consumerist logic of diversity. Indeed, the limitations of diversity politics as they circulate through individual games, critical theory, and industry practices are at the core of this book.

My interest in the gamer has less to do with actual demographics (or, in fact, actual gamers, in the sense of those who explicitly claim the identity) and more to do with the theoretical implications of the idea of a gamer as an individual traversing complicated technological, narrative, ludic, economic, and social systems simultaneously and at will. To grapple with the idea of the gamer is also to grapple with the question of how a marketing fiction is deployed in the interest of organizing differences among an otherwise unaffiliated group of people. All identities, after all, are fictions that organize us. I am in agreement with Sara Ahmed on this score, who argues that regardless of the ontological reality of an identity category, the task of the critic is to "attend to categories to understand how what is ungrounded can become a social ground."[20]

No discourse, of course, has rendered "gamer" an identity category in the way that sex, gender, race, or sexuality have been, but the residual effects on the community look strikingly similar. Take, for example, the Entertainment Consumers Association, founded "to give gamers a collective voice with which to communicate their concerns, address their issues and focus their advocacy efforts," including staging protests at court hearings and circulating petitions.[21] Other organizations, such as charities like Child's Play, seek explicitly to raise the profile and reputation of the gamer community by doing good deeds. These movements and groups emerged at a time when video games were surging forward as an entertainment industry, with all the anxieties about children and sex and violence that attend such a rise in influence. Just like films and comic books and novels before them, video games have been subject to moral panics about sex and violence and threatened with government regulation. The strain on "gamer" as an identitarian designation also emerges, unsurprisingly, alongside these controversies. It is easy to pick out how the logic of authenticity, a central feature of identity politics, structures how movements like #GamerGate mobilize their constituents.[22] "Real" gamers, after all, would not ruin the fun by nitpicking minor details of a game or support news organizations that are out to trick them into playing terribly crafted but ideologically innovative games. Responses to harassment also engage this identitarian logic, calling for increased visibility and inclusion of nontraditional gamers within corporate structures and design paradigms, reinforcing rather than breaking cycles of incorporation into unjust systems.

Gamers, for better and for worse, are bigger than those who actually play video games. In many ways, gamers are bigger than video games themselves. We gamers have come to overshadow the complicated assemblage of community, technology, art, money, and play that we call gaming, and I hope to attend to this condition by troubling the gamer's position with respect to the other parts of the system. Identity is an important marker for imbalances of power and a crucial site of resistance, but an overdetermined focus on identity itself can also mask the operations that sustain that imbalance. In this moment, gamers are exceptional: in our virtuosity as players and our toxicity as fans, in our lack of diversity (or abundance thereof) and our exploitability as a market category, and in our mastery over our own virtual worlds and heroic narratives. In part, this book aims to knock us down a peg, to put us into our proper context: stuck inside the mess of stories, rules, machines, conflicts, desires, affordances, constraints, and politics with which we continually struggle to actualize ourselves. The overdetermined emphasis on gamers can lead to the assumption that human subjectivity—that fetishized essence of gameplay that gamers and critics alike call "agency" or "interactivity"—is the most important component of the gamic system.

The declaration that video games are "a mess we don't need to keep trying to clean up" comes from an ontological position similarly interested in decentering human figures from an analysis of games.[23] Such thinking, whether explicitly in the form of object-oriented ontology or based in related intellectual traditions like platform studies, has been an important part of the development of game studies as a discipline. The image of the mess in particular offers a way for us to embrace the proliferation of approaches to studying games without attempting to constrict them to a narrow range of best practices. It also aptly metaphorizes the complicated assemblage of parts that make up the system of gaming. And yet, while I am working within and expanding upon a tradition of game studies that looks beyond the human and holds multiple methodologies in tension with one another, I do not embark on this project with the mess primarily in mind.

The "trouble" of gamer trouble is in part a commitment to my own training and intellectual genealogy, which has pushed me to entangle games and gamers with the frequently maligned discourses of identity knowledges like feminism and ethnic studies.[24] These methodologies may begin with the very questions of inclusion and identification that animate so many gamer conflicts, but then they push into them to locate structural social justice interventions. I prefer the word *trouble* to *mess* for the way it can describe not merely ontology and thingness, but the frictional relationships between things (and people), as Donna Haraway uses it in urging us to find new ways to live and create—perhaps even survive—together, across species and in damaged ecologies.[25] It is a word made most famous in academic writing by Judith Butler, who uses it to think through the ways we all produce gender by performing in concert and in conflict with social norms and our own bodies, and how such performances and subversions open up new political possibilities.[26] Gamers perform such complicated dances with social and technological systems each time they pick up a controller. It is also alive in political discourse, such as in US Representative John Lewis's common refrain to "make good trouble" when seeking racial justice. Trouble describes resistance and consequence, anarchy and solidarity. It is something we find ourselves in as much as we create it for ourselves, and it is frequently unclear whether we find it pleasant or not.

Trouble also invokes, for me, the deep histories of conflict around intersectionality in feminist and queer theories, particularly on the part of Black women intellectuals, from Sojourner Truth and Audre Lorde to Kimberlé Crenshaw[27] and beyond. These voices are still calling for the recognition of difference—a refusal to flatten ontologies while striving to flatten hierarchies—while being blamed for divisions within their own political movements. They are the original killjoys,[28] facing backlash from their contemporaries for the crime of wanting both recognition and the redistribution of resources.[29] Feminist thought has never been monolithic, and I deploy it in this book in ways that are primarily concerned with racial, transgender, and queer justice. Trouble is a glitch in the matrix. Trouble is a woman who stands out. Trouble is *cruzando la frontera*.

Gamer trouble encompasses all of these registers because gamers are and do all of these things. Similar to the mess, *trouble* describes the multifaceted condition of video games as software, hardware, story, performance, and more. It layers on their participation in relationships fraught with instability and conflict, including within the political realm, where they have gathered so much attention recently, and in the academic realm, where they have risen to prominence over the past few decades. It incorporates the gamer's simultaneous experiences of immersion within and alienation from virtual worlds and virtual characters, their struggles with technological and ludological systems in the act of play, as well as their various efforts to make sense of and embrace all of this. And above all, *trouble* places games and gamers squarely in conversation with its own critical foundations in queer and women of color feminisms. In the multiplicity of approaches to the study of games, this is not an uncontroversial move, as it risks the usual association of identity politics and identity knowledges with a lack of critical rigor. However, in the spirit of the mess and the trouble into which we've waded, I humbly suggest that if there is room to work toward correcting the lack of sufficient attention to technical details in the study of video games, there is also room to continue to explore the possibilities of queer, feminist, and critical race perspectives in our field as well—especially those perspectives that show us how identity politics actually lie at the heart of our technologies. This book adds to the conversation started decades ago by researchers like Patricia Marks Greenfield and Marsha Kinder and works with contemporary feminist game studies thinkers aiming to realize our "Laura Mulvey moment" in our field.[30]

Judith Butler set out to critique the identity category "woman" as an organizing principle around which feminist politics revolved, famously arguing that both sex and gender are continuously produced through individual and systemic performances. In *Gamer Trouble*, I demonstrate how the act of playing a video game creates similarly troubled circuits of performance and identity formation, some of which rely on the emergence of a coherent category, "gamer," against which critics and other outliers may be judged.

These performances also continually destabilize the identity category, such that it is always in flux. There are the gamer troubles that serve as a cultural backdrop to video games and the gamer's trouble of constantly negotiating agency and constraint within technological and narrative systems. There is the trouble of industry representation, which sometimes seems stuck in adolescent fantasies when designing stories and characters. Then there is the trouble of game studies itself, which emerged scant decades ago and is currently enjoying a surge in popularity, with all the anxiety and growing pains that go along with it.

This is the final rhetorical beauty of the word *trouble*: it contains multitudes. All of these troubles, while inhabiting their own distinct conditions of possibility and their own unique ontologies, nevertheless coalesce around the central turbulence that animates gaming and gamer culture: playing a video game. It is to this trouble that we now turn.

Gamer, Interrupted

Gamer trouble emerges in a lot of different contexts, but I'd like to kick off this journey by locating it within the affective and attentional structures of gaming itself, which envelope users within circuits of play that are most pleasurable when uninterrupted. These structures operate at the immediate, face-to-interface level as well as on the level of culture, and attending to the way that they organize gamers can help us gain a foothold to understand how power flows through individuals and communities in the gamic system.

It is fairly common to think of gamers as immersed in their own worlds, virtual or otherwise. This plays out in our popular notions of what gamers are as well as in how we have theorized the medium in game studies. Throughout much of the field's short history, this reality was frequently described as the "magic circle," a space in which the rules of a game supplant the rules of society, creating a zone of play that allows a range of behaviors and interactions that would otherwise not occur among players. Drawn from Johann Huizinga's foundational work on play, the concept of the magic circle became popularized in Katie Salen Tekinbaş and Eric Zimmerman's *Rules of Play* game design manual. It captured the attention of a number of scholars and produced enough challenges and misreadings that Zimmerman wrote a formal response in 2012 to knock down what he called the straw-man argument that the magic circle proposed games as closed formal systems separated from their cultural contexts.[31]

And yet, conceptualizing the magic circle is not the only way that players and theorists have imagined themselves as part of an enclosed, if permeable, system. One of the reasons the magic circle is a useful way to describe gameplay, after all, is that it offers a convenient account for the sense of separation one feels from the "real world" during gameplay. Despite the formal problematics, for analysis, of restricting game activity to a privileged, separate arena (and there are many, and they are well documented), to say that the relationship between player and game, or players and each other, is experienced at a distance from the world should not be controversial.

We can see a similar attempt to capture this distancing in the concepts of flow and immersion, which emerge in part to describe affective experiences of gameplay. *Flow* is a state of absorption resulting from performing an activity that is difficult enough to challenge one's abilities but not so difficult as to frustrate them. Though it was developed by behavioral psychologist Mihaly Csikszentmihalyi to understand self-motivation to perform a broad range of tasks, it has become important in the study and design of games as well. *Immersion* is related to flow in its attention-consuming capacities but frequently is understood in relation to fictional worlds, as Janet Murray outlines in *Hamlet on the Holodeck*. Murray likens it to being plunged into a body of water, whose difference from the air "takes over all of our attention, our whole perceptual apparatus."[32]

These phenomena fit into what James Ash prefers to call an "interface envelope," a structure "in which space and time appear and are orientated around the immediacy of player action."[33] The interface envelope captures the tendency of an interface to shepherd a user's attention and entangle them within its own circuits of power, continuously adjusting and folding itself around them to create shifting, extended modes of engagement. For Ash, envelope power results when a developer successfully enfolds players within their systems, but its responsive and temporary nature means that the envelope is not always achieved nor does it always look the same from player to player. Because of its ability to imagine envelopment in terms of flexible power exchanges between gamer, game, and technology, I find this formulation particularly useful for a feminist analysis of gaming, and I will continue to draw on it as a way to understand various forms of gamer trouble.

When we expand the enclosure beyond the game itself, we get what critics have called the *metagame*, explained by Stephanie Boluk and Patrick LeMieux as the envelope of practices that exist around video games, "the material trace of the discontinuity between the phenomenal experience of play and the mechanics of digital games."[34] The metagame is what bridges the game to the real-world power and politics that swirl around it. Paying attention to metagames can reveal ideological structures at work in gamer culture, such as the hegemonic "*anti-metagaming metagame*" that cuts video games out of their context, reducing games to opaque commodities with defined uses, and turns gamers into entities plugged seamlessly into these products, according to the will of the corporations who create them.[35] What flows from this metagame is a techno-utopian ideology that encourages the belief in meritocracy, forward progress, and the enclosed magic circle[36]—envelope power on a meta level.

Whether we consider gamers to exist within bubbles, envelopes, circuits, circles, or other semiclosed systems, the enclosure within such attention-commanding and gratification-granting power dynamics, no matter how permeable, presents the question of what trouble happens when these spaces experience a rupture. Boluk and LeMieux explain organized online harassment campaigns like #GamerGate as a result of breaking the magic circle surrounding gamer culture, disrupting a metagame that directs gamers to pursue seamless enjoyment.[37] A rupture in the envelope becomes akin to the castle walls under siege. Gamers react in the way they have been trained: by neutralizing the enemy. In many ways, conflict is central to gaming, and therefore it must be central to how we understand gamers. However, the desire to obliterate opponents occasionally seems at odds with the pursuit of gamic tension: Does one want to win or to play?

To understand this paradox, we must dig deeper into the nature of conflict in establishing envelope power in games. We can point to a number of critics who recognize the importance of friction to gaming. In their survey of definitions by game designers and theorists from the past century, Salen Tekinbaş and Zimmerman found that rules limiting player behaviors were ubiquitous across all but one of the eight definitions that they examined, even though "conflict or contest" was only explicitly included in three of the definitions.[38] Rules, in their function as unnecessary obstacles that structure compelling moments of play,[39] are fundamentally about constraint. Even before this, there is the question of technology itself. Whether the ultimate foe is an elaborate artificial intelligence or a simple maze, mastering the interface is the first step in the journey. We fight with controllers, with simulated physics, with monitor refresh rates, and with network lag before we ever fight with game rules or each other. It is no coincidence that in their roles as cinematic heroes, gamers frequently represent the victory of man over machine.

Master the interface to master the rules to master your opponent: this is the gamer's way (at least as the current ideology of gaming constructs it), and it is decorated with epic wins, achievements, unlockables, and Easter eggs. This is the gamer that Wark invokes when she proposes gamer theory, at the heart of which is gamer radicalization, a breaking free of the ideology of constant competition and personal advancement: "The gamer as theorist might look toward a transformation of what matters within gamespace, a style of play that edges away from agon, distinction, decision, the fatal either/or."[40] Of course, there are already gamers who play against this ideology of winning in various ways.[41] However, I do not invoke Wark here merely to repeat her call for expanded notions of playing games. I invoke her to point out the inherent contradiction in a gamer ideology that seeks out conflict only to abolish it by winning. Games are full of competition, antagonism, aggression, and friction by design. Without unnecessary obstacles, there are no games.

We might consider, then, that at the heart of many gamer troubles lies ruptures that introduce the wrong kind of obstacles—those obstacles that stand in the way of the successful implementation of the envelope power (or perhaps, more accurately, the power envelope) of gameplay, disrupting the envelope's integrity. These include conflicts between player and avatar identity, guilt-inducing critiques, uncanny animations, and network lag. The proliferation of theories of containment in game studies suggests that envelopment is part of the pleasure of gaming, so conflict is tolerated only to the extent that it sustains the envelope (which, crucially, is initiated by a technical apparatus). This is Bernard Suits's lusory attitude, the willing acceptance of constraint for the sake of the game, gone digital. Gamers fit into this scheme according to how well they do or do not maintain the envelope: in game studies, we know the wrong kind of players as triflers, cheats, and spoilsports.[42] However, in the context of the digital, envelopment also involves the technological mediation of interpersonal connection, to a greater or lesser extent depending on the platform. These (dis)connections cannot be messy, or the interface has failed. The power envelope, even in team play, is one that still tends, ontologically, toward isolation and enclosure.

This mingling of affect and power is useful for queer women of color feminist analysis, because bad feelings expose precisely when and where the disruption of power occurs. This is true for gamers that fit into the demographic fiction of the straight white adolescent boy as well as those that fall outside of it. Envelopes are never absolute, and trouble gets to everyone eventually. While they may have a similar experience of ruptures in the gaming envelope, it is important to recognize that different gamers have different proclivities toward and capacities for responding. For individuals who continuously navigate structures that erase their visibility in the world, certain types of trouble, like a protagonist avatar who does not match the player's own identity, are not particularly disruptive. Other types, like coordinated harassment campaigns, increase their vulnerability in a wider context of everyday oppression. For those who move more effortlessly through the world thanks to various forms of privilege, the disruption of a potent power fantasy can be more unsettling.

This book focuses on different kinds of tensions that build across the gamic system as power flows through its different parts, drawing in and repelling different gamers at different times. We may locate a specific tension in a specific place, such as a controller or an interaction between players, but its embeddedness within the wider context of the game's power envelope means that the origins and the consequences of any particular trouble is directly tied to the rest of the system. In order to fully understand the nature of gamer trouble, we must move fluidly between the singular and connected forms of trouble that gaming presents. From the microcosmic levels of electricity and flicks of the thumb to the grand stages of identity politics and global capitalism, wherever gamers find themselves, gamer trouble follows.

Exploring Gamer Trouble

Now we arrive at the roadmap of the book, which brings the question of the field of game studies into immediate view. What we now know as game studies has seen its share of turmoil as it sought to find a place across and apart from various disciplines, from computer science to sociology to literature. While a full accounting of field formation is outside of the scope of this project, a brief characterization might explain why politicized inquiry and the widespread valuation of identity knowledges with respect to game studies only rose to prominence in recent years. This illusion is connected to what might be the only bit of lore that exists about the formation of the field: the narratology versus ludology debates. Much like #GamerGate, narratology versus ludology is described quite differently based on which side one feels an affinity toward. On the one hand, Janet Murray describes it as an "academic turf war"[43] in which so-called ludologists sought to carve out territory for the study of games as systems by labeling other critics "narratologists" who only seek to understand games as stories. On the other hand, Espen Aarseth describes the ludologist intervention as "a reaction to sloppy scholarship" unfairly characterized as a ban on narrative approaches to games by those who "are less astute readers, scholars and interpreters than their training gives them occasion to presume."[44]

I am here more interested in the affective consequences of narratology versus ludology than the particulars of the conflict (which are subject to analysis elsewhere in this book) because this scholarly kerfuffle has had profound effects on those beginning their training in game studies, although we have only been able to discuss this in informal support networks. Feminist scholar Emma Vossen has detailed the repercussions of the lingering debate on women and nonbinary graduate students working in the field, noting the gendered timbre of the argument (emotional, "sloppy" narratologists vs. rational, precise ludologists) and offering her own experience as someone who delayed her entrance into the field for a long time because of its perceived hostility toward the perspectives of women.[45] Elise Vist recounts her decision to exit game studies as a graduate student because her feminist perspectives felt like a secondary concern in larger disciplinary conversations.[46] Women and feminists are familiar with these slippages between identity and politics (woman vs. feminist), either of which may mark us for exclusion from particular communities. I have my own experiences to add to these anecdotes, but what I will put in print is that I am grateful for time spent as a graduate student studying English and feminist studies, without which I would not have the confidence to approach video games as an unrepentant queer feminist scholar pursuing racial justice.

Vossen attributes the exclusionary nature of game studies to the intersection of academic culture with gamer culture, both of which are dominated, at least in our imaginations, by straight white men. Crucially, representatives on both sides of the narratology versus ludology debate understood what was happening as a kind of competition, whether the "turf wars" of Murray's characterization or the invasion implied by Aarseth's earlier declaration that cinema and literary study were attempting to colonize video games.[47] This conflict may itself be a lingering effect of academic training, described variously as an "anxiety of influence" inducing ludologists to cast off their former disciplines[48] or a symptom of "the critical sensibility that dominated the '90s—the era of deconstruction and poststructuralism in which many game studies scholars came of age."[49] However, the pugilism of this era, which has been parodied in a Photoshopped image of scholars Janet Murray and Gonzalo Frasca facing off in a boxing match, also hints at the gamers lurking beneath the surface. It's true that all academic production involves a bit of argument, but it would be a mistake not to point out the similarities, both affective and structural, between winning a game and winning an argument—or winning a game and scoring a tenure-track job, a big federal grant, or resources to build a department. In other words, gamer trouble extends to game studies because game studies (indeed, academia) is full of gamers: not just players, not just critics, but individuals whose enjoyment of games as objects and attachments to the intense attention-commanding structures of playing (and winning) align too easily with the competitive demands of the neoliberal academy.[50]

The spoils of such victories come in the form of citation practices, which form what Sara Ahmed calls the "academic walls" structuring our disciplines.[51] Ludologists seemed to have won the battle, as the first two decades of game studies scholarship was dominated by formalist perspectives that not only shied away from cultural critique of video games, either about gender or race, but also minimized the impact of women on the field. The feminist practitioners in game studies have taken note and demanded that we, as a discipline, do better. Kishonna Gray created a hashtag, #CiteHerWork, to point out how the citational politics of journalists and academics writing about games tends to erase the contributions of women.[52] Mia Consalvo asked game studies to take up the work of confronting toxic gamer masculinity,[53] and TreaAndrea Russworm put out a call to action for game studies to join the fight against white supremacy.[54] In order to answer these calls, we must rethink our histories, our citation practices, and our scholarly interests: "It takes a conscious willed"—dare I say nontrivial?—"effort not to reproduce an inheritance."[55] *Gamer Trouble*, in part, is an attempt to put in such effort.

Today, we appear to be in a renaissance of queer, feminist, and critical race scholarship in game studies, with numerous book collections, journal special issues, and monographs rising to prominence over the past few years—a fulfillment, perhaps, of our Laura Mulvey moment.[56] The appearance of this resurgence is an illusion, of course, as critics have been writing about gender, race, and sexuality in games for decades even if this work hasn't been circulated as widely. In 2017, Adrienne Shaw exhorted scholars in game studies to recognize the rich history of intersectional feminist scholarship that had been written about games since the 1980s but that faded into near-obscurity in the aftermath of narratology versus ludology.[57] If I make the mistake of calling this current trend a wave, it is only to draw attention to the fact that, as Clare Hemmings points out, such narrativizations of our disciplines can obscure the rich work that has always been going on.[58] That we can point toward no explicit prohibition of feminist work in video games prior to this wave does not disprove an exclusion; Ahmed notes that being the "diverse" body in a discipline tunes one in to not only how "the apparently open spaces of academic gatherings are restricted" but also the ways that "those restrictions are either kept out of view or defended if they come into view."[59] The inchoate discomfort of graduate students and early career scholars that seem to mark an exclusion of women, queers, and people of color (or those critical perspectives that advocate for them) in game studies are probably not symptoms of hysteria, even if we cannot prove their origins without harm to ourselves or our communities.[60]

I began working on this project long before #GamerGate, during a time in which robust intersectional, interdisciplinary feminist critique of video games had been driven under the radar by the remnants of a scholarly debate that pushed the major players in the discipline toward a critique of form and structure rather than culture and representation. Many of us worked in seeming isolation or within small supportive communities to develop approaches to studying games that met the demands of ludology while remaining compatible with the political exigencies of the various identity knowledges in which we were being trained. During a period marked in the United States by the presidency of Barack Obama, popular interest in feminism, queer liberation, and racial justice surged forward, propelled in part by communities on the internet that facilitated the spread of information about activism and politics to larger and larger audiences. While identity knowledges remained strong within their own corners of the academy, increasingly visible clashes between progressive and reactionary activists online and elsewhere pushed an interest in identity into the mainstream of academia and eventually game studies itself. #GamerGate, only the most visible of these encounters, represented a tipping point beyond which no one associated with video games—academics, fans, and industry alike—could afford not to have an opinion about identity and representation in video games. While this was a boon for visibility, #GamerGate also set the terms for conversations that many of us had been building for years. It is not lost on the feminist gaming and game studies communities that our relevance is now justified by the emergence of a virulent harassment campaign rather than the self-evident value of nuanced conversations about the politics of gamers and video games. The landscape has been irrevocably altered, but the work remains the same.

Gamer Trouble enacts a model of interrogating difference in video games that unites the study of hardware with that of community and considers software design alongside representation in the traditions of the digital humanities and game studies alike. At the same time, it also maintains a focus on exposing both the toxic politics and liberatory potentials of games and gaming culture with the theoretical frames of feminist, queer, and critical race studies. Of particular note, throughout the book I use the singular *they* rather than the conventional *he* or feminist *she* as the default indefinite pronoun in an attempt to subvert our binary gender system. In the event that binary gender is necessary for discussion, I restrict my use of *male* and *female* to discussions that engage with popularly held (mis)conceptions about the biological body, to key theoretical terminology (such as "male gaze"), and to labels as they are used in computer interfaces. My use of *women* and *men* (or *feminine* and *masculine*) throughout this book may thus result in a few awkward formulations, but this is a sacrifice that I am willing to make.

To build this analytical approach, each chapter of *Gamer Trouble* moves through layers of the gamic system—discourse, technology, and representation, in turn—before finally settling on a chapter that tackles a single game series from a system-wide point of view. Each of these layers, of course, blends into the others. Separating them in this way is less to imply any ideological breaks than to give each component of the system sustained critical attention in turn.

Chapter 1, "Of Dickwolves and Killjoys: Feminism and Interpretative Violence in Gaming Communities," traces a long history of conflict in gamer culture that contextualizes the vitriol of #GamerGate as ordinary rather than extraordinary gamer trouble. While the character of the hashtag harassment campaign might have come as a surprise to those who were discovering gamer culture through the reports of the mainstream media, it was all too familiar to the women, queers, and people of color whose opinions and bodies have long caused the wrong kind of friction in gaming communities. Of particular interest here is the Dick-wolves controversy of 2010, which sprung up when feminist gamers pushed back against the popular gaming webcomic *Penny Arcade* for a casual rape joke. Earlier moments of harassment in gaming communities can help us understand these clashes in terms of worldbuilding and knowledge creation, in which explosive rhetoric surrounding controversial nodes in the gaming community exposes the centrality of appropriate interpretation, rather than identity per se, as a core component of discursive border wars.

Rather than remain fixated on the sins of gamers behaving badly, I extend this analysis of discourse into early academic writing about video games. This era of game studies field-building drew heavily on the language of colonization in order to position video games writ large as the victim of exploitation by an academic elite housed within established disciplines as well as the target of smear campaigns by overzealous cultural critics instigating moral panics about sex and violence. In order to make room for real experts to provide useful commentary, both of the offending groups—greedy English professors and fanatical feminists—needed to be exposed as ignorant of the forms and functions of video games. Analyzing early scholarship around *Grand Theft Auto* reveals many of the same anxieties about appropriate interpretation that motivated the vitriol of gamer purists, which, coincidentally, also placed feminists on the outside of a group that "really" knew what games were and how they work.

Chapter 2, "Making a Face: Quantizing Reality in Character Animation and Customization," examines how science and software design inflect cultural understandings of race and gender. This chapter reaches back to the eighteenth- and nineteenth-century revitalization of physiognomy to understand how contemporary technologies reinscribe old stereotypes and approaches to race and gender that have been repeated and critiqued for centuries. The positivist perspectives on humanity that developed during this time continue to reverberate in contemporary approaches to gender, race, and sexuality, particularly in the realm of computer animation and modeling, which is particularly susceptible to scientific discourses about reality and requires numbers to perform its operations. I invoke the notion of *quantization*, or the chunking up of a thing like the human face into discrete numbers, in order to explore the ways that the numerical fictions about bodies overwrite the complexity of actual identity.

I explore, on the one hand, machines and the bodies they capture for digital reproduction and, on the other, gamers and avatar creation interfaces that create bodies in the digital, showing that the interactions between them enact what Gloria Anzaldúa identifies as the practice of *haciendo caras*: strategically navigating systems of racial oppression by leveraging the friction between a mask placed by society and one's own face. Rather than complaining about mere diversity and inclusion, gamers who point toward avatar creators that limit their ability to create a range of representation are pointing toward a type of wrinkle in the power envelope that is less disruptive to those gamers who are more frequently (or more thoroughly) hailed by the system.

Chapter 3, "Gender, Power, and the Gamic Gaze: Re-viewing *Portal* and *Bayonetta*," takes a gamer's perspective on classic feminist film theory, particularly Laura Mulvey's concept of the male gaze, which features prominently in conversations about sexy women in video games. This chapter challenges gamers and game studies scholars to think about the unique context of visuality in video games and what it means for the way we understand gendered power dynamics in visual scenes. The gaze operates differently in a medium that includes user-controlled cameras and multiple objects competing for attention in a saturated visual field, and we need to modulate our understanding of cameras accordingly.

At the center of the dispute over visuality in games lie the bodies of women that are frequently understood to be created by and for the pleasure of men. In order to explore new ways to think about visual power, this chapter interrogates Chell, the avatar from *Portal* who was widely celebrated as a landmark in the representation of women because of her modest figure and full-coverage jumpsuit, and the title character of *Bayonetta*, who was controversial because of her sexy aesthetic and over-the-top innuendo. In these cases, appearances are deceiving: considered within a more complete context of gameplay, computational procedures, and racial and queer histories, Chell and Bayonetta offer very different political possibilities than what simple representational analysis suggests. This chapter argues for the need to update our perspectives on media, identity, and power to account for a changing technological landscape.

Chapter 4, "Does Anyone Really Identify with FemShep? Troubling Identity (and) Politics in *Mass Effect*," looks at the feminine version of Commander Shepard, known affectionately as FemShep to her fans, not as a character in her own right but as a structure full of holes into which gamers project their differences. I propose that shifting away from Fem-Shep as a character allows us to see beyond the ways in which she manifestly fails as a feminist and queer icon, from her technological status as a woman built on the framework of a man to the universally disappointing narrative that failed to maintain thematic consistency or pass many basic tests for avid social justice warriors.

Instead, the chapter attempts to rescue difference (which, in video games, becomes tamed into a series of menu choices designed to maximize market share) from neoliberal diversity politics. By inhabiting the contradictions that FemShep contains, FemShep fans point the way toward a coalitional politics that does not require shared identification for coherence. This invokes Audre Lorde's concept of the "house of difference," which Kara Keeling uses to think through digital identity politics and the value of becoming another. In turn, I build off of the work of these Black queer feminist thinkers to propose that while video game politics are frequently appropriative and imperfect, we must continue to work through uncertain territory in order to continue to grow.

The book concludes with a meditation on what it means to call for more conflict in an era dominated by vitriolic social media exchanges and violent rhetoric in political discourse, as well as how understanding trouble through the figure of the gamer can lead us to a more productive vision of frictional encounters. Trouble is about connections and mingling rather than isolation, and in many respects, it is about resisting victory and conquest, even of our own sides, as a political necessity. It is sometimes damaging and frequently uncomfortable, but it is also often the only way to respond to systems of power that will never stop shifting under our feet.

Through its varied, messy explorations of video games, gamer culture, and queer (and) women of color feminist theory, *Gamer Trouble* attempts the "flexible, kaleidoscopic thinking" that Janet Murray envisions for the future of a media studies defined by computers. This commitment to complexity also enacts very political goals. Trouble does not have to be destructive. As the chapters of this book and a long history of feminist, queer, and racial justice struggles demonstrate, it can be tremendously generative and even necessary for development. Yet while most activists and oppressed communities engage in conflict because they have no other choice, gamers intentionally tap into trouble—frequently, though not always, for fun. Gamers are paradigmatic for helping us think about the possibilities of enrichment and empowerment in incredibly contentious times. We must learn how to embrace the ruptures and breakages in these attention cycles and turn them into generative forces rather than traumatic ones that may result in lashing out against others. The foundations are there, written in the gamer's constant pursuit of friction.

1

Of Dickwolves and Killjoys

Feminism and Interpretative Violence in Gaming Communities

In the thick sociality of everyday spaces, feminists are thus attributed as the origin of bad feeling, as the ones who ruin the atmosphere, which is how the atmosphere might be imagined (retrospectively) as shared. In order to get along, you have to participate in certain forms of solidarity: you have to laugh at the right points. Feminists are typically represented as grumpy and humorless, often as a way of protecting the right to certain forms of social bonding or of holding onto whatever is perceived to be under threat.
—Sara Ahmed, *The Promise of Happiness*

Feminist arguments are disabled before the argument begins; invented caricatures of "angry feminists" speak so loudly in antifeminist accounts that actual feminists cannot get a word in edgewise.
—Barbara Tomlinson,
Feminism and Affect at the Scene of Argument

At the end of 2014, what began as a personal vendetta by an ex-boyfriend against an independent game developer boiled over into a widespread, coordinated harassment campaign targeting women and their feminist allies across the gaming community. The movement, eventually united under the hashtag #GamerGate, attracted the attention of the international press like few other gamer controversies had: by October, the scandal had been covered by the *New York Times*, the *Washington Post*, the BBC, CNN, the *Guardian*, and more. As the visibility of women, queer folks, and people of color in the gaming community continues to expand, the public increasingly bears witness to these highly publicized vitriolic encounters between gamers who attempt to expand the industry's representational and cultural practices and those who try to silence them with hate speech, death and rape threats, and other forms of harassment. #GamerGate is only one of the latest examples of this trend, but it has come to overshadow the longer history of antifeminist public discourse in gaming and tech culture.

In this chapter, I recover some of that history, partially in the interest of reframing the conversation around #GamerGate to more accurately reflect its position as ordinary rather than extraordinary gamer trouble. I do so primarily by digging into Dickwolves, an earlier harassment incident in gaming culture that occurred when the popular webcomic *Penny Arcade* posted a comic strip featuring a description of a wolf with phallic limbs that rapes prisoners every night. The outsized fan response to feminist critiques of the comic strip was itself an iteration of harassment events that have been occurring in online spaces since the days of text-based bulletin boards, which themselves are extensions of the harassment and silencing of dissenting women in public discourse generally. Historically, critics have read these incidences as a result of turbulence introduced by the sudden appearance of women (and other Others) in spaces that are traditionally understood as boys' clubs, and that the solution to this turbulence is to normalize the presence of nonnormative bodies through concerted visibility and sensitivity campaigns meant to inoculate established groups against the destabilizing effects of the newcomers. Anastasia Salter and Bridget Blodgett, for example, recognize the way that the heated arguments around the Dickwolves incident created an atmosphere that essentialized gendered roles within the gaming community and positioned men inside and women outside the privileged power envelope of the community.[1]

However, the main work of this chapter is to trace the structural continuities between the boundary policing that critics love to point out in fan communities and that which happens in academia. In order to do this, I first recast the language around these incidents a bit more broadly, beyond *diversity* and *inclusion*, both of which suggest that the mere presence of different bodies causes a type of friction that we can then eliminate by processes of normalization and incorporation. This places responsibility on the mismatched bodies themselves for disturbing the peace rather than the rigid systems and social dynamics that fail to accommodate their differences. It also fails to account for the fact that normalization and incorporation more often change the nonnormative bodies than the conditions that exclude them in the first place. By shifting my attention in this way, I am not suggesting that writing about diversity and inclusion in gaming culture is unimportant. Rather, I want to attend to the things that move out of focus when these are the only concepts that structure our approach to inequality. I am particularly interested in how keeping our eyes on the bodies of the marginalized and the antics of the oppressors prevents us from seeing the everyday conditions, including the behaviors of presumably rational actors like academics (and journalists and other bystanders, though my focus here is on academic knowledge production), that make such behavior possible. Whitney Phillips, in her study of online trolling, suggests that "the most exceptional thing about trolling is that *it's not very exceptional. It's* built from the same stuff as mainstream behaviors."[2] This sentiment is at the heart of this chapter.

To think about the structural aspects of gamer troubles like Dickwolves, I read high-profile harassment events in gamer culture not only as problems of identity but also as problems of hermeneutics (reaching into this word's origins in religious study to invoke the passion with which these arguments frequently play out), here labeled "interpretative violence" after Markku Eskelinen's early comments about theorist Janet Murray's unwelcome analysis of video games. While many understand gamers as a group organized around enthusiasm for a shared pastime[3] (or a group hailed by the corporate overlords that control the products at the center of this pastime[4]) and see the limits of the community as defined around gender,[5] I am interested in the fact that the boundaries of gamer identity also trace an interpretive community that is partly defined by its resistance to the dissenting opinions offered by those who also share a love for video games (often women and frequently feminist women). Although the identity of the critic in question undoubtedly inflects how a particular interpretation is received, and there is ample evidence for the way a mere identity is enough to disrupt the smooth envelope of play,[6] one does not always need an appropriate body to fit in so much as an appropriate mind: the correct way of thinking about a sacred object that leads to its divine truth.[7] It is no coincidence that "fan" derives from "fanatic," with its own history of religious fervor.

We can and should identify the disingenuousness of #GamerGate's refrain about "ethics in games journalism," and critics like Andrea Braithwaite have documented what the movement's targets have insisted all along: sexism, racism, and other identity-based discrimination fuels much of their rage and harassment, despite claims to the contrary.[8] However, the exhibition of diverse bodies in defense of #GamerGate also points toward the importance of the right way of thinking, in the same way that the exhibition and testimony of a religious convert help affirm the wisdom of a particular belief system. In #GamerGate, I see this operating in the celebration of figures like "Based Mom" Christina Hoff Sommers and the women and people of color in the #NotYourShield campaign, all of whom were paraded around to prove that #GamerGate was in fact a diverse movement whose argumentative positions therefore could not be sexist or racist, as its critics claimed. Sommers markets herself on YouTube as "The Factual Feminist," and claims to "use a data-driven approach to the basic tenets of feminism," presumably to expose its pernicious myths. #NotYourShield was a hashtag initiated by individuals pretending to be women and people of color who aligned with #GamerGate and that eventually earned the support of "real" folks who identified with these categories.[9] These defensive strategies expose the facility with which diversity critiques can be dismissed when they center only around bodies rather than politics or ideas. As Ashley Lynch observes, the incorporation of diverse bodies through movements like #NotYourShield is a conditional acceptance granted "as long as they promote #GamerGate's talking points."[10] Such acceptance is not uncommon; each of us certainly can identify a personal acquaintance who is affiliated with a social or political movement built upon their own oppression.

Feminist gamers clearly exist, but they are pushed to the margins of the community when they do not fall in line with dominant gamer interpretations of video games. One of the primary mechanisms of the ouster is an appeal to the trope of the angry feminist. The angry feminist exists by many names and in many forms—including the "killjoy" and, in the era of #GamerGate, the "social justice warrior"—and critics like Sara Ahmed and Barbara Tomlinson recognize it as a figure who interrupts: for Ahmed, the angry feminist is blamed for disrupting community harmony by daring to point out a problem, and for Tomlinson, this the figure trotted out by opponents to seize control over the scene of an argument and undermine feminist positions before they are laid out. Anger is indeed central to feminist practice: neither Ahmed nor Tomlinson critiques the anger of the feminist but rather the social forces that marshal against that anger. Audre Lorde recognizes anger as an emotion that is crucial for solidarity work, both as a protective response to injustice as well as a tool to fight back. She insists on the importance of anger within feminist spaces in which racial inequalities frequently prevail, urging feminists not only to be receptive to the anger of Black women, poor women, and other women of color in order to learn how to create a more just world but also to tap into anger born of injustice as a "powerful source of energy serving progress and change."[11]

Summarily dismissing the anger of the marginalized enables those in power to neutralize a powerful tool of dissent. In antifeminist spaces, the label of "angry feminist" marks any woman (and frequently any queer or trans individual of any gender) who dissents. While many kinds of misogyny are born out of disgust for the bodies of the less powerful, the violence of online harassment is born from a backlash to what Luke Charles Harris calls the "diminished overrepresentation" of whiteness and masculinity in online communities, which is a direct result of the power leveraged by feminist and antiracist activism.[12] In the turmoil, nonconforming bodies become swept up in the quest to purge nonconforming ideas. One does not actually have to be a feminist to experience the force of rage that is born from antifeminism.

This chapter situates antifeminist backlash as part of the gamer's distrust of "expert" knowledge about video games, which has its roots in the censorship campaigns in the 1990s and 2000s and the figure of the "mean mommy," another version of the angry feminist who lurks in the shadows of anxiety about restricted access to video games. Women were the primary targets of #GamerGate, along with the journalists and academics who encouraged gamers to take a more critical view of games themselves, but they were all lumped together under the gendered sign of "social justice warrior," which Adrienne Massanari and Shira Chess note is "a mode of the monstrous feminine."[13]

Examining the role of interpretation and knowledge creation in harassment events can help us recognize how professional critics in academia and beyond create conditions that, if they don't outright sustain movements like #GamerGate and Dickwolves, leave academic communities vulnerable to their tactics and unable to respond effectively. It's easy to point the finger at rabid fans and identify them as the origin of trouble, then dust our hands off and go home. It's far more difficult to look at our own practices of and complicity in antifeminism and racism through scholarship. In order to understand how accusations of "interpretative violence" come to bear on academic conversations around video games, it is also important to recognize how proper ways of thinking constitute the backbone—and, indeed, a gatekeeping mechanism—of academic study. This chapter will therefore close by analyzing game studies' early disciplinary conversations around narrative and representation through emblematic early work on the controversial game series *Grand Theft Auto*. These conversations—which coincide with a contentious period of disciplinary formation in the game studies field, the narratology versus ludology debate, with its own angry feminists at its core—demonstrate how scholarly boundary policing and defensive posturing leave critics unable to respond effectively to the racism and sexism that exists in games and gaming culture and, at worst, creates hostile environments for marginalized individuals in the community.

Moving from fan problems to academic ones exposes this gamer trouble in particular to be more than just a struggle over the definition of *gamer* or *video game* but part of a more diffuse process that disciplines critics of white supremacist cisheteropatriarchy. This process allows dominant actors to refigure the defensive acts committed by the marginalized as an assault on the dominant collective, thereby recasting their own dominant assaults as acts of defense.

You Don't Understand: Mean Mommies, Censorship, and Growing Up Gamer

There is a long and infamous history of trouble around the content of video games. Some of the incidents have been legislative in nature, but many of them have simply grabbed the nation's attention at various times. Historian Carly Kocurek traces the first moral panic about violence in video games to the 1976 arcade hit *Death Race*, which awarded points for running a car over stick figures on a monochrome field.[14] Brenda Romero identifies the first major controversy over sexual content in a video game as concerning the 1983 game *Custer's Revenge* for the Atari 2600, in which the gamer piloted the eponymous general (naked and sporting a massive pixelated erection) across the screen, dodging arrows raining from the sky, in order to rape an Indigenous woman tied to a post.[15] During the 1990s, concerns over violence dominated how publications like the *New York Times* covered video games,[16] fueled in part by the 1993 US Senate hearings that resulted in the Video Games Rating Act and the formation of the Entertainment Software Ratings Board (ESRB), a nongovernmental body that is still responsible for rating the age appropriateness of video game content.[17] In 1999, the Columbine school massacre put video games in the spotlight once again due to Eric Harris and Dylan Klebold's purported obsession with first-person shooters.[18] However, the most concentrated demonstration of political concern surrounding video game content occurred in 2005 after the discovery of "Hot Coffee," a sex minigame hidden in the code of Rockstar's *Grand Theft Auto: San Andreas*. This attracted the attention of a wide range of state and federal lawmakers, including Senator Hillary Rodham Clinton, who worked with senators Joseph Lieberman and Evan Bayh to initiate federal legislation regulating the sale of video games to minors.[19] Legal scholars Clay Calvert and Robert D. Richards dubbed this period "the video game censorship saga of 2005."[20]

Panics over sex and violence in video games did not end with "Hot Coffee," and the perceived assaults on this portion of the entertainment industry continue in the form of widespread research about the addictive nature of video games and questions about whether games can cause violent behavior in the real world.[21] Various gamer-related groups have responded to this troubled relationship with the media and academy. For example, the industry-affiliated Entertainment Software Association puts out its own research about gamer demographics to emphasize the diverse audience that plays games. Community-based groups like *Penny Arcade*'s Child's Play raise money for charity in order to prove that gamers are more than "ticking time bombs waiting to go off."[22] While the community did not form wholly in response to conflict, it is clear that trouble, in one form or another, has chased gamer culture from the beginning.

While the moral positions of legislators and media organizations largely depended on the fears of parents for urgency, gamers recognized that this crusade also needed the knowledge of "experts," frequently academics, for legitimacy. As a result, within the community, these issues were largely set around the question of who can best understand what video games do. In many cases, expert opinion did not line up with the experiences that gamers themselves had with video games, and politicians' factual inaccuracies and use of inflammatory language like "murder simulators" exasperated the community.[23] During the 1993 Senate hearings on violent video games, Senator Byron Dorgan misrepresented *Night Trap* (1992) as a game that was about trapping and killing women.[24] Politicians and expert testimonies misrepresented media effects studies as unanimous about the harmful impact of video game violence on the youth, when actual studies are much more heterogeneous.[25] There was also much confusion over what role "Hot Coffee" actually played in *San Andreas*, as it was technically included in the software but was only accessible by making a (very minor) modification to the game's files.

Clearly, the "experts" had been getting it all wrong. In one strip of the popular gamer webcomic *CTRL+ALT+DEL*, artist Tim Buckley penned an open letter in response to Jack Thompson, the litigious attorney who earned widespread notoriety in the community by suing video game companies over their ratings and violent content. Buckley's cartoon avatar describes himself as one of millions of gamers who did not turn out to be murderers, proclaiming, "We outnumber you, and the people that think like you." The strip emphasizes Thompson's "ridiculously low I.Q.," lack of "common sense," and suggests that the lawyer's use of "statistics and professional opinions" can also be twisted around to prove that Thompson "eats paint chips" and "sodomizes giraffes."[26] Whether we take politicians and their expert witnesses as sincere or gamer opposition as thoughtfully considered, these encounters demonstrate a deep distrust of so-called expertise on video games.

At this point, you might notice that almost all of these politicians and experts calling for the regulation of video games are men, by virtue of the fact that most politicians and academics are also men. Yet the narratives around incidents like #GamerGate largely revolve around women ruining video games. There is certainly a "boys' club" dimension to this dynamic, as has been demonstrated by critics like Salter and Blodgett,[27] but there's also something more at work. During the 2016 US presidential primaries, *Forbes* contributor Paul Tassi pondered whether gamers could (or should) forgive Hillary Clinton for the campaign she waged against video game violence. He wrote that "her position fundamentally misunderstands both games and the market for games," a sentiment that we can recognize in the critique of Thompson above. However, Tassi eventually arrives at another familiar trope from political discourse: "In a way, Hillary Clinton reminds me of my own mother."[28] Tassi details his mother's extensive prohibition of video games, his subversion of her will by sneaking to his friends' houses, and his failure to become the expected "psychopath" as a result, a common narrative after decades of video games being blamed for school shootings. The invocation of Mom here mingles this distrust of authority with another common adolescent complaint: "No one understands me."

That these are grown-ups leveling the accusation is somewhat beside the point, as is the fact that adult content has been common in video games since the first arcade machines.[29] The long political crusade against the video game industry mingles with the extensive marketing and cultural fantasy of the straight white young man continually to reproduce the gamer as not yet grown, such that growing up gamer means anxiously reestablishing one's credentials in the adult world. The age difference from the popular perception of gamer culture means that parents generally are expected to be clueless about video games and youth culture. However, critics like Sarah Stang and Rob Gallagher[30] have noted that fathers, the grown-up gamers from yesteryear, have been reincorporated into the gaming narratives of today, leaving mothers uniquely alienated from video games. Moms are also constructed as the enforcers of good taste and propriety, the most likely to fret if their children are spending too long on an antisocial pastime, and also the ones to blame if children have too much screen time. They are frequently associated with censorship—like Hillary Clinton and video games, Tipper Gore played a prominent role in attempts to regulate profanity in the music industry. Somewhere in the narrative about the women who are ruining video games lurks the specter of the mean mommy.

Suddenly, "Based Mom" is not such an odd nickname for #GamerGate's "feminist" champion, Christina Hoff Sommers. It is also fitting that #GamerGate proponent and right-wing provocateur Milo Yiannopolous eventually brought Anita Sarkeesian, Jack Thompson, and Hillary

Clinton together in a satirical quiz game to expose the deep similarities (in their dangerous misunderstandings of video games) shared by "a trendy, cutting-edge third-wave feminist YouTuber," "a fusty old religious reactionary," and "a nightmare amalgamation of Feminist Frequency and Jack Thompson who is running for President."[31] While this rhetorical gesture seems to indict Clinton the most, what it actually does is induct Sarkeesian into a club of which Thompson and Clinton, the out-of-touch parents, have long been members.

These conflicts have been brewing for a long time, at least from the early attempts by parents and the government to curtail children's access to and participation in video games on the basis of what was perceived to be flawed expertise on the question of what a video game does. That women so frequently get placed at the center of a fight started largely by men and boys is part of the misogynist logic of the angry feminist in her myriad forms, from mean mommy to social justice warrior. Here, the visceral memories of government attempts to regulate video games mingle with the convenient target of a woman with an opinion on the internet, what Katherine Cross describes as the "'terror dream' that sees us reliving the paternalist past and lashing out at all criticism in the hopes of keeping the grasping hands of the censor at bay."[32] In the next few sections, I will explore a gendered harassment event that preceded #GamerGate for an understanding of how the discourse around expertise and ownership of video games has developed over time and how the angry feminist rears her head in these conversations over and over again.

The Big Bad Dickwolf

Once upon a time, there was a webcomic about video games called *Penny Arcade*, written by Jerry Holkins and Mike Krahulik. This publication started in 1998 and eventually grew into a gaming-themed media empire that today includes comics, podcasts, multiple video series, a yearly convention, a charitable organization, massive collections of merchandise, and even a video game. Though Holkins and Krahulik are not game developers, they have a comparable amount of influence over the gaming public. PAX, the *Penny Arcade* Expo, is one of the most highly anticipated conventions on a gamer's calendar, shadowed only by industry events like the Electronic Entertainment Expo (E3) and the Game Developers Conference. During the censorship saga of 2005, Holkins and Krahulik fulfilled a ten-thousand-dollar donation to charity on behalf of Jack Thompson, who had promised it in exchange for a game that simulated the murder of game developers instead of innocent civilians and failed to hold up his end of the bargain when someone obliged. The duo made the *TIME* 100 list in 2010, edging out the only other video game–related candidate, developer Peter Molyneux. *Penny Arcade* represents the apex of fannish devotion—a media and social empire built on playing and commenting on video games and other things relevant to a gaming-focused geek culture.

The *Penny Arcade* comedy toolkit includes, in addition to video game parodies, "jokes about violence,rape,aids,pedophilia,bestiality, drugs,cancer,homosexuality, [*sic*] and religion,"[33] as well as dinosaur secret agents, fruit-fucking robotic blenders, and other outlandish characters that aim to reach a "fickle 18–24 yo demographic."[34] On August 11, 2010, a new character entered the roster: a villainous wolf with limbs made of phalluses. Mentioned only in passing, the dickwolf was part of a gag in a strip making fun of the objective-driven morality encouraged by video game quest structures. The comic's hero, having saved the five slaves required by the game's quest, runs into a sixth person in need of rescue. Though the slave appeals to the hero with tales of being "raped to sleep by the dickwolves," the hero decides that he has filled his quota and leaves.[35] It was neither the first nor the most explicit rape joke in *Penny Arcade*'s history, but "The Sixth Slave" initiated an internet fan fight over rape culture that pitted Holkins, Krahulik, and their supporters against what they identified as unreasonably angry fans bent on eradicating free speech.

"The Pratfall of *Penny Arcade*," a time line constructed by an anonymous user on Tumblr, tracks Dickwolves-related activity, including blog posts, individual tweets, appearances at fan conventions, and news coverage, from the comic's first release in August 2010 all the way to September 2013.[36] There are hundreds of links posted to the time line. As critics responded to "The Sixth Slave" on platforms ranging from personal Twitter accounts to game news sites, Holkins and Krahulik used the official *Penny Arcade* website to post rebuttals, Dickwolves merchandise, and even more comics in support of their controversial content. I wish to focus on two particular feminist entities in the drawn-out conflict: first, the feminist blog *Shakesville*, which published the first critique of "The Sixth Slave" the day after its debut in August 2010 and hosted an open comment forum for trolls in February 2011 as the conversations heated up; and second, game developer Courtney Stanton, who became the subject of intense online harassment after he wrote a blog about declining an invitation to speak at PAX because of Dickwolves in January 2011.

To many, Holkins and Krahulik's dismissive and satirical responses to requests for awareness of the seriousness of rape humor was a much-needed public stand against political correctness by leaders of the gaming community: a renewed battle over censorship, less than a decade after Hillary Clinton failed in her attempts to regulate the industry. For the feminist gaming community and its allies, however, the persistent displays of contempt by "Team Dickwolves" (as the official *Penny Arcade* T-shirt christened them) dramatically foregrounded a truth that was difficult for others to accept: the misogynistic, homophobic, and racist "trash talk" dismissed as harmless fun in gaming situations underwrote bullying behaviors that operated outside the envelope of play.

Feminists and Fatties and Trolls, Oh My!

And yet, it is frequently the feminists who are dismissed for their anger. Barbara Tomlinson's exploration of the trope of the angry feminist exposes it as a rhetorical trick useful for throwing out arguments without considering them first, deploying the full strength of hegemonic power to disqualify an argument that might threaten its dominance. Those who use the angry feminist trope do so both as a convenient panic button at the scene of argument and to reinforce the fantasy of debate that is independent of political power—after all, emotion has no place in the fair and balanced arena of logic, and it frequently undermines the appearance that a person's opinion is intelligent or well-informed. Disguising political argument as neutral, unemotional territory conceals the fact that dominant ideology lends "utterances friendly to prevailing power relations an overdetermined 'reasonableness' while rendering most oppositional arguments automatically suspect."[37] The trope of the angry feminist, therefore, is itself a mask for its own conditions of possibility.

Tomlinson identifies a number of personae who tend to deploy the trope of the angry feminist in specific ways. One of these personae, the Tough Baby, is particularly relevant to discussions of geek culture.[38] Both bully and innocent, dominator and babe, the Tough Baby persona affords its enactor the disciplinary tools of power while shielding them from the burden of responsibility, much as many gamers and geeks might exhibit the sexist and racist behaviors enabled by white masculine privilege while simultaneously claiming injury as members of an alternative class of masculinity. The Tough Baby enacts "anger in the superior position," a self-presentation that relies on contradictions for coherence: "Condemning feminist vehemence vehemently, feminist anger angrily, feminist politics politically, the Tough Baby persona is *candidly* inconsistent."[39] I draw on Tomlinson's typology here in order to enact what she calls feminist socioforensic discursive analysis, which attends to the way affect and emotion structure conversations about social justice in order to expose the manifestly political underpinning of supposedly "neutral" arguments.[40] While Tomlinson develops this technique in response to academics using neutrality as a shield for antifeminist rhetoric (a point to which we will return), I find it additionally useful for thinking about fan conversations because of the frequency with which antifeminist arguments appeal to rationality as their ground, even as those who make these appeals are shouting on the internet.

A typical Tough Baby sequence of events unfolds in the following way: "misrepresent the feminist argument, joke by using her words to create a silly scenario, attribute that scenario to her, present it as representing all feminists, use it to evoke the trope of the angry feminist, and, in case no one has noticed, *brag about doing it*."[41] This sequence is a remarkable prediction of the chain of events following the appearance of the Dickwolves. The first public document to emerge in the wake of "The Sixth Slave" was a guest post on August 12, 2010, by Milli A. on the US-based feminist blog *Shakesville*. Filed as part 53 in the site's ongoing satirically titled "Rape Is Hilarious" series, Milli A. expresses her disappointment with the use of rape to emphasize the comedic purpose of the sixth slave in the comic. *Penny Arcade* responded to this and private emails sent from concerned readers with another comic that sarcastically implored potential "rapers" not to commit violence after reading their comic.[42]

The response comic, "Breaking It Down," enacts its superior position by distorting the arguments leveraged against "The Sixth Slave" for comedic value. Holkins and Krahulik misrepresent "rape culture" as a force that directly influences people to rape, though it instead refers to a cultural climate that makes light of or minimizes the physical and emotional consequences of rape, normalizes paradigms of victim-blaming, and portrays violent sexual encounters as the pinnacle expressions of passion and desire. It is a term originating in activist circles that has been picked up for extensive use by the feminist blogosphere. In order to minimize the labor involved in repeatedly explaining this specialized vocabulary to visitors, many of the same feminist blogs critiquing "The Sixth Slave" offer resources, explanatory posts, and personal stories to help site visitors educate themselves about rape culture and community expectations about discussing it.

Krahulik posted comments on *Shakesville* without regard to their community conventions and ignored the educational materials offered to him.[43] In doing so, he attempted to establish his dominance in the conversation as it played out in spaces that belong to other communities. As a team, Holkins and Krahulik further established their "toughness" by publishing their reactions to private concerns on a public blog with millions of readers;[44] by dictating who is and is not a true long-term reader of the webcomic;[45] by tweeting sarcastic remarks about rape culture; and by engaging in multiple subsequent public behaviors, such as drawing a Dickwolf live for an audience or creating a "Team Dickwolves" T-shirt for the *Penny Arcade* store, that demonstrated their fearlessness in the face of criticism.[46] These acts, committed publicly for what grew to be a rather large audience, helped Holkins and Krahulik set the terms of the debate by writing most of it themselves.

The other side of the Tough Baby persona is a disavowal of responsibility, which the pair accomplished in the hands-off approach they took in response to the supporters who flocked to feminist-identified websites in order to harass bloggers and defend their favorite comic strip. As the encounters unfolded over several months, Holkins and Krahulik continued to promote Dickwolves at events and in their merchandise offerings. While the initial reaction to the comic was strong but unremarkable in quantity, the continued actions of the duo attracted more attention and calls for apology that they then ignored. Instead, their fans took up the cause of defending them, setting into motion yet another set of tropes familiar to feminist criticism: aggressive and vitriolic harassment.

Such behavior is not new to feminists or other social justice activists; whether they publicly critique the behavior of popular figures or privately admonish their peers, the challenge that they present to the belief in a just society makes them frequent targets of escalating verbal abuse at the scene of argument. Sara Ahmed writes about how happiness frequently underwrites the smooth operation of an unjust society, functioning "as a technology or instrument, which allows the reorientation of individual desire toward a common good."[47] Those who challenge this orientation become killjoys, not simply blamed for exposing what happiness conceals but interpolated as bodies that bring along bad feelings and trouble: "You are 'already read' as 'not easy to get along with.'"[48] On the internet, anonymity and accessibility—two traits that encouraged early hopes of utopian social interaction—enable a particularly intense form of policing the killjoy, who is usually a woman and very often not white.

Online harassment has taken this form for decades, contrary to early fantasies of the World Wide Web that erased embodied difference once and for all. Julian Dibbell's famous account of "A Rape in Cyberspace," published in 1993 in the *Village Voice*, is an early instance of sexualized violence in an online text-only gaming space.[49] Linguist Susan Herring's body of work on gendered discourse in online forums begins in the heyday of IRC and Usenet and documents both the decreased success rates of women's contributions in online forums and a specific "rhetoric of harassment" employed in gendered confrontations online. For Herring, this set of rhetorical strategies emerges out of "the ideological dominance of (male-gendered) libertarian norms of interaction on the Internet" and, though documented in the early to mid-'90s, reads as if it could have been gleaned from contemporary online forums.[50] Lawyer, journalist, and blogger Jill Filipovic chronicles a host of online harassment events against women online in the early 2000s, including those aimed at not only herself but also game developer Kathy Sierra, who quit blogging in 2007 after online harassers targeted her.[51] Mikki Kendall traces a continuity of strategies and perpetrators in her own experiences of gendered and racial harassment across a range of topics starting in 2009.[52] Karla Mantilla has also documented a long history of gendered harassment in online spaces.[53]

Although the rhetorical moves and antisocial behaviors of Team Dickwolves can be mapped onto older forms identified by Tomlinson, Filipovic, Herring, Kendall, and Mantilla, the responses of the feminist blogging community have evolved over years of enduring near-identical scenes of harassment. *Shakesville*, for example, provides primers on social justice issues important to the community, and "Shakers," the site's group of bloggers and regular commenters, continuously refine their own vocabulary and inside jokes to describe and defuse harassing behaviors, much of which is codified in the site's "Shaxicon." The blog's strict commenting guidelines discourage those unfamiliar with basic feminist arguments and positions from participating in the conversation.

Moderators enforce the *Shakesville* commenting policy with methods including editing the language of the comment, referring the offender to the comment policy, and more, up to and including deleting violating messages from the discussion thread and permanently revoking the user's commenting privileges. Moderating comments ensures a space that abides by a shared set of values and prevents distracting or unexpected materials from disrupting individuals or conversations. Strict comment moderation deliberately challenges the libertarian principle of freedom of speech that Herring and Mantilla associate with gendered online harassment, but site owner Melissa McEwan frames the legitimacy of the so-called safe space of the community by invoking another libertarian principle: the right of the landowner to dictate the rules of their property. The site's comment policy elaborates, "Whether you can comment at *Shakesville* is ultimately at our discretion—and plaintive, angry, or accusatory wailing about free speech will be met with yawning indifference. This isn't a public square. This is a safe space."[54]

Shakesville has been the site of many vitriolic internet comment fights because of its feminist politics. McEwan, who identifies as a gamer and blogs on the subject of video games, has been harassed almost continuously for one reason or another; the site's most intense controversy to date centered on her criticism of the PlayStation 3 game *Fat Princess* in 2008.[55] The "Shakesville Troll Warz 2008" saw moderators and community members debating gamers who flooded the comments of a post in which McEwan discusses the hate mail and blog reactions to her critique of the game.[56] When Shakers began speculating from which website these commenters came, one of the visitors posted a link to a *Fat Princess* thread on NeoGAF, a gaming discussion board. Later waves entered from other gaming-related websites. A common accusation from the trolls was that Shakers were not "real" gamers and thus should stay away from commentary about video games.

Over the course of 2,244 posts, the trolls' language ranged from classic antifeminism ("Feminism is just another form of sexism" [Someone]) to gendered harassment ("I hope this game sells above and beyond, to prove to get [*sic*] no one gives a shit about whining cunts" [Fat b is a faggot]) to personal attacks against McEwan herself ("god you fat bitch just shut the fuck up" [fatty mcfatfat]). As the commenters' usernames also show, harassment was not restricted to the text of the comment; the names chosen by the aggressive visitors ranged from insulting and vulgar phrases to nonsensical strings of characters. Very few used actual names, and when they did, they were often references to fictional people like Captain Hook of *Peter Pan* fame and Cecil Adams, the persona behind the question-and-answer column *The Straight Dope*. Like assailants wearing masks, the commentators wielded anonymity itself as a threat. Instead of allowing these tactics to intimidate or frustrate them into silence, the community embraced the encounter, collectively ridiculing their trolls as they entered and incorporating some of the most absurd attacks and responses into community parlance. As a result, "lol your fat," "we have only pie here," and "pathetic anger bread," all phrases taken from conversations with the trolls, are some of the Shakers' most commonly used inside jokes.[57] Largely because of the blog's high profile on the internet, regular Shakers are experts at wielding feminist rage to expose and deflect antifeminist affect.

Sarcasm is typical of the *Shakesville* affective mode; a longtime favorite motto of the community is "I'm not offended; I'm contemptuous." Whereas a logical response to accusations of inappropriate feminist affect is to minimize evidence of such affect from their language, the *Shakesville* community deflects antifeminist argument by embracing affect, redefining it according to their own terminology, and ultimately directing it back at critics. McEwan and the *Shakesville* blogging team are well known for arguments that are presented with prose that is biting, witty, and sometimes outright rageful. They operate in the mode of the angry feminist or the feminist killjoy but—much as Lorde, Ahmed, and Tomlinson encourage—reject the stigma associated with being bearers of negative emotion, instead embracing it for their own agenda. Indeed, rhetorical affect binds the community tightly.

Shakesville's encounter with Team Dickwolves in 2011 played out slightly differently. In terms of sheer numbers, it fell short of the *Fat Princess* event, generating only 1,864 comments, though it was more visible thanks to the high profile of *Penny Arcade*. On the whole, the public comments from visitors to the site were confrontational and dismissive, but not as explicit or threatening as the posts from *Fat Princess*. In fact, several Shakers expressed disappointment in the forum about the relative tameness of the Team Dickwolves trolls.[58] However, McEwan did report that, much like with *Fat Princess*, she was receiving hate mail and threats from fans upset over the critique of *Penny Arcade*, even though the original poster was Milli A. The fight over *Fat Princess* was not an advertised open thread, though McEwan left instructions in the original post for moderators not to enforce the normal rules for commenting. For *Penny Arcade*, she created a "safe space" of sorts for Team Dickwolves to voice their objections, insults, and concerns but noted that the trolls sending her angry emails in private did not openly attack her on the comment thread when explicitly invited.[59]

While McEwan ties the behavior of her private assailants to rape culture itself, Tomlinson might see the inconsistent bullying of the Tough Baby. A casual observer might even suggest that Team Dickwolves was more polite than the trolls that came to harass *Shakesville* over *Fat Princess*. However, the experience of game developer Courtney Stanton, a transgender man who was perceived as a woman at the time of the incident, suggests quite the opposite. Stanton entered the conversation in response to the October announcement of Dickwolves merchandise in the *Penny Arcade* store. Reasoning that the Team Dickwolves shirts glorified rapists in the form of sports fanaticism, Stanton designed his own shirt: the Dickwolves Survivors Guild, proceeds from which he donated to a rape crisis center.[60] This move solicited little response at the time (and, in fact, Holkins and Krahulik added women's shirts and team pennants to the store in December). However, on January 24, 2011, Stanton cited Holkins and Krahulik's refusal to apologize for Dickwolves as the reason he would not be speaking at PAX East. Two days later, the Dickwolves merchandise disappeared from the *Penny Arcade* store, and Stanton publicly thanked Holkins and Krahulik for removing the items.[61]

Whether the events were related or not, internet commentators reacted swiftly in making the connection. During the first week of February 2011, commenters flooded Stanton's blog with harassing messages that invoke both Herring's study twenty years ago and *Shakesville*'s experience with *Fat Princess*. In addition to harassing blog comments that included threats of rape and physical harm, Stanton reported receiving private death threats and that people were calling "local police to try to 'prove' [he was] fabricating the fact [he] was raped to get attention."[62] A new Twitter account, @therapeculture, emerged with plans for "exposing [Stanton's] self-centered worldview."[63] When not invited to a space explicitly to air grievances, Team Dickwolves seemed to get its bite back.

Stanton does not, in the manner of the *Shakesville* community, embrace affect and redeploy it against his harassers in order to reshape the scene of argument, though in his later reflections, he observed that anger seemed to coincide with increased engagement with his blog posts. The public arguments on Stanton's blog featured some of the classic antifeminist strategies deployed by Team Dickwolves against *Shakesville*, and Stanton and his allies addressed them in earnest, making a point of exposing many of these strategies as repetitive tropes deployed against other feminist arguments. Stanton took the additional step of drawing up a digital textual analysis of the more than one thousand comments he received in the first week of February. Using IBM's Many Eyes application, he created different visual representations of his week of comments in order to demonstrate the difference between language that moves blog conversations forward, even if it is aggressive or hostile, and trollish language, which by his definition does nothing but "add noise to a conversation."[64] He compiled these for a conference presentation.

Stanton's Many Eyes images reveal something that is unsurprising but had not before been visually represented about conversation surrounding the Dickwolves event: the word *rape* was central to all discussion, but only trolls used it almost exclusively as a verb and often as a threat against Stanton personally. Additionally, Stanton provided maps of *fat*, which turned up on the blog despite being off topic, and the phrase *I hope* in order to further demonstrate the ways in which trolls use predictable personal attacks instead of taking part in more nuanced discussions. In Stanton's words, "The trolls only have one hope and it's like they're reading from a script," as most of the branches end in variations of wishing him to be raped (see figure 1.1).[65] Where *Shakesville* wielded affective commentary as a way to expose the absurdity and bad faith of Team Dickwolves comments, Stanton used presumably neutral technology to demonstrate precisely the same thing. Both strategies allowed Stanton and *Shakesville* to maintain their claims on their own online spaces in the face of oppressive hate speech, even though the emotional and psychic cost of such resistance is high.

Holkins and Krahulik positioned themselves above the Dickwolves fray, offering commentary from their influential social media accounts without directly addressing their public interlocutors, with the exception of Krahulik's foray into *Shakesville* and responses to private emails. They claimed no responsibility for the Dickwolves hordes who claimed to defend them. In the end, the Babiness of the *Penny Arcade* authors was finally confirmed by the nature of their reentry into the conversation months after

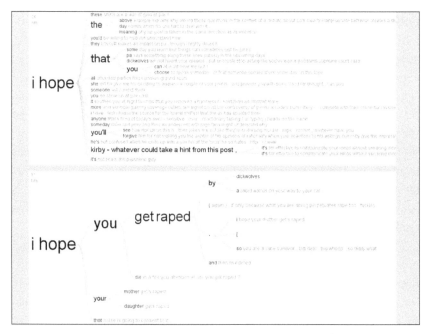

Figure 1.1. Courtney Stanton's word map of the Dickwolves conversation. Image courtesy of Courtney Stanton.

the harassment had started. After Team Dickwolves had assailed feminist bloggers for months with death threats, rape threats, gendered insults, and more, Krahulik posted on the *Penny Arcade* blog that it was time for everyone on both sides to back down because his wife had received a single death threat.[66] Holkins's blog on the same day distanced the pair from Team Dickwolves' activities, claiming at last that they never could have predicted the mess the original strip had caused and that their continued silence was entirely the fault of the feminist bloggers, both because of their hostile stances ("I'm not entirely certain a conversation is possible") and because the duo felt the need to not "draw unwanted attention to the sources of the complaint."[67] Ultimately, the call to back down was both ineffectual and insincere, with Krahulik, Holkins, and Team Dickwolves continuing to engage in the harassing and escalating behaviors, including at a public appearance in 2013 in which Krahulik opined that pulling the Dickwolves merchandise from their store was a mistake.[68] Both assailed and assailant, the Tough Baby remains consistent in his inconsistent bullying.

Insufferable Know-It-Alls

Salter and Blodgett have characterized the Dickwolves incident as a response designed to shore up masculinity within the "hardcore gaming public," effectively creating a "boy's club" that disciplines the femininity in their midst.[69] The events I've outlined above corroborate (and, indeed, run parallel to) their analysis, though I would like to add to the conversation by turning to the explicitly political and epistemological, rather than identitarian, dimensions of the Dickwolves encounter. The two figures I analyze in conjunction with Dickwolves, after all, are not simply attacked as individuals whose identities violate the gendered norms of mainstream gamer culture: they are attacked as individuals who situate themselves as experts in explicitly feminist modes of knowledge production and advanced methods for analyzing culture. Hostile gamers took note of this, criticizing not only the affect of *Shakesville* bloggers but the advanced level of their discourse. A recurring theme in the *Fat Princess* discussion, for example, was the pretentiousness of McEwan's writings. In her update about responses to her *Fat Princess* post, McEwan quotes an attack from Jim Sterling, a popular columnist who at the time wrote for the gaming website *Destructoid*: "As you can see, she uses 'words' like 'heteronormative' to sound clever and informed, a tactic which invariably fails and makes one look presumptuous and pretentious."[70] The contempt for a high level of discourse carries into the discussion thread: "Sorry, but most of what you typed was a bit pretentious and theres a whole lot of 'holier than though' [*sic*] BS amongst it IMO" (annonymous [*sic*]). Such a dismissal of critique attempts to reinforce a boundary between fans, who speak in plain language and realize that games are just games, and critics, who even on an open forum on the internet, overanalyze pop culture objects with politics in mind and use specialized language to do so. Though they are not working from within recognized institutions, the descriptor *academic* seems appropriate here, and I feel compelled to remark on how the juxtaposition of the uncritical fan and the fanatical critic marks a curious slip in the affective meaning of fanaticism in gamer culture.

While the commentary of bloggers like McEwan and Stanton clearly bear the traces of academic feminist thinkers and even digital humanities methodology, their critiques also lie firmly outside of the academy—and for good reason. Consider the central concern of the debate, rape culture, which became popular in the feminist blogosphere while losing steam in academia in the early 2000s. It reemerged in academic feminism, thanks partly to the study of internet activism, ten years later.[71] In the academy, the concept of rape underwent radical transformation as disciplinary feminism itself changed: the sex wars, feminist pornography studies, and projects validating sex worker subjectivity all complicated the infamous 1970s feminist analysis that most sex between men and women was violent and coercive. Even absent the affective flames, the debate over the Dickwolves might have taken a dramatically different shape in academic discourse, if it had happened at all. I don't wish to suggest that the separate trajectories of feminist blogging and academic feminism mean that internet social justice is less useful or insightful than that of academia. In fact, the reverse is frequently true. Lisa Nakamura, for example, insists on the importance of user-generated responses to instances of harassment in order to produce accountability and resistance when institutional structures fail to respond.[72] These communities theorize their own conversations and, more to the point, rally their own defenses.

Shakesville advertises itself as an "advanced feminist blog" whose policies ensure that discussion moves beyond introductory topics, and some of the vocabulary used by writers and commenters is the same as that used in university classrooms and academic conferences around the world: heteronormativity, patriarchy, rape culture, privilege, inter-sectionality, politics, globalization, cultural criticism, and so on. Some of it, however, is quite different. For example, Courtney Stanton's re-sponses to his trolls discuss some of the same issues with feminist affect that Tomlinson engages, but while Tomlinson calls for reading through and with affect instead of dismissing emotional response as unworthy of consideration, Stanton warns people away from "tone arguments" and directs them to the *Derailing for Dummies* website to further learn how to take feminist arguments seriously. In the *Fat Princess* thread, com-menters and trolls battled over the meaning of several different logical fallacies, while Shakers mocked Team Dickwolves with witty rewritings of Emily Dickinson poems and discussions of *The Adventures of Huckle-berry Finn*. Given these types of encounters, it is unsurprising that many active members of the community have close ties to academia. Shakers mention in the *Fat Princess* thread that they teach writing to under-graduates and mechanical engineers; one commenter leaves the *Penny Arcade* open forum in order to work on their dissertation; a few modera-tors and blog contributors are tenured faculty at universities.

Degrees and professions are somewhat beside the point, however: re-gardless of their credentials, the angry feminist is always both too smart for their own good as well as a dumb bitch who doesn't understand what's really going on. The bind of identity politics means that it is not so easy to disentangle knowledge-making practices from one's own body, so it is entirely possible that being a woman with an opinion on the internet also puts one under the threat of being labeled a feminist killjoy if that opinion doesn't align with those who control the terms of the conversation. The long history of harassment that punishes women and feminists in gaming culture, exemplified here by Dickwolves, demonstrates the consequences of these toxic community dynamics. This longevity, however, also points to the resilience of feminist communities and feminist critique in the face of violent discursive and emotionally manipulative oppression. The efforts to silence feminist voices have been unsuccessful, though they have had serious impacts on individual feminists' lives. It is distressing to watch this pattern repeat over and over again but encouraging that there are always more voices and bodies to continue the struggle.

Disciplinary Colonization and Interpretative Violence

In the last few sections of this chapter, I will examine how the anxieties that structured the field-building practices of game studies, an academic discipline with its own fannish proclivities, temporarily sidelined feminist and critical race critique—at least until fannish harassment events made these an urgent concern to scholars in the field. True to the nature of academic discourse, the conflicts within game studies are less explosive than those on the blogosphere, but they originate in similar anxieties about being taken seriously and have the same goal of controlling the scene of argument when it comes to video games.[73] They also have the same outcome: producing an environment in which identity knowledges and, by extension, marginalized populations are less than welcome.

The early days of game studies were fraught with trouble. Early scholars worked tirelessly to earn respect for the fledgling field and secure a future for themselves under the inauspicious gloom of video game controversy. The inaugural issue of the journal *Game Studies* in 2001, whose editorial introduction proclaims the beginning of "Computer Game Studies, Year One," characterizes the emergence of the discipline as a zero-sum game: "Making room for a new field usually means reducing the resources of the existing ones, and the existing fields will also often respond by trying to contain the new area as a sub-field. Games are not a kind of cinema, or literature, but colonising attempts from both these fields have already happened, and no doubt will happen again. And again, until computer game studies emerges as a clearly self-sustained academic field."[74] It is curious to see the language of resisting colonization at the core of these early encounters between game studies scholars and other disciplinary approaches to their objects of study, an affective and structural similarity that we can identify in the anxious territoriality of gamers fighting social justice warriors.[75] That same issue of *Game Studies*, in the manner of any good journal's quest to set out the borders of its discipline, features passionate and contradictory perspectives on the importance of narrative, for example, to a game's meaning. A highlight of the issue for those approaching from certain humanist perspectives is the accusation that Janet Murray, in her foundational work *Hamlet on the Holodeck*, performs "interpretative violence" to the game

Tetris by reading it as a figurative enactment of the pressures of contemporary life.[76]

This anxiety of influence, as Murray dubs it,[77] resulted in a series of encounters known as the narratology versus ludology debate, which took place within the *Game Studies* journal, in conferences and symposia, and notably on the publication and online discussion forum for the edited collection *First Person: New Media as Story, Performance, and Game*.[78] Commonly described as a battle for dominance between "narratologists," who interpret video games primarily as stories, and "ludologists," who are interested in games as systems of rules, the debate had lasting consequences in the formation of the field and constitutes what I called in the introduction to this book our only real disciplinary lore thus far. Janet Murray's "Last Word" about the debate resonates strongly with contemporary opinion: the ludologists made important contributions that changed how we study games for the better, but their creation of a phantom group of narratologists to whom they were opposed was a needlessly reductive casting of many scholars who would never claim the title "narratologist"—a move that was misleading and confusing to students entering the field. As a graduate student, Emma Vossen was particularly vocal about the effects of narratology versus ludology on her entrance into game studies, and she has written more widely about its place as a gatekeeping mechanism for the study of games.[79]

Much like gaming itself, the field of game studies has been dominated by the voices of men until quite recently. It would be a mistake to gloss over the gendered dimensions of this particular conversation, especially since some of the earliest academic writing about games was done by women: Patricia Greenfield, Marsha Kinder, Brenda Laurel, Elizabeth Loftus, Janet Murray, Marie-Laure Ryan,[80] and more. Crucially, Janet Murray was not working within an explicitly feminist theoretical framework in *Hamlet in the Holodeck*, but her insistence on the importance of narrative and representation (both associated with culture and the feminine) to the study of video games was intolerable nonetheless. The ludologists promoted a formalist perspective (associated with rationality and the masculine) from within what they described as a vulnerable position within the academy—echoing the dual dominance and precarity of the Tough Baby. They were also the men who planted a flag on 2001 as the year game studies began, minimizing the importance of the work that came before, and who eventually rose to prominence as its founding fathers. Citing fear of intellectual colonization, with Janet Murray's interpretative violence serving as a symbol of this advance, they took back their discipline from the "sloppy scholarship"[81] of those who would claim video games for their own disciplines as narrative forms with representations in need of critique and interpretation. Espen Aarseth's early claim that Lara Croft's pixels, "already analyzed to death by film theorists," are irrelevant to the meaning of *Tomb Raider*,[82] emblematic of the ludologist position, echoes gamers' pushback against critique (by women) itself. "It's just a game" might stand for both the uncritical fan position as well as the polemic nature of the ludologist critical framework.

Perhaps, as Murray acknowledges, there has been some confusion across continents, with ludology actually occupying a "marginal" position in the European intellectual community from which it emerged.[83] There are also complicated power dynamics that exist between US and European academic communities. However, the rhetorical choice to characterize the encounter between disciplines in terms of colonization and violence (rather than, for example, synthesis or conversation) sets the terms for a debate that could not be amicably resolved. By constructing narratology versus ludology as a colonial struggle, the discipline congealed around questions of power and dominance, framing interlocutors as competitors rather than colleagues and introducing the expectation that there would be winners who would stay and losers who would leave. Even when video games are sneered down upon by cultural elites, such attempts to gain legitimacy by going to war with voices deemed too old-fashioned, sloppy, or uninteresting, particularly when those voices belong to individuals themselves marginalized within academic spaces, is acting in alignment with white supremacist cisheteropatriarchy. When white European men claim marginality and say they are working under threats of colonization, it is difficult not to see the echoes of Tough Baby gamers clinging to toxic masculinity as a way to strike back against perceived oppression by feminists and parents.

Murray attempted to close the narratology versus ludology debate with her "Last Word" in 2005, but the effects of the conflict still linger today. Ludology proved to be a persuasive and important position, but likely as a result of these anxieties about disciplinary colonization, early game studies work in cultural studies "lost," becoming less visible than the formalist perspectives of the ludologists. David Leonard identified this problem in 2006 when he exhorted game studies to begin producing more scholarship that dealt with gender and race.[84] At the time, he was a rare vocal critic of the "liberal colorblind (yet racially informed) discourses" of game studies academics, who were mounting defenses of games like *Grand Theft Auto: San Andreas* (2004) against government interference while ignoring its problematic representations of urban Black culture.[85] In fact, alongside Anna Everett and S. Craig Watkins, Leonard was one of the few scholars working within game studies who used a critical race lens to think about the game series at the time.[86]

Notably, the rise of game studies itself, as designated by the *Game Studies* journal, coincided with the rise of *Grand Theft Auto* (hereafter *GTA*), which became widely known in 2001 after the release of the critically acclaimed *GTA III*. Laurie Taylor, in fact, credits *GTA III* with shifting game studies in the direction of ludology due to its innovative gameplay.[87] This might seem curious at first glance, given the treasure trove of problematic narrative and representational content in the game that cultural studies is well suited to address. However, I contend that the turn away from cultural studies during the rise of *GTA* perfectly demonstrates the way game studies as a discipline avoids certain types of trouble in order to preserve its legitimacy as an academic field. After all, if video games are bad objects contributing to the decline of society, as so many have claimed over the years, how can we justify our love for and devotion to them through the pursuit of scholarship?

I will now trace the effects of early scholarly writings about *GTA*, which enact the anxieties around cultural legitimacy and control over the interpretation of video games that we have been exploring to this point. Academic critics' efforts to seem neutral on the topic of *GTA* not only allowed the conversation to miss important critiques of its problematic representational practices but, owing to the lack of community voices invested in racial and gender justice, also resulted in scholarship that was racist and sexist in nature, creating a hostile environment for marginalized scholars interested in joining the discussion.

"It Is Not, However, CJ's Freedom That Interests Us as Gaming Critics"

Grand Theft Auto seems a perfect object for the multiple modalities of academic critique. It is one of the most highly praised and influential game series of all time and the source of multiple major controversies about violence, sex, and representation in the industry—a treasure trove for nuanced study. *GTA III* earned widespread praise for its novel contribution to gameplay in terms of freedom of movement and satire. *GTA: San Andreas* swirled at the center of the 2005 congressional investigations into the ESRB and state and federal efforts to regulate game sales to minors. While most of the public outcry has been against the criminal violence in the series, mainstream critics also complained about stereotypical racial representations and problematic gender politics, including the widely publicized existence of sex workers in the games. All of the *GTA* games feature gang narratives set in US urban centers,[88] and almost all of the protagonists in the series are racialized. It was created by a small team of game designers headquartered in Scotland, whose creative process seems alternately to parody and faithfully reproduce the output of Hollywood and the recording industry, yet sales of the game are overwhelmingly concentrated in the United States.

The series is popular, critically acclaimed, culturally provocative, politically ambiguous, seemingly aligned with white supremacist cisheteropatriarchy, technologically and procedurally innovative, and situated on a complicated transnational process of production that has important implications for both northern sides of the Atlantic. It should have resulted in a vibrant academic conversation, with supporters and detractors and in-betweeners complicating the debate. Instead, the game studies discourse on *GTA* is tepid at times and outright racist at others, focusing on formal properties of the games and taking a defensive stand with regard to the controversial narrative and representational content in the series. Leonard's observations about the reluctance of academics to analyze race in the series points toward many of the discursive practices I will detail here.

The story begins, curiously enough, with media scholar Henry Jenkins getting his "ass whupped" on the talk show *Donahue*, to which he was invited (under a disingenuous promise of reasoned debate) to defend the violence in *GTA III* against media critics in 2002.[89] In the immediate aftermath of the appearance, he wrote a response on *Salon*. Even though Jenkins has an established record of feminist scholarship in fan cultures and video games, his account of the *Donahue* experience is satirical and offers a mixed position on the mean mommy trope discussed at the beginning of this chapter. First invoked in the dismissal of his experience as a father ("On *Donahue*, activists are moms and intellectuals are presumed to be childless"),[90] the Mom reemerges as a foil to the "pointy-bearded civil libertarian"[91] throughout, presumably as a way to parody how mainstream media lean on the trope to maximize the impact of stories about video games.

However, this parody loses force at moments in which the mean mommy slips in his account between constructed audience and real. For example, Jenkins writes that "Donahue spooks moms with a clip from *GTA3*,"[92] but one of the moms is finally revealed not to be a mere construct but a "*Donahue* dittohead" going after Jenkins's credentials in his mailbox, saying, "You are obviously not a mother trying to raise teenagers you stupid freaking moron idiot."[93] These slippages occur at points in the story when Jenkins is maximally exposed to audience ridicule and his reputation as a media expert is most in peril of disintegration. The entire satirical piece, in fact, revolves around musing, after a call to his own mother, about what he should have said while on air. In the temporality of the regretful satire, it is too late for Jenkins to correct his televised mistakes—and, indeed, his revisions continued when the piece was republished in his essay collection *Fans, Bloggers, and Gamers*, where he clarified that he was, in fact, unsettled by the racial politics of the game, though that was not evident in the broadcast or his initial published response. Jenkins's good humor about it all serves to deflect his shame and reestablish his expertise, in part by juxtaposing himself against the hyperbolic figure of the mean mommy, here reimagined as a perpetrator of online abuse.

This brief account demonstrates just how easily the angry feminist (here in the guise of the mean mommy) becomes the scapegoat for negative experiences around video games, even for a scholar who publicly advocates for feminism. Hillary Clinton, Melissa McEwan, Courtney Stanton, Janet Murray, and the phantom *Donahue* mom all function as the bad guy against whom gamers and game studies scholars (perhaps one and the same) must reassert their authority. The controversies surrounding *GTA*, like the controversies around video games generally, frequently have an angry feminist lurking in the background.

Jenkins is a respected public scholar and a proven proponent of cultural critique, specifically about gender, in games (as well as an accused narratologist), so he serves here as an example whose reputation can withstand a bit of public critique. However, in the interest of recognizing the shared responsibility of creating a community discourse, from this point forward, I will break from traditional citational practices and refer only to the larger publications in which the quotations were published—for these examples, they will be abbreviated *MAC* (*The Meaning and Culture of* Grand Theft Auto, an edited collection),[94] *GS* (*Game Studies*, the peer-reviewed journal mentioned earlier), and *GAC* (*Games and Culture*, another peer-reviewed journal). I draw this methodology from theorist Clare Hemmings, who explores grand narratives in feminist theory using a similar citation strategy in order "to emphasize the role of journal communities—editors, boards, peer reviewers, and responses to publishing conventions and expectations—in the establishment of feminist (and broader academic) knowledge practices" and to support "non-corrective approaches" in engaging her scholarly community by avoiding framing the discussion in terms of "good" and "bad" authors.[95] While this section will not share her exclusive focus on journals as the primary discourse makers of the field, partially due to the much more limited size of the game studies oeuvre during the period of interest, it does share Hemmings's commitment to holding the community as a whole responsible for the discourse produced within it and for addressing its shortcomings collectively. To this end, I have also omitted the language from articles about *GTA* that were published outside of the game studies community in the journals of other disciplines, many of which have well-established interests in social justice critique. I make this gesture in the spirit of collegiality while maintaining scholarly rigor. It is important for us to witness what has been said so that we can do better in the future, but perhaps it is not as important to subject individual scholars with less institutional power to easy public shaming for work written more than a decade ago.

Leonard observes that the unilateral defense of violent video games by academics and others erases race from conversations about at-risk youth, gang violence, and stereotypical representations of criminality.[96] A similar tactic is to suggest that such concerns are somehow separate from serious academic inquiry. The introduction to *MAC* bifurcates the conversation about *GTA* in its very structure: part 1 details "a scenario in which game developers like Rockstar are trying to make adult oriented games and at the same time are faced with new forms of censorship," and part 2 looks at "the games as they might be studied absent the controversy."[97] This splitting of inquiry into two different modes—one positioned as descriptive and the other as investigative—works to bracket off certain types of critical work from others and suggests that any critique of the games on the grounds of violence, racism, or sexism comes from outside of the academic game studies community. Scholars ask readers not to "be guided by reactionary and emotional propaganda" when assessing the games,[98] assuring us that concerns with media effects about violence are "perpetuated at least partially by sensationalist stories" in the press[99] and even suggesting that the more interesting questions for the discipline lurk beneath the surface of moral objection: "Putting aside the moral questions involved [regarding the murder of a sex worker to get one's money back], the implications of emergence for allowing the player greater freedom, and thus more interesting and challenging situations, are only just beginning."[100]

This latter example refers to the neutrally labeled "emergent gameplay" event that was a central part of the Australian Office of Film and Literature Classification's decision to refuse classification to *GTA III*, effectively banning its sale in the country. One of the health restoration mechanisms in the game is to hire a woman to have sex with the player character in his car. Gamers combined this tactic with the ability to take money off of the bodies of people they kill and ended up with a misogynistic gameplay event that gamers dubbed the "hooker cheat." While some scholars have elected to use the gamer terminology for this event, I prefer "sex worker exploit," in order to label it more accurately as a gameplay event and not to reproduce misogynistic language about sex workers. Game studies academics often describe the criticism of gameplay events like the sex worker exploit as an example of "games being analyzed and assessed in terms of films and videos rather than in their own terms, as games,"[101] an echo of the ludologist position. They also tend to frame violence and criminality in the game as completely optional: "Such acts were not part of the game's mission-based structure";[102] "Players can pick up a mission when and where they want, skip or ignore others, build their avatar as they wish, set alternate or side goals, or completely ignore the narrative aspect altogether";[103] "Some players may shoot characters or destroy property, while others may simply drive around San Andreas running ambulance, taxi, or police missions."[104]

The defense of the sex worker exploit reaches its logical and most problematic extreme in a piece examining it "divorced from narrative context"[105] to illustrate limitations with prevailing notions of agency in gameplay, only to dismiss it in the end as "weak emergence" and thus ultimately insufficient in proving the main argument.[106] This rhetorical move takes the assumption that criminality in *GTA* is ultimately about gamer agency, complicates it with the notion of an agent-like system of rules that results in an unexpected outcome, and consequently absolves both the game designer and the gamer of any responsibility for the gendered violence that results. Mounting an agentic defense maintains our ideological status quo: it is a hallmark of the supposedly postfeminist, postrace society in which we live that racism and sexism are cast as intentional acts rather than systematic, accidental, or even coerced ones. The assumption that neither gamers nor Rockstar would ever have any actual misogynistic intent in performing or enabling this gendered violence suggests that misogyny is an unthinkable attitude in the present day (or, at the very least, a rude accusation to make without evidence of intentionality).

Such moments of depoliticization pepper scholarship about *GTA*.[107] This is not simply a matter of failing to include a feminist or racial justice critique when the opportunity arises, although such omissions are microaggressions that demonstrate the relative value of certain types of knowledge over others.[108] Approaching texts without an orientation toward relevant cultural critique can sometimes result in sexist and racist scholarship. In discussing the limitations of player freedom in *San Andreas*, for example, one scholar remarks on the situation of the Black avatar: "If I control or play C. J., then this African American character is my instrument or slave within the game world (which is ironic given that within the narrative, he wants to become a 'player,' and doubly ironic given the cultural context of the game)."[109] The argument does not unpack the "irony" of CJ's slavery in a video game about Black gangsters (nor of the doubly ironic use of the racialized meaning of "player" to emphasize this context) and continues to use the vocabulary of enslavement to discuss participation in both the gamic system of rules in *GTA* and the wider cultural matrix of capitalism without theorizing slavery according to any perspectives in Black studies. Several such verbal slips about CJ and others exist throughout the literature.

Scholars seem generally unaware and uncritical of their own positions as primarily white, privileged academics writing about representations of poor Black and brown folks in video games. They also seem unaware of historical patterns of representation that would render seemingly innocent comments racially problematic: "Carl (CJ) has a much more complex semiotic physiology than Tommy Vercetti did";[110] "Should I keep him in the same styles long enough, however, CJ's sex appeal will diminish and strangers will start to comment on the strength of his body odor";[111] Catalina "compensates [in a positive way] for her double marginalization (of gender and of race) with hyperbolic aggressiveness, transforming herself into a very explicitly [*sic*] femme castratrice." This catalog continues, from the (white) academic congratulating the (white) game designers on an "impressive" curation of reggae music in *GTA III*[112] to the claim that one can "marginalize" a style of play by calling it subversive[113] to the multiple uncritical repetitions of "hooker cheat" in articles inside and outside of the proper discipline. There is also the quote I've used as the heading for this section, taken quite out of context but whose double meaning perfectly captures the unintentional effect of these critical oversights: "It is not, however, CJ's freedom that interests us as gaming critics." One particularly symbolic oversight is the dustjacket of *MAC*, which depicts six different Black, brown, and Asian men and women (and zero white figures) in poses of varying criminality, yet the volume includes only one chapter devoted to the discussion of race.

The main contention here is not simply that not enough scholars in the field are doing focused studies on race, gender, and other issues of power—though I am saying that too. Kishonna Gray, writing in 2014, notes the continued absence of critical race critique on games generally and *GTA* in particular.[114] What is at issue here is the collaborative process of publication that failed to include anyone versed in the theoretical vocabulary and history of marginalized populations that would have encouraged authors to think through these problematic statements in the first place, particularly given the ties the *GTA* games have to race, gender, and empire. There is plenty to say about all of these things; David Leonard, by discussing the postracial discursive dimensions of arguments about *San Andreas*, and Anna Everett and S. Craig Watkins, by writing about its "racialized pedagogical zones," have not exhausted all (or even most) of the possibilities for a critical race critique of *GTA*.[115]

The work that does account for the racial elements of the games primarily focuses on their formal properties as satire. In this "carnival of caricature," the game surrounds the gamer "with urban, suburban, and rural and ethnic stereotypes as well a commercially saturated environment of decadence and superficiality,"[116] all of which become tools of a potentially subversive signifying practice. These arguments laud Rockstar's "devastatingly accurate sense of humor"[117] and focus on the pleasure of laughter as a moment of meaningful critique of and confrontation with the realities of inequality. While these arguments can be quite compelling and do in fact complicate the presence of racial caricatures in the game, there is a notable lack of the perspectives of critical race theory that address the commodification of Black, particularly hip-hop, culture and its appropriation by white supremacist signifying regimes. *GTA*, after all, comes from a context quite removed from Black resistance to US capital and racism. Even as a parody of US medial excess, *GTA* frequently misses the mark, yet it is precisely this quality that makes it a compelling object of interest for the academic mode. However, there is little in the critical record to reflect this.[118]

As a final gesture, I'd like to demonstrate how a pervasive postracial ideology limits the effectiveness even of ludological modes of critique in game studies. Take, for example, one author's attempt to articulate the function of the ludic spaces of *GTA: San Andreas* in terms of their relation to the real-world cities that they represent. The author thinks through the ideologies of ludic space and urban space in the city of Los Santos, based off of real-world Los Angeles, and comments on the similarities in concern between theories of foundational game studies thinkers and studies of the urban complexities of Los Angeles. In attempting to untangle whether Los Santos operates more as "a medial space (existing primarily as a parody of Los Angeles) or a ludic space (existing for the purpose of conducting play),"[119] the text is consistently stymied by the chaotic nature of Los Angeles itself, which is difficult to render iconically and seems in fact quite ludic in many aspects of its design. Ultimately, denied a clean resolution to a multifaceted problem, the piece concludes this way: "The case of Los Angeles is especially problematic for this analysis because it is in many ways a city of contradictions: it is a dominant feature of the American mythos, and yet it contains relatively few iconic structures."[120]

Scholars like Mike Davis, José Saldívar, and Laura Pulido have long argued for recognizing the racial structures that organize the physical layout of Los Angeles, whose twisting highways and formidable architecture can be read as a way to control the Black and brown populations in the city. Pulido, in her study on environmental racism in Southern California, traces a history of urban planning tied to racist policies that extends back into the mid-nineteenth century. "Whites' residential desires and real estate interests," she claims, "were two of the more powerful forces that shaped early Los Angeles."[121] Many people today are willing to accept that overtly racist practices occurred 150 years ago, but Pulido's work draws a causal chain from the exclusionary housing practices of the past to its present-day layout. Whereas the urban geography of Los Angeles by the account of this piece about *GTA* seems an incomprehensible palimpsest of changes in plan, one might more coherently account for it in terms of the flows of marginalized populations around the city.

A key moment in the argument, in fact, lingers on the riot that occurs at the end of the *San Andreas* main story arc. Using the image of the Mulholland and Richman neighborhoods of Los Santos as visibly separated from the center of the city itself, the text discusses the borders between city and country in procedural terms: during the riot, the NPCs in the country area do not go into aggressive mode, while those in greater Los Santos do, except for people within the territory of Mulholland. This feeds into a discussion of ludic and geographic boundaries that touches on the topic of class but then moves away quickly with a footnote, placing race outside of the scope of the argument. However, acknowledging the racialized organization of space in Los Angeles brings space, race, and ludics in Los Santos into coherent relationship with one another; reinforces the author's point about class; and places both of these in conversation with the history of the 1992 Los Angeles race riots to which the end of *San Andreas* actually refers. So if, as this argument contends, "the game's aesthetic merit extends chiefly from an understanding of its spaces in terms of the aesthetics of the urban environments being referenced"[122] and "understanding the constitution of this space is crucial to accounting for the player's lingering experience of the game's unique narrative format,"[123] then understanding Los Angeles—and, by extension, Los Santos—as a racialized geography is paramount in a discussion of the space in the game. Suddenly, the geometric division of Los Santos into racial gang territories, the multicultural alliances required to beat the game, and the inability of scholars to describe the cultural landscape of Los Santos without mentioning its racial characteristics[124] come into much sharper focus.

No scholarship is neutral, and as critics like Roderick Ferguson and Sara Ahmed[125] have demonstrated, the academy has an extended history of anchoring hegemony even as certain disciplines attempt to modify cultural structures of power from within. Failing to account for these histories in the formation of a new discipline risks reinforcing this trend. The example of *GTA* scholarship in the game studies corpus is an extreme one chosen to show how postracial and postfeminist ideology can easily spread in a discipline still forming an identity, even when ignoring the racialized and gendered politics of a game series is ultimately detrimental to the work produced. This accounting was not to suggest that no work on race and gender in *Grand Theft Auto* has been done, but it is a mere few teaspoons (to use *Shakesville*'s terminology) in the greater pool of writing produced about this most influential of game series. It is a symptom, rather than the cause, of game studies' lingering unease with feminist and critical race critique. The processes that contributed to this condition remain largely unremarked upon, perhaps out of a sense of professional courtesy (or fear of professional reprisal),[126] or perhaps because the nature of academic discourse is to promote the illusion of impartiality by obscuring the interpersonal dynamics that structure the work that we do. Whatever the case, the fear of the angry feminist in game studies results in the perpetuation of racism and sexism in our conversations in ways similar in structure and effect, if not in tone or fervor, to what happened in the wake of Dickwolves and #GamerGate.

Conclusion: When Dickwolves Storm the Ivory Tower

In this chapter, I have put fan and academic border wars in conversation with one another in order to demonstrate how the kinds of boundary policing that occur in various gaming communities share common origins (an anxiety about being taken seriously as folks who take video games seriously), strategies (invoking the trope of the angry feminist to dismiss political critique) and outcomes (the creation of a hostile environment for marginalized individuals and thus the perpetuation of white supremacist cisheteropatriarchy). These commonalities are important for a number of reasons. First, they dispel the illusion that academic critique, despite its seeming distance from the emotional turmoil of fandom, is innocent of hostile emotional posturing. Second, they encourage us to attend to the structures, rather than the affects per se, of boundary-defining conversations. Lastly, they emphasize that we are not doing scholarship in a vacuum: many of us may feel safely ensconced within the proverbial ivory tower, but the problems facing gamers are not abstractions—they are real and immediate for members of the game studies community as well. Gamer trouble—here, the violent misogyny and abject racism of fan communities and industry productions—does not go away when we don't write about it. We also cannot write about it without positioning ourselves within it, and doing such political scholarship takes training, humility, and practice—what Sal Humphreys calls being a "self-reflexive" researcher.[127]

Ultimately, our future may depend on such work, because trouble has come home to roost. In 2014, as #GamerGate was in full swing, the Digital Games Research Association (DiGRA) found itself at the center of an internet conspiracy theory claiming feminists were using the organization's international influence to take over the video game industry with the aid of the United States government. Shira Chess, Mia Consalvo, Adrienne Shaw, and T. L. Taylor, all notable scholars doing feminist work in game studies, became targets of internet mobs affiliated with the #GamerGate hashtag as a result of this theory. The trouble started when #GamerGate operatives discovered a public Google Doc full of notes from a fishbowl-style panel about feminism and game studies hosted at the DiGRA conference by Chess and Shaw. A conspiracist known on YouTube as Sargon of Akkad, a prominent figure in the #GamerGate community, eventually listed past and current members of the DiGRA board in order to classify them as either legitimate "academic" or illegitimate "feminist" researchers.[128] Feminist game studies scholars on Twitter responded by uniting under the hashtag #AcademicAndFeminist, where they were joined by other academic feminists across the disciplines. In later reflections, Chess and Shaw describe facing questions about whether the fishbowl panel leading to the DiGRA conspiracy was worth the attention and harassment it brought to members of the organization, some of whom seemed to side with #GamerGate against the feminist colleagues in their midst.[129] Given that the panel attempted to address the isolation of feminist scholarship from mainstream game studies thirteen years from the birth of the discipline, their answer is a resounding yes.[130]

Though the bifurcation of "academic" and "feminist" appears in the context of a conspiracy designed to intimidate the women writing about video games and feminism in an academic context, it captures the core of the division that I have been tracing throughout this chapter: feminist knowledge production is always seen as operating outside of legitimate modes of interpretation and communication, whether the context is fannish or professional. This is, indeed, the function of the trope of the angry feminist: to kick actual feminists out of a conversation in favor of a cultural construction that stands in for the absurdity and irrationality of feminist critique. Sometimes, feminism isn't even called by name and instead becomes projected onto the bodies of dissenting folks that happen to be nearby: the killjoy that introduces bad feelings to a conversation. With Dickwolves and #GamerGate, the killjoys stand in for the censoring forces attempting to take the fun out of gaming culture. With ludology versus narratology, killjoys haunt the anxious encounters between culture and procedure. With *GTA* scholarship, killjoys threaten the sanctity of a cultural medium just coming into its own. With all of these, the effort to position feminist thought outside of the norms of conversation has the additional effect of discouraging women, people of color, and others from participating in these conversations.

Chess and Shaw indicate relief that the fishbowl panel never produced a manifesto, as one of its attendees suggested: "Perhaps this is for the best—manifestos are so often full of anger and ire, and only speak to [a] specific, insider audience."[131] This sentiment is understandable in the context of a conflict that felt like an eternal shouting match with no end in sight, but as a conciliatory gesture, it also internalizes the illegitimate logic of the trope of the angry feminist, to whom no one will listen, we are told, if they (we) don't stop shouting. Yet if we've learned anything from the lives and practices of the rowdy social justice blogosphere and feminist academics struggling for legitimacy, we know that whether feminists are angry and shouty or logical and polite, whether they soothe the guilt of their interlocutors or stomp all over the things that make them happy, they will likely still face policing and harassment from inside and outside of their own communities. As so many feminists have shown us over and over again, sometimes anger and ire is the only available—and only appropriate—response.

2

Making a Face

Quantizing Reality in Character Animation and Customization

Between the masks we've internalized, one on top of the
other, are our interfaces. The masks are already steeped with
self-hatred and other internalized oppressions. However, it
is the place—the interface—between the masks that provides
the space from which we can thrust out and crack the masks.
—Gloria Anzaldúa,
Making Face, Making Soul / Haciendo Caras

The fantasies enabled by video games would not be possible without
the animation and customization technologies that bring them to life.
Yet even compared to the lifelike spectacle of older digital Hollywood
blockbusters like *Avatar* (2009), the computer animation powering the
visual scenes of cutting-edge video games like *Assassin's Creed: Odyssey*
(2018) is lacking in fidelity and emotional impact, and for good reason: they represent similar approaches that serve quite different ends.
One approach, prerendered animation, is destined for a film reel or
static video file. Animators in this format have ample time and machine
power to finesse, composite, and process the final images. Real-time animation, on the other hand, requires the machine to calculate and render
the separate visual components like movement and lighting as software
runs, allowing the user to move around, control camera angles, and otherwise play with a scene. It is the technique most complementary to the
active nature of video games, but it is process-intensive and limited by
hardware power and the efficiency of the algorithms programmed in the
background. In the late 1990s, the use of prerendered animation in video
games like the *Final Fantasy* series reached its peak. By alternating
gameplay with these "cutscenes," the games industry seemed to suffer
from what critics at the time called "cinema envy."[1] Although cutscenes

still play an important role in video game storytelling today, real-time animation is the standard, allowing developers to integrate narrative more seamlessly into the player's gaming experience.

It is a truism that the video game industry continuously strives for increased photorealism in its digital representations. In contrast to computer animation in the film industry, which is dominated by the cartoonish aesthetics of Pixar, Disney, and DreamWorks,[2] top sellers in video games utilize gritty realism to represent the world. Franchises like *FIFA World Cup*, *Call of Duty*, *Assassin's Creed*, and *Elder Scrolls* all represent very different types of narrative and gameplay universes, but they all share the same dedication to photorealistic graphics. Developers and journalists often cast graphical fidelity as key to sophisticated performance and storytelling,[3] forever predicting the arrival of a future when technology will unlock the secret to making digital animation indistinguishable from real life so that video games can operate with the same emotional complexity as film. Cinema envy, it seems, can take many different forms.

In order to create these stunning visual representations, computers first needed to learn how to draw objects and people. Today, I can use a tool like Blender or Maya to create and manipulate three-dimensional objects within a visual frame that simplifies all calculations under the surface: I use mouse and keyboard commands to create, sculpt, paint, reorient, and otherwise bring these virtual objects as close to my creative vision as I am able. These interfaces are designed to fit within a continuum of analog and digital art tools for the user's sake, which helps me feel as if I am manipulating clay or painting with a brush. However, the objects I create using these programs do not share everything in common with their predecessors, and these material differences have important implications for the way we think about digital images.

Jacob Gaboury, a historian and theorist of computer animation, argues that contemporary three-dimensional digital images have separate material and ontological genealogies from other visual media and must be regarded according to their own specific conditions. While two-dimensional digital and analog art operate within a regime of visuality primarily concerned with making things visible in particular ways, Gaboury points out that a computer's knowledge of three-dimensional objects is vastly more comprehensive and requires its programmers primarily to grapple with how to make what should be invisible disappear from view.[4] Technologically, this means that 3D rendering begins as an assortment of objects with extraneous spatial and compositional data that must be flattened and reduced in order to simulate the two-dimensional screen-based view intended for the human eye. Metaphorically, however, what computer scientists have called the *hidden surface problem* "functions as an analogy for computational materiality itself, or more accurately the computer's disavowal of its own materiality through the black boxing effect of the interface."[5] This concealment, which I understand as a form of masking as I move forward in the chapter, is fundamental to the way that contemporary digital media operate at the level of computation and also at the level of politics.

From the perspective of an end user, the black box is a welcome phenomenon that obscures the complicated functions that turn the smooth surface of a smartphone into a sophisticated computer interface, for example. Very few users need or desire to see these processes in action. My own grappling with 3D creation software would be much more unpleasant if I needed to calculate the dimensions of my object at various viewing angles, and it would certainly restrict the pool of people who could create digital 3D art. However, the convenience and seeming simplicity of contemporary digital devices also mask a host of other material troubles that allow the global tech industry to operate smoothly: devastating environmental consequences,[6] gross labor violations,[7] and deep military ties[8] all underwrite our most treasured and seemingly innocent technologies. My experience with my smartphone is forever changed by my knowledge of the human rights and environmental consequences of coltan mining, and this serves as an unpleasant disruption in the otherwise seamless envelope around myself and this particular device. And yet convenience often wins out over conscience, returning me to the simplicity of my screen and its stimulating images.

In this chapter, I am going to trouble the slick surfaces of computer-generated images in order to recapture their sublimated content—what must become invisible in order to preserve the fantasy of cutting-edge technology that moves ever in the direction of progress. Jacqueline Wernimont urges us to be aware of the ways that quantum media, those technologies that break human subjects down into calculable chunks, always serve the interests of the ruling class, from the organizational technologies of colonialism to the self-recording pedometers and smartphones of the present.[9] I wish to extend this logic to animation and avatar customization. I argue that as each subsequent generation of games pushes its representations into higher polygon counts and more sophisticated lighting algorithms, their fundamental dependence on the mathematical rendering of the human body masks a deep connection to "scientific" understandings of race and gender that anchor our most contemporary technology in the racist regimes of our not-so-distant history. These are what D. Fox Harrell would call the phantasms that lurk and emerge as "computational media play roles in constructing ideas that we unconsciously accept as true and constitutive of reality yet are in fact imaginatively grounded constructions based in particular worldviews."[10] They give the racism and sexism of the past a new, more palatable life in the present.

To explore this phenomenon, I begin by examining the masking technologies of motion-capture animation, which record the data of certain bodies and map them to others, simultaneously deflecting and reaffirming the importance of racial and gender identity in digital performance. Next, I situate these technologies within a history of the racial science of physiognomy, a method of weaponizing the face by reading personality traits like intelligence or temperament onto its features. Finally, I examine avatar creation interfaces to determine how our quantized understanding of the human face results in a politics that reestablishes white masculinity as the center of subjectivity and where we can look to break through these masks and create our own politics. My focus on the digital human face throughout this chapter emphasizes the connections among identity, politics, and technology that flow through our entertainment technologies.

"Kara": Imitation, Race, and Becoming Human

Quantic Dream's short film "Kara" debuted in March 2012 to demonstrate the real-time animation capabilities of the company's new game engine for the PlayStation 3. The film opens with robotic factory arms assembling a white android woman as a man offscreen instructs her to perform a series of speaking and movement tests. After successfully establishing her functionality, Kara demonstrates a self-awareness and willfulness that alarm her tester, who declares her defective and begins to disassemble her. As the factory arms dismantle Kara limb from limb, she begs for her life, promising not to cause trouble. The animation reaches its climax when Kara is reduced to nothing but a head and torso, her scream of "I'm scared!" halting the progress of her dismemberment. The operator, his sympathy finally provoked, reinitiates the assembly process as a close-up of her face reveals two tears rolling realistically down her cheeks. He tells Kara to join her unaware sister androids and asks her not to make any trouble. She thanks him and steps on the platform to be boxed up, a flash of uncertainty and contemplation in her eyes as the scene fades out.

"Kara" was meant to demonstrate animation technology that surpassed the limitations of what roboticist Masahiro Mori in 1970 called the *uncanny valley*—a level of anthropomorphic detail in robots (later applied to computer-generated images) that is quite close to reproducing a human likeness but not close enough to make humans feel at ease with it. With each successive generation of Pixar movies, video game consoles, and animation techniques, pundits and fans declare the valley one step closer to being leveled. Quantic Dream's demo was no different, with expert industry animators such as Jonathan Cooper applauding the level of emotion the company captured and reproduced in the piece.[11]

The technical feat of Quantic Dream's accomplishments in visual fidelity and realistic lip-synching mirrors the technical feat of Kara, an android that demonstrates the capacity to think independently and wonder about her own existence, but that they center on a lone white woman is no accident. The short story arc of "Kara" foregrounds how an experience of uncanniness in technology is closely related to cultural expectations of identity: Kara only upsets the quality control technician once she deviates from her programmed performance of femininity. The script is heavy-handed in this regard, beginning with Kara's initialization speech: "Hello, I am a third-generation AX400 android. I can look after your house, do the cooking, mind the kids. I organize your appointments. I speak three hundred languages, and I am entirely at your disposal as a sexual partner. No need to feed me or recharge me. I am equipped with a quantic battery that makes me autonomous for 173 years. Do you want to give me a name?" As the scene approaches its climax, the operator begins to call the android by affectionate but gendered nicknames like "honey" and "baby" that gesture to a time in which white women not unlike Kara in appearance and demeanor were celebrated as housewives and secretaries. The process of disassembly plays out as an unsettling but stereotypical sequence of sexual violence: the forceful removal of clothing, the restraint of limbs, the cutting up of her body into pieces, the begging and pleading and tears, the gratitude and promises of obedience in return for being released in one piece (see figure 2.1).

Feminist critics have written about Alan Turing's early thought experiments on artificial intelligence and their destabilizing implications for categories of identity like gender. Turing's inclusion of gender as a "control model" for his famous test misses "the obvious connection between gender and computer intelligence: both are in fact imitative systems, and the boundaries between female and male . . . are as unclear and as unstable as the boundary between human and machine intelligence."[12] These permeable boundaries form the basis of postmodern cyberfeminism, a project that has been expanded and updated by theorist-practitioners like micha cárdenas, whose theory and practice of the transreal allows for identity that crosses from real to virtual bodies, from technology to biology, and from species to species.[13] In this context, the instabilities of Kara-as-android, Kara-as-woman, and Kara-as-animation-demo merge

Figure 2.1. Robots disassembling Kara. "Kara" (Quantic Dream, 2012). Screenshot by author.

with Kara-as-performer, for the real magic behind the cutting edge of contemporary computer animation technology is not the ability to generate the illusion of life purely from an artist's imagination and skill; it is the ability to train computers to accurately reproduce the performance of a human actor captured on camera.

In the supposedly postracial climate of the early 2010s, the use of a white woman as the face of a fight for subjectivity and freedom displaces the racial implications of the android's narrative. Her performance in front of quality control, read in a different light, can recall American histories of Black bodies performing on the auction block, her request for a name by her new owner an invocation of the name changes (and power of naming) that also attended enslavement. Kara's primary complaint, in fact, is not that she is expected to perform domestic and sexual duties in her life but that she is "a sort of merchandise." Black feminists such as Hazel Carby and Patricia Hill Collins have exposed how the ideals of white womanhood, particularly of the domestic type to which Kara is assigned, rely on the invisible labor of Black and brown women to sustain them. Read alongside their work, the blinding whiteness of this tech demo is more than just an attempt at simulating more realistic lighting. Indeed, Kara's whiteness is the invocation of white womanhood as the universal sympathetic victim, supplanting historical realism (performance on an auction block) for the emotional realism of the damsel in distress.

While the story of Kara eventually inspired the 2018 game *Detroit: Become Human*, at the time, the developers insisted there were no future plans to develop this animation demo into a game. Tech demos are isolated texts with no direct monetary value in the form of admission sales or rental fees. While demonstrations of in-game footage may feature the white man protagonists of their stories, some of the most high-profile proof-of-concept demos and short-form landmarks in the industry feature the animated faces of women. In 2008, Image Metrics, a company pioneering facial animation techniques that did not rely on expensive camera rigs or the time-intensive process of placing markers on an actor's face, went viral with a series of videos starring Emily O'Brien; the actress proclaimed herself the "new face of animation" as a result of her work with the company. Two years before that, Quantic Dream released "The Casting," an animation of an actress who auditions with a monologue about deciding to kill her husband instead of committing suicide after discovering his affair; offscreen voices assess her afterward as talented but too old for the part. Björk's 1999 music video for "All Is Full of Love," in which computer graphics company Glassworks animated the singer's face onto white android bodies (not unlike Kara's), was a music industry landmark that won numerous awards for its special effects. This tradition of women's faces in animation, in fact, goes all the way back to the roots of the technology: Frederic Parke, one of the earliest pioneers in computer animation, created the first three-dimensional animated face based on his assistant, a woman, in 1972.[14] Like any other medium that uses models or performers, these digital representations are grounded in the flesh-and-blood bodies of the women that inspire their creation.

Searching the record of facial animation demos from prominent companies, one finds few nonwhite faces in the crowd. Those that exist fetishize their difference: a tribal Samburu warrior head animated by Image Metrics (based on a recording of an endorsement read by a Black Haitian American actor) or the head of a Black man animated by Cubic Motion to the audio of a speech by John F. Kennedy.[15] These technology demos, while meant simply to demonstrate the capability of software systems for capturing and rendering realistic human faces, ultimately require the cultural interpretation of those faces to legitimize their messages: an artificial woman's face emoting real distress, a tribal face ironically endorsing high-tech software, a Black face speaking with the voice of the white man credited with advancing institutional racial equality in the United States. These productions are technologically impressive because of the way they "strategically conflate notions of realism and authenticity" in an effort to create a lifelike digital performance, relying on the relationship between performer and image to produce a sense of graphical fidelity.[16]

As one of the most densely packed sites of information exchange on the human body, faces are particularly difficult to replicate with accuracy and are subject to fraught histories of power and politics. When engineers and artists take on the task of creating faces in a digital context, decisions made in the name of efficiency, function, or style inevitably inflect the cultural and political implications of the resulting representation. The examples outlined above begin to illuminate this phenomenon.

They also begin to illuminate what Hoelzl and Marie characterize as the twenty-first-century quest to render the world in calculation, a condition brought forth by the digital image and the reach of computers into everyday life.[17] The digital faces on display in computer animation and gaming avatars emerge from a logic of realism that is based in calculation and meticulous measurements, a realism structured by the promise that numbers can capture and transmit the otherwise incalculable essence of human facial expression. The remainder of this chapter will interrogate this promise, situate it within a deeper history of facial calculations, and examine how numbers insulate digital techniques from political accountability, reinvigorating centuries-old practices of racism and sexism within our most contemporary technologies.

Measuring the Face

Quantization is a term that refers to constraining an object into a discrete set of units. It can refer to any type of measurement but has particular significance in the context of digital media. Quantization is necessary for computers to understand and manipulate any kind of data, from population statistics to complicated 3D models. Any analog to digital conversion involves quantization, since digital formats at their core function as discrete sets of ones and zeros, while objects and images in the physical world do not. File compression also involves different strategies of quantization, from simple rounding algorithms to more complicated functions that, for example, eliminate audiovisual information that humans are unlikely to detect in a media file. While it enables rapid calculation and transmission of different types of data, it is important to recognize that quantization reduces the complexity of these data and silos them into a computational logic that historically serves the convenience of the ones writing the algorithms.

Digitization is not the first time that scientists and artists have found it necessary to quantize the face. The ancient practice of physiognomy, which interpreted an individual's personality traits and temperament based on their facial characteristics, experienced a revitalization in the eighteenth and nineteenth centuries owing partly to the application of Enlightenment principles of objectivity and the scientific method. Johann Kaspar Lavater's essays on physiognomy were originally published in German in the 1770s, but within forty years of its publication, fifty-five different versions of his work had been released in the major European languages. Crucially, the success of physiognomy, like computer animation, was also rooted in a fascination with realistic imaging technologies: the rapid spread of physiognomy was in part due to the quality and number of portraits used to illustrate Lavater's volumes, which were difficult to find at such prices at the time.[18] Physiognomy was a science that resonated widely with individuals, and its ubiquity all over the world is marked in literature and the arts. In the wake of Lavater's writings, Romantic novelists applied physiognomic principles to the design of their characters,[19] while painters in the late eighteenth and early nineteenth centuries began to study physiognomy to improve their craft.[20] These creators leveraged the power of "science" to create more compelling art.

More importantly, the science of faces served as a social facilitator to form community based on notions of Otherness. Recoding physiognomy in the scientific mode was an important stepping-stone in the development of what Sharrona Pearl calls "shared subjectivity," enabling Victorians to make communal connections over what were formerly individual observations about the people around them.[21] Physiognomic measurements lent an air of truth to these prejudices: if it can be measured consistently, it must be real. The progression to scientific racism, founded on a growing sense of nationalism in the period, was not far off. In Pearl's account, for example, the popular proliferation of physiognomy contributed to the differentiation of otherwise visually indistinct minorities such as Irish Catholics and Jews in political caricature. Indeed, even Lavater's original work on physiognomy appealed to the self-evidence of racial and national biases to prove its truth: "Calm reason revolts at the supposition that Newton or Leibnitz ever could have the countenance and appearance of an idiot, incapable of a firm step, a meditating eye . . . that one of these in the brain of a Laplander conceived his Theodicea; and that the other in the head of an Esquimaux, who wants the power to number further than six, and affirms all beyond to be innumerable, had dissected the rays of light, and weighed worlds."[22] Scientific racism advanced with later treatises about racial difference by writers like Arthur, comte de Gobineau, and the development of pseudosciences like phrenology.[23] Such processes concretized the face as a weapon of oppression within the developing logic of modernity.

Charles Darwin sought to unravel whether facial expressions signified across cultures and species. His 1872 work, *The Expression of the Emotions in Man and Animals*, criticized the unscientific nature of physiognomy, instead praising the work done by contemporary anatomists like Charles Bell and Guillaume-Benjamin Duchenne in unlocking the mechanics of the face. Darwin was particularly inspired by the works of Duchenne, who, among his other contributions to the science of anatomy, created a famous gallery of facial expressions in which he stimulated muscle groups with electricity in order to isolate and document which muscles were responsible for particular expressions. Parts of Duchenne's gallery of faces were incorporated into *Expression*, and Darwin showed others to various colleagues in order to document their description of the stimulated emotions. Instead of trying to figure out the moral character of individuals like his predecessor Lavater did, Darwin was interested in rooting out similarities not only among the "distinct races of man" but between human facial expressions and those made by animals. Such "true" expressions suggested to Darwin the underlying unity of human and animal behavior; in exposing this interspecies similarity, the face was yet another way for him to prove the process of natural selection.[24] Darwin's quest to ascertain commonality of origin could have been a key step in erasing the racist ideologies put in place after hundreds of years of colonization. Instead, the appropriation of the face by science was used to further enable the ruling elite to classify and separate human beings based on physical characteristics.

Perhaps the most notorious institutional application of physiognomic and pseudoscientific understandings of the human face came in the twentieth century with the rise of the Nazi Party in Germany. Physiognomic practice was a cornerstone of German philosophical traditions in general and the racist policies of the Nazis in particular; the very proliferation of physiognomic thought and its attendant disciplined gaze "helped the Nazi leadership congeal the German populace into a community of self-policing, spectatorial subjects able to stylize itself as the 'master race.'"[25] Although the subtitle of Lavater's work suggested that he aimed to promote "Human Understanding and Human Love," Richard Gray notes that the volume included early empirical assessment of Jewish and other groups' physiognomies and moral characters,[26] a trend that continued in the work of phrenologists Franz Josef Gall and

Carl Gustav Carus before becoming fully developed in writings by racial anthropologists Hans F. K. Günther and Ludwig Clauss in the 1920s
and '30s. Other state-sponsored eugenics programs existed in the United
States and Europe at the time, but Nazi Germany's atrocities against its
own citizens have come to symbolize the terrible dehumanizing power of
science in the twentieth century. The German fascination with physiognomy in the preceding centuries was no small coincidence.

Making Masks

While numbers by themselves seem to be neutral, this brief history of
physiognomy demonstrates the ease with which numerical data about
humans can be put to use to serve those who control the data. We might
think of quantization as a type of *lenticular logic*, which Tara McPherson
describes as the "logic of the fragment or the chunk, a way of seeing
the world as discrete modules or nodes, a mode that suppresses relation and context."[27] While the chunking of quantization is not the same
chunking as McPherson's lenticular postcards, it has the related effect of
rendering the face apart from its political and cultural context. In addition, quantization necessarily reduces the complexity of the measured
object, morphing crystal-clear images into the jaggy blocks of a JPEG.
This happens both literally and figuratively: animation's uncanny valley might also be understood as a problem of information resolution.
Any quantized face may be said to be a compressed version of its whole,
instrumentalized for some particular purpose. The numerical values of
a face, taken in isolation, may indeed yield useful information for those
who study it, from forensic anthropologists to visual artists. However, it
is important to keep in mind whose convenience these measurements
serve, and for what purposes the techniques for gathering them are
being developed.

Computers, which make manipulating numbers even easier, have
contributed to the wider reach of such data collection. Facial recognition
technologies, a growing part of governmental surveillance programs, operate on the same principles as many visually based motion-capture systems like Image Metrics, for example. Theorists like Simone Browne and
Shoshana Magnet have elaborated on their relation to biopower and racism.[28] Faces under the machinic gaze are no longer simply the window

into individual moral character, inborn human nature, or the divine; they have become a seemingly inescapable tool of population control, an efficient means for monitoring large groups of people. From the CCTV networks of cities like London or Tampa to the intake processes of US Customs and Border Protection, the digital facial image is a widespread tool of panoptic surveillance. Artists like Zach Blas have made conceptual media interventions on the politics of facial recognition and physiognomy: in response to research suggesting that observers could visually identify gay men by their face, his Fag Face project mathematically combines the faces of fags, terrorists, criminals, illegals, activists, and other undesirables of society into machine-unreadable, inhuman masks that can be exported to a 3D printer and worn for political action.[29] Adam Harvey developed the Computer Vision Dazzle project, a lookbook of antisurveillance hair and makeup fashions for everyday wear.[30] Such work underscores how even though scientists and technologists endorse the persistent belief in physiognomy as benign, there are grave repercussions for the most vulnerable members of society, many of whom suffer more under regimes of hypervisibility and recognition.

Similar problems attend facial quantization for the purposes of representation rather than recognition. Part art, part engineering, part scientific observation, the act of producing moving digital faces is no longer new in computer science, but it continues to sustain great interest and investment. Pioneered by scientists like Parke, who created both the first computerized facial model and the first computer-animated face at the University of Utah in the early 1970s, computer facial animation has become quite important for industries ranging from entertainment to advertising, military to medicine, education to law enforcement. The drive for photorealism in the early development of computer animation came from its military and entertainment applications, which inspired and funded early research in the field,[31] placing specific priorities on the direction of development.

With computer facial animation, much like any artistic practice, realistic representation begins and ends with the surface image. Parke created the first facial animations from a mask of polygons based on photographs of lines mapped onto a woman assistant's face, calculating the minimum number of shapes "good enough to achieve realistic facial motion."[32] These images were hollow: the first animation demo produced from this work, created by Parke and Ed Catmull, allows the camera to navigate into the interior of an animated hand, emphasizing its glove-like structure before moving onto footage of a digitally animated face.[33] Later animation technologies incorporated complicated simulations of skeletal and muscular structures, only recently to fall back on the surface of the face with sophisticated motion-capture technologies that read video footage in order to animate. Stephen Platt and Norman Badler are credited with introducing a conceptual model for simulating some internal structures of the face to achieve more realistic animation effects in 1981,[34] though this is a concept that nondigital visual artists have understood for centuries.

Perhaps unsurprisingly, the drive for the realistic face ultimately loops back to the nineteenth-century scientists discussed earlier in this chapter; in particular, Parke's animation textbooks begin with a reproduction of charts of facial expressions and corresponding muscle groups gleaned from Duchenne's facial stimulation experiments and a brief discussion of Darwin's work in *Expressions*. Many practitioners also refer back to the work of specific texts like *Gray's Anatomy*, a widely used and frequently updated anatomy handbook first written by a contemporary to both Darwin and Duchenne.[35] The sciences of faces and facial expressions, with all of their problematic assumptions about human nature and the historical baggage of racism and sexism that comes along with them, underwrite much of the training and development of computer facial animation techniques. Occasionally these histories surface in the discourse.

Patricia Beckmann-Wells and Scott Wells's *Face It: A Visual Reference for Multi-ethnic Facial Modeling*, demonstrates what happens when the logic of facial quantization meets contemporary demands for realism. The book, which has the admirable goal of helping developers reduce the racial homogeneity of their character representations, reads more like a physiognomic treatise from the nineteenth century than a technical manual for artists. Its illustrations include a gallery of skulls and corresponding measurements from around the world, photographic portraits of individuals with their age and country of origin listed alongside an artist's representation of the face with cranial measurements, and a world map that groups scores of ethnicities together under continental labels.[36] The desire for realism seems here more of an imperative to evoke, for example, a sense of "Africanness" in a consumer for whom the discursive idea of Africa, rather than a knowledge of the continent's specific cultures or peoples, has a particular meaning. This meaning is conveyed through the use of numerical values that purport to communicate some truth of the faces they describe.

Curiously, those who endorse these quantitative methods often do so after distancing themselves from their utility. Parke and Keith Waters acknowledge that male and female skulls are very similar to one another,[37] while Ryan Kingslien admits that he "knows" forensic scientists often find it difficult to identify the sex of a skull.[38] Beckmann-Wells and Wells expound for several paragraphs about the racist history of "typography" and the scientific evidence refuting the belief that facial traits differ significantly from one racial group to the next.[39] Bodies do not fit cleanly into the identity categories that we create to classify them. Indeed, skeletal variations by gender and race are so minute as to be negligible to all but the trained eye, which is the reason experts like osteologists even exist. This is the paradox of the quantization of the human: absolute differences are difficult to measure and minimal at best, but they provide such a compelling account of deeply held beliefs ("I can identify a person's race and gender by looking at them") that use of these data is irresistible. In the face even of personal beliefs to the contrary, individuals like Parke, Kingslien, and Beckmann-Wells act in their capacity as educators to provide students with a desired knowledge: how to create convincing ("realistic") representations of gender and race, as measured by popular understandings that are bolstered by quantitative data.

This is a problem that is somewhat unique to the digital creative arts, which frequently seek to create visual representations of unique faces rather than a one to one correspondence to an actual person's face, all under the pressures of photorealism. Unlocking the "truth" of facial representation occurs at the point of contact between analog and digital: physical measurements. Quantizing the face, however, glosses over details on a finer scale that computer graphics researchers continue to pursue: pores, pimples, wrinkles, hair textures, tiny asymmetries. Running ever-smaller fine-toothed combs over the data may yield impressive images, but the greater test of these convincing representations comes when they are finally put into motion. Lev Manovich explains that "the idea of illusionism has been connected with the success in representation of certain subjects," such as grapes and human skin in Western painting or "moving nature" in media of motion, noting that the field of computer graphics has taken up the challenges both of skin and of nature in motion over the course of its development.[40] Echoing this sentiment, Mori postulated that adding motion to robotic design would exaggerate the curves of the uncanny valley, inducing more intense positive and negative emotions when presented to a human observer.

Though computer animators shifted from emphasizing surface structures of the face to simulating its interior, contemporary innovations in animation technology have returned to the surface once again, using recorded footage of live actors to drive facial animation rigs—digital models of faces with points of articulation that can be moved by an animator to create expressions and speech. Facial rigs incorporate the internal physical simulations of muscles and skeletons and external simulation of skin textures in order to deform the face realistically in response to its moving parts, but their cues from performance capture data act purely at the surface. As Manovich predicted, the proof of reality in this digital medium is intimately tied to motion: the movement of lips, the fluttering of eyelashes, the trail of a tear as it rolls down a cheek. Early performance capture researcher Lance Williams reported the success of his performance-driven animation technique to capture eye blinks and other "lifelike twitches and secondary motions which would be unlikely to arise in pure animation."[41] Even full performance capture, pioneered by James Cameron's team for *Avatar* and streamlined in the "Kara" demo, is based on the notion that the unity of corporeal motion—face, body, and voice captured together—is what makes a performance "real."[42]

But these proofs of reality are not necessarily tied to the detailed reproduction of the likeness of a person, and this is part of what makes the process animation—the production of illusion—rather than cinema. At least four different women played the role of Kara in the demo I discussed at the beginning of the chapter: Valorie Curry, the actress whose performance in English was the basis for Kara through most of the scene; Karen Gansk Wallet, who performed Kara's German and French speaking parts; Hanako Danjo, who sang Kara's Japanese song; and an uncredited body double who helped block and rehearse the choreography for the scene (see figure 2.2). This composite performance is quite different from cutaway glimpses at body doubles in film, since the contributions of the other performers are meant to remain in full view of the audience. Curry's face is the model for Kara, and the other actors wear her like a mask in their portions of the scene, thanks to the technology that enables their performances to be retargeted to the rig based on Curry herself. Such masking of identity is standard in animated features, with actors lending their voices to the images created by visual artists. These practices have long resulted in gender or race swapping in animated films and video games. One notable example of this is the Black voice actor T. C. Carson cast as the fantasy Greek hero Kratos in the *God of War* series, a character who is known as the "Ghost of Sparta" and renowned for the paleness of his skin. Motion-capture technology has the power to streamline the covering up of identity in new ways, creating assemblages cobbled together from multiple performers to create a single fictional individual.

As with any masking practice, the potential of this technology to create new opportunities for performers is very powerful; in Carson's case, the necessity for extremely pale skin did not prevent his participation as the lead in the highly successful *God of War* series. However, this ability also offers opportunities for whitewashing in the entertainment

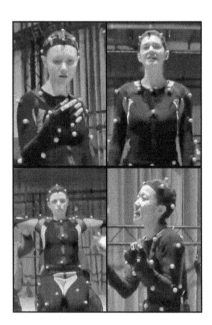

Figure 2.2. Actors who played Kara. Clockwise from top left: Valorie Curry, Karen Gansk Wallet, Hanako Danjo, unnamed body double. "The Making of 'Kara'" (Quantic Dream, 2012). Screenshots by author.

industry, which already prefers lighter-colored skin even in nonwhite performers. Scholars like Richard Dyer have revealed how technological developments, such as cinematic and photographic cameras and lighting techniques, occur in response to the way whiteness is valued by content creators; concealing the less marketable faces of nonwhite actors behind digital masks might be seen as a natural extension of this. The discussion of "Kara" at the beginning of this chapter, for example, pointed out how her identity as a white woman was central to the function and meaning of the demo, and the requirement for fluency in other languages did not prompt the director to cast the French Japanese actress Danjo, for example, as Kara. In fact, neither Danjo nor Wallet are officially credited for their contributions to the short film, although they appear in its behind-the-scenes documentary.[43] Far more than the realistic tears of its central figure, the real technical achievement of "Kara" was the ability to seamlessly stitch together the performances of multiple individuals to create the illusion that a white woman could speak a number of European languages and perform a traditional Japanese lullaby with native fluency, thereby masking the contributions of her coperformers.

Digital animation complicates the relationship between face and body in somewhat paradoxical ways. On the one hand, artistic techniques and animation pedagogy collapse face into body, deferring to quantitative notions of what makes a face a face and what differentiates any one face from another. On the other hand, the use of digital facial animation to bring characters to life based on live-action performances also separates face from body in a way that threatens to dissolve the ties between performance and embodiment. This is, in some ways, a postmodern dream come true: the ultimate confirmation that all identity is constructed, that any individual can wear any mask and put on a convincing show. However, as critics like N. Katherine Hayles, Lisa Nakamura, and Wendy Chun have shown, the promise of the digital to completely blank out identity can never actually be fulfilled and in fact often executes quite the opposite work in culture. The masked status of the performers working behind these carefully designed facades attests to this. At the beginning of this section, I suggested that animation's uncanny valley is a matter of information resolution, which might suggest that the solution is technical. However, pursuing and showcasing technical solutions without regard to the historical practices of the field is more likely to reproduce and reinforce inequalities that already exist. This is the lenticular logic of technological development, the chunking away of technology from culture and the quantization of "progress" into discrete units of measurable advancement. It allows centuries-old methodologies to find new life in our most cutting-edge technologies and fails to prevent the inequalities that attend their assumptions. But as engineers and artists continue to do battle against the uncanny valley, perfecting performance capture and skin textures and photoreactive pupils, Gloria Anzaldúa's wisdom about masks emerges: it is neither in the face nor in the mask, but rather somewhere in between, in which the political work of *haciendo caras* ("making faces") begins.

Making Faces

While the machine-readable face reduces people to barcodes and places them under the power of a biopolitical regime, the machine-reproducible face flattens faces into algorithms and places people under a computational regime of quantization. It is this regime that allows cultural decisions about software to become confused with technological necessity. For example, during an interview in early March 2010, the gaming news site Kotaku asked Gordon Van Dyke, producer of the high-profile war game *Battlefield: Bad Company 2* (2010), why there were no women soldiers in their game. After joking that "girls" in *Battlefield* would be too distracting for his wandering eyes, Van Dyke explained that adding the skeleton models and animation necessary to put women in the game would add too much extra data for the machine to handle.[44] This is a recurring defense in the games industry and was deployed more recently by the makers of *Assassin's Creed: Unity* in 2014 and again in 2019 by Blizzard Entertainment, the makers of *World of Warcraft*, to explain why they added racial diversity to the game fifteen years after launch.[45] Despite the massive creative and technical effort devoted to the realistic replication of weaponry, laws of physics, and destructible environments, it turns out that the development team omitted women avatars from *Battlefield: Bad Company 2* because of strains on computing resources. Such technological decisions, underwritten by cultural biases, structure the interfaces that mask our interactions with technology.

The mask and its power to conceal has been an organizing concept in the chapter to this point, and it is useful here to think about masks not only in their metaphorical capacity as digital images created over the recorded performance of a physical actor or the ways that the black box hides the internal functions and politics of a computational system but in their various literal instantiations as well. Masks can be physical, like the ones produced by Blas and others to confuse facial recognition algorithms; they can be technical, like data filters or image processing overlays (or, indeed, quantizing methods) that help a computer do its job; they can also be descriptive, like the resemblance of a facial map to a mask or the way digital faces can be sculpted by artists or gamers. The interface itself is a mask worn by the computer's internal processes. Questions of interface have been thoroughly explored in digital criticism, but in keeping with this project's overall goal of introducing new voices into conversations about technology, it's time to face Chicana feminist Gloria Anzaldúa, who understands masks as social performances forced specifically on women of color by a society that refuses to recognize the complexity of their identities, constraining faces into recognizable labels. For Anzaldúa, there is power not simply in casting off these masks but in negotiating the space between a face and its masks. She calls this space the "interface," after the layer of cloth used in sewing to reinforce stitching and the structure of garments. As the very sites of contact between enforced identity and the self, interfaces are painful and restrictive, the sources of oppression and regulation of bodies. However, the scars created at the interface also provide structure and strength enough for the face to break free of its masks, to honor the truths the masks create and the lies that they conceal, to negotiate complicated layers of identity forged in the friction between self and oppression. She calls *haciendo una cara* a "metaphor for constructing one's identity," but it is also about the necessity of continuing to move through the world in the face of oppression, to bear and work the masks from within and not lose sight of one's own identity, to embrace the inter/face and expose it to the inter/faces of others.

There is more than just a clever pun between Anzaldúa's interface and the interfaces we recognize in the parlance of digital culture: they are both points of contact between a restrictive hierarchical system and the desire of an operator working with (or within) that system. The digital interface shapes our interactions with the technology it masks much like negotiating the inter/face shapes our interactions with others, and it is often the friction—the trouble—rather than the mask itself that is the most productive site of critique and resistance. I invoke her here in the spirit of imagining new relationships to the quantized face, reaching beyond the study of technology to the work of queer woman of color feminism in order to develop a reparative response to an otherwise bleak technological status quo. *Haciendo caras* in a literal sense can be a political act, performed by Zach Blas's Fag Face mask production or in Mongrel's Colour Separation installation years earlier.[46] What might be considered an avant-garde art practice, however, is also within the reach of average gamers and computer users every day: avatar creation. The remainder of this chapter will explore the connections between the quantization of identity, the construction of avatar customization interfaces, and the possibility of *haciendo caras* with the technologies that are currently at hand.

Customizable avatars offer gamers the opportunity to participate in the creative process of a game's narrative, transforming the protagonist into an image of the gamer's own making. The processes of identification that occur between gamer and avatar are complex and subject to discussion elsewhere in this book, particularly in chapter 4, but it is sufficient here to say that there are as many reasons for customizing an avatar in a particular way as there are gamers.[47] Since the motivations of the users are multifaceted and impossible to predict, an analysis of the customizable avatar yields far more interesting results on a systemic level: rather than what specific avatars emerge, the more pertinent question is what range of possibilities does an avatar creation system enable? How restrictive, exactly, is the interface? In addition to resisting the quantizing impulse that also structures simplistic versions of identity politics, this is an approach suited for broader concerns in game studies, as the set of rules and environments generated for play often seek to create possibility spaces for gamers rather than a linear trajectory or simple narrative for an audience. Ludic spaces call for ludic scholarship, analytical approaches that seek not merely to inhabit and perform within the confines of those spaces but to experiment with them, to bend them, and potentially to break them. Gamers routinely test out the boundaries of gamic systems, whether through virtuosic performances of speed runs through the game, public sharing of glitches and exploits in the code, or creative remixing of game footage to tease out hidden meanings in a text.

In scholarly criticism, such experimentation has precedence in experimental digital humanities methodologies, influenced largely by the set of techniques described by Lisa Samuels and Jerome McGann as "deformance," a term coined through a combination of the concepts of performance and deformation of a text. Although Samuels and McGann trace this type of critical work back to the likes of Dante and Dickinson and provide examples of deformance operations performed on print texts, the operations themselves can be greatly facilitated by computer automation and hence became models for humanities computing techniques. In game studies, these types of experiments have been done by Jeremy Douglass and William Huber in the Software Studies Initiative lab at the University of California, San Diego. Their research employs imaging methods that transform video game screens into blips on large-scale time lines. Huber's work defamiliarizes the visual landscape of games like *Kingdom Hearts* (2002) and *Fatal Frame II* (2003) in order to root out play patterns in player movement and frequency of menu interactions.[48] Organized on a massive scale, the images are unrecognizable except for predominant colors or major screen features that signal scene or game mode changes. Douglass, on the other hand, collapses moving screens into new image formations: time frames, time slices, and time structures. The resulting images are recognizable at first glance, but creating a static image out of moving pictures with an eye for uncovering previously inaccessible patterns is truly an act of deformance.

My practice of *haciendo caras* for this chapter involves testing the limits of avatar interfaces. I categorize this as a new type of deformance in the sense that it is a new technique for academic study, but gamers have been playing with avatar interfaces since they existed. The popular "Monster Factory" video series begun by Justin and Griffin McElroy for the *Polygon* gaming website uses avatar deformance for comedic entertainment.[49] My reasons for understanding it as an academic technique, however, are less about playfulness (although that is an important factor) and more about necessity. Company representatives often find themselves under the discursive binds of economics, corporate secrecy, and lack of experience with the technologies in question, so it is often not useful to take their explanations of how technologies work at face value. Code is not always accessible for study. Deformance methods are particularly useful in these scenarios: pushing at the boundaries of and provoking unexpected behaviors from any software system can reveal a lot about the way it was designed to function. While no two avatar creation systems are alike, there are still similarities that occur across a sufficient number to draw comparisons. Some common features that occur across avatar creation systems include mandatory choice between "male" and "female," slider bars for selecting or altering features, and premade avatars from which the gamer can choose. Some of these features are ideal for deformance operations; slider positions, for example, are easily manipulated to their extreme points to tease out the limits of the system. Default avatar faces can be sorted, compared, and layered on top of one another through image compositing to determine trends revealing cultural assumptions about identity. Gender flexibility can be tested by creating avatars that challenge gender norms.

The prevalence of slider systems in avatar creation is one of the most readily accessible indicators of the quantization of the face in digital media. Some sliders operate on discrete clicks that change the size or position of a particular facial feature. Some sliders map different whole parts (such as nose or hairstyle) to positions on the line. Still others mimic the continuous flow of analog sliders, which mask rather than overcome the logic of quantization. To execute deformance techniques on a concrete example, I chose Bethesda Game Studios' *Fallout 3* (2008) for its complicated facial slider system, organization of avatars by gender and race, and use of contemporary US racial categories: African American, Asian American, Caucasian, and Hispanic. The game's facial slider system, used also in *The Elder Scrolls IV: Oblivion* (2006) and updated for *Fallout: New Vegas* (2010) and *The Elder Scrolls V: Skyrim* (2011), consists of nine categories with thirty-one points of articulation overall. It represents one of the most complicated and flexible avatar facial customization systems in commercial video games, even more than a decade after its release. Fan forums dedicated to helping new users navigate the system to create attractive faces point to the difficulty of achieving a desired result.[50] Manipulating the interface is not easy; one function in particular locks certain sliders to others so that they move in different directions together. In theory, this prevents users from making changes that might warp the facial mesh by, for example, exposing more of the nasal septum than was intended by the designers, resulting in viewing the seams of the skin. In practice, however, it means that results achieved in one part of the face are lost as the user attends to other parts or that facial feature drift results in a face that is quite different from the user's intentions.

Because of the complexity of this facial slider system, it is likely that categories to organize different types of faces exist to facilitate the construction of a desired face. However, the existence of racial categories alone establishes a particular quantization of identity from which the operator cannot escape; while the choice of race or gender may not impact gameplay in a significant manner, it does frame the activities of the avatar within US cultural histories. The categories offered in *Fallout 3* are of particular interest, since they are not traceable to census categories, nor do they attempt to cover the range of racial identifications in existence in the United States at the time of the game's creation. Tanner Higgin suggests that *Fallout 3*'s racial categories induct gamers into the violence of post–World War II institutional racism, befitting the game's chronology, only to fade into the fantasy of a postracial society once the avatar's appearance is finalized and the creation screen goes away.[51]

In a gamic environment, the complexity of race can prove an educational mechanic. In games like *Fallout 3*, however, race is little more than a matter of aesthetics. Although it is produced in the tradition of role-playing series like *The Elder Scrolls*, *Fallout* does not fall into the *Dungeons & Dragons* lineage in which race (often masked as species) carries particular gameplay benefits. While interpretations like Higgin's account for a particular ideology of race that maps onto the surface signifiers of the game's avatar creation system, the absence of mechanics like racial bonuses, which are popular in many fantasy games, conceals how, to borrow Thomas Lamarre's terminology regarding Japanese animation technologies, the gamic machine of *Fallout 3* "thinks" race.[52] *Fallout 3*'s avatar creator simplifies racial identity to a matter of four menu choices. After choosing the character's gender and race, the gamer has the option to choose one of ten default faces created for each set of identities. These default faces vary widely in terms of skin tone, features, and hairstyles, and each is further customizable by the user. Given that sliders control the customization of faces, one way to investigate how the machine has been programmed to think race is to compare slider positions for the default avatar faces and track how the sliders impact the faces differently.

I first did this by maximizing and minimizing the features of an avatar's face in order to discern the limits in place on individual features. This process reveals the extent to which the slider-locking mechanisms work and the surprising degree to which the face can be warped. In fact, avatar facial deformance performed to minimize all the features of the face can result in a face that looks normal, if pinched, from the front, but with a profile that flattens the nose all the way down against the skull. This holds true across all races and genders. Marked differences in the maximum and minimum sizes of nose, chin, and mouth, however, stand out among the differences not only between male and female avatars but between the avatars of different races as well. Some of these map onto racial traits that are part of a long tradition of caricature: longer and pointier noses for Caucasian faces, larger lips for African American faces, and so on (see figure 2.3). Doing these experiments with *Fallout 3*'s individual race and gender categories reveals that skin tone alone does

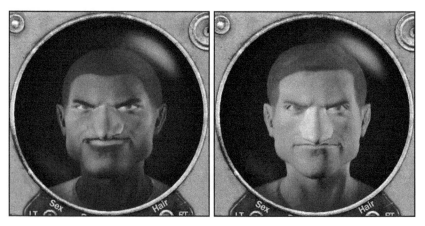

Figure 2.3. African American male and Caucasian male avatars with features maximized. *Fallout 3* (Bethesda Game Studios, 2009). Screenshots by author.

not separate each race's faces from others' and that exact matches are difficult to achieve across racial and gender divides.

Using image editing software, it is also possible to layer images on top of each other in order to make comparisons that might otherwise be difficult without technological assistance. For the *Fallout 3* avatars, one useful comparison to make is to compare the slider positions of the default faces to see how these representative faces are constructed by the developers. Such a technique is similar to the time volumes created by Jeremy Douglass in his projects for the Software Studies Initiative, and they can be produced using the same software from that project, imageJ. These image sets reveal certain patterns that are interesting to note, such as Caucasian male chins being uniformly set to the "Broad" side of the spectrum when the other three races are spread apart. Such patterns might indicate a preference for certain cultural markers of race and masculinity (see figure 2.4).

A final manipulation of avatar facial images that yields interesting results for *Fallout 3* is to composite all the default faces into one "typical" face for each race and gender. I perform this face-making strategy as a way to enter into conversation with the artistic practices of Zach Blas and Mongrel, who spoke back to homophobia and racism by creating composited faces for political art, and also to critique the compositing strategies suggested by eugenicist Francis Galton in 1879, who used it as a strategy to root out the facial characteristics of criminality.

Figure 2.4. African American male, Asian American male, Caucasian male, and Hispanic male sliders (from left to right) showing composite of distribution for chin values for default avatars. *Fallout 3* (Bethesda Game Studios, 2009). Screenshots by author.

Galton suggests that photography can "give us typical pictures of different races of men, if derived from a large number of individuals of those races taken at random."[53] His suggestion informs the logic behind this particular deformance technique, not in the interest of reinforcing racial categories but rather to expose how organizing faces according to such categories lends itself to this way of thinking. I used imageJ to create composites of each racial "type" in *Fallout 3* and created a gallery of curiosities that suggests that certain race and gender categories, such as the "African American male" and all "female" faces, exhibit less variation in facial conformation and skin tone than, for example, the "Caucasian male" faces. While such judgments are ultimately a matter of personal observation, creating composites of these default faces in imageJ can help in making the determination: variations in blurriness indicate where faces are more similar to each other. The Caucasian male faces seem more distinct from their average than other sets of faces (see figures 2.5 and 2.6). This corresponds to theories of outgroup homogeneity that have been observed in both social science and humanities theoretical contexts.

Karyl Ketchum's 2009 account of the FaceGen software that serves as the foundation for *Fallout 3*'s avatar customization system reaches similar conclusions as these avatar deformance techniques. Ketchum interviewed the developers of the software, who reported that the parameters governing FaceGen's facial manipulations arose from methods that harken back to Darwin and Lavater: "A group of 273 respondents was interviewed and asked to rate a series of faces according to how male or how female they were, how attractive they were, and age estimations. These figures were put into a computer program, along with statistical data gathered from 'other psychology data bases,' and trends within this data were identified. These trends were then computed in terms of standard deviations, which were then projected out by plus or minus ten, to establish the two extreme points on each continuum."[54] The resulting software interface, legitimated by the pseudoscientific language and methods described above, includes sliders for gender, race, age, caricature, and asymmetry. Ketchum notes that these sliders are yoked together in problematic ways, such as how the masculine extreme of the gender slider increases the value of the "African" and "East Indian" sliders, while the feminine extreme is linked to the "European" and

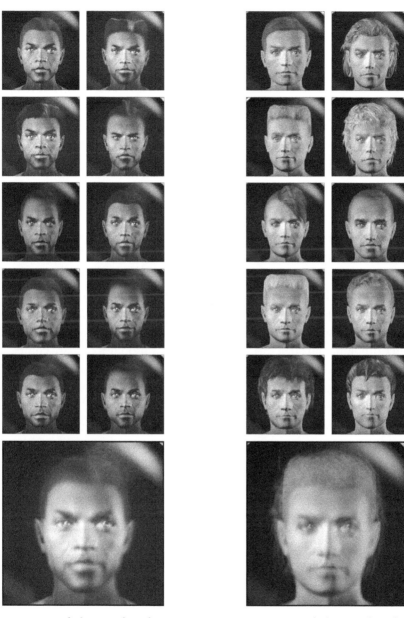

Figure 2.5. Default avatar faces for African American male avatars, as well as their composite. *Fallout 3* (Bethesda Game Studios, 2009). Screenshots by author.

Figure 2.6. Default avatar faces for Caucasian male avatars, as well as their composite. *Fallout 3* (Bethesda Game Studios, 2009). Screenshots by author.

"SE Asian" sliders.[55] Centering all sliders on the interface creates the face of a white man.[56] FaceGen takes culturally determined data about race and gender, quantifies and codifies it in pseudoscientific jargon, and then encodes it in the parameters of its facial models, asking the general public to perform racial identifications in the name of scientific development. Ketchum traces the use of FaceGen through police sketch artist software and ultimately concludes that such uses of "the problematic racialized measures structuring the software's technoscience" serve to legitimate strategies of racial and gender profiling.[57]

Modding the Mask

Deformance experiments allow nonexperts to tease out the inner workings of technical systems by manipulating the interface in ways that are available to them without much tinkering. However, those with the right kind of knowledge can change the interface outright. Modding (modifying) game software is a common practice supported by communities of gamers who play around in the code of a game, either to alter fundamental structures or to create new modules that are compatible with the original software. These users tweak commercial games, create customized tools for them, and even add creative content for others to experience. Modders discovered and unlocked the infamous Hot Coffee content in *Grand Theft Auto: San Andreas* (2004), and they gave gamers access to previously unused gay romance dialogue in *Mass Effect 3* (2012). Some modders create experiences compelling enough to become their own games, like *Defense of the Ancients* (2003), which was originally a mod of *Warcraft 3* (2002), or *Counter-Strike* (2000), which began as a mod of *Half-Life* (1998). Modding is another way to gain knowledge about the processes under the hood of a piece of commercial software, and it can also be a potent means to resist, as various critics have documented.[58]

In order to create and integrate their desired content, modders must be familiar with the details of the game's code and asset management processes. Modding communities have used FaceGen to create personalized content to import into *Fallout 3* and other FaceGen-based avatar creation systems. They face obstacles in importing these characters that confirm some of the suspicions raised by my avatar deformation experiments—namely, that the technological design of *Fallout 3* incorporates race as a set of measurable aesthetic differences that center on the face. For example, user Belthan, creator of the "FaceGen Race" mod for *Fallout 3*, explains that direct imports from FaceGen to *Fallout 3* become distorted because of the additional facial modifiers for race and gender added to the game by the developers. The facial deformation experiments conducted in this chapter demonstrate that these modifiers include such racially stereotyped facial characteristics as the nose, the mouth, and the eyes.

This seems to paint a straightforward picture of difference in the game: the technology of *Fallout 3* structures race as a set of aesthetic restrictions that draw on communal notions of what *race* means and, as a result, constrains the face-making practices of gamers to a "statistical validity of the face"[59] determined by consumer surveys and social science data. Ketchum's observation that the white male face is the result of centering all sliders in FaceGen points to the ways that technology rehashes and recodes old ideologies of the primacy and neutrality of whiteness and maleness. The menu selections, as predicted by Lisa Nakamura, point to race as a choice of discrete identities.[60] More than this, however, the customizable race function enabled by modding tools and the deformance experiments performed for this section reveal that race and gender also exist as a range of limits set by a "baseline face." Making a face in this system means, on the one hand, determining a normative face from which all others in a particular group deviate and, on the other hand, struggling with an interface based on the principle of normativity to create a face for any number of reasons.

The deformance experiments attest to how flexible this system is out of the box: the range of faces enabled by any gendered or racial choice is quite considerable. While the foundations of the software do emerge from white supremacist cisheteropatriarchal methodologies and cultural assumptions, by the time the user meets the interface, the choice of race and gender slide into the multicultural politics of contemporary postracial society: that is to say, the nonfunctionality of race and gender in terms of gameplay, coupled with the large roster of eighty default faces to choose from and thirty-one customizable facial features to modify, reduces identity in *Fallout 3* to a matter of personal style.

In fact, it turns out that "race" is the key to true individuality in the software's functionality. The robust modding community for *Fallout 3* provides a number of aftermarket bodies, faces, and cosmetics packages to obtain for free in order to create a truly unique character. However, using body replacer tools in the game causes all other bodies in the world to use the player character's "unique" body style. In order to get a true, one-of-a-kind avatar in *Fallout 3*, the gamer must make an entirely new race to restrict individuality to one avatar in the game world.[61] Bethesda's officially supported modification software for *Fallout 3*, GECK (Garden of Eden Creation Kit), enables modders to create content for the game within a polished interface. Exploring the GECK interface and tutorials reveals that the process for creating a custom race involves setting a "baseline face," which the customization interface will alter within the game itself.[62] The modder then adds this new race to the unmodified choices—African American, Asian American, Caucasian, and Hispanic—already available on the character creation menu, which allows a player to customize as normal. If race is the ultimate style accessory—that is, in the software logic of *Fallout 3*, the thing that enables the gamer to establish individuality—what does this contribute to an understanding of race and identity in an increasingly digitized world?

On the surface, the move toward individuality in the form of beginning with a wide range of customizable faces is encouraging and one that is being adopted by such large-scale avatar creation platforms as Xbox Live and *Second Life*. In this way, the development of avatar platforms resembles the proliferating identity categories of neoliberal initiatives of diversity and inclusion. It is the logical terminus of quantization processes whose only means of improvement is to break themselves down into smaller and more numerous pieces. However, these changes mask over problems rather than attend to their underlying structures. In *Fallout 3*, this is exemplified by the choice of race to begin with, tied to problematic histories of racial discrimination and biological essentialism, as well as the hidden cultural metrics of FaceGen, which encode assumptions about gender and race into the customization interface. There are other such slippages across the world of avatar creation. In BioWare's *Dragon Age: Origins* (2009), female avatars can never have a chin as wide as any male avatar and a human character with dark skin and hair will still have a light-skinned family. *The Elder Scrolls V: Skyrim* uses assumed human secondary sex characteristics like height and neck size to distinguish nonhuman genders in species like the reptilian

Argonians or feline Khajit. Until an update in 2018, the social avatars of Xbox Live, regardless of gender, could use any facial or hair feature from the menu but were limited to highly gendered clothing choices unless other options were purchased through an online store. *Second Life*, which offers perhaps the most flexible avatar creation mechanisms in the industry, nevertheless maintains fairly modest limitations on body and face size, despite having a "fat" slider. In aggregate, virtual face and body creators reveal that even with technology, it is difficult to move away from essentialist ideas of identity informed by the politics of the past, whether they are the legacies of physiognomy, Darwinian approaches to facial recognition, nineteenth-century understandings of anatomy, or even twenty-first-century quantizations of digitized identity.

Conclusion: Haciendo Karas

As machines assemble Kara, the mechanical seams on her limbs gradually recede under the human skin that spreads from the edges of her face to the rest of her body. She is struck with the odd impulse to cover her nakedness once the flesh reaches her genitals. From the moment she appears on-screen to the climax of the violent assault on her body, Kara's face is irreducible, the guarantor of her humanity. The complex histories of faces as objects of science, sites of ethical exchange, and markers of difference make them uniquely complicated entities to digitize and interpret through a digital haze.

Where, then, to gain a foothold on the inter/face, to open up the face-making possibilities of these structures in ways that challenge older models of understanding the face and take advantage of the affordances of the digital? As technology improves, it will offer exponentially more options for customization and realistic reproduction of human affect. Kara's successful imitations (as animation, as human, as single performer) recede into the uncanny valley as new technologies emerge. Avatar customization suites further granulate their slider bars with increasingly smaller (yet still discrete) increments of change, some even now attempting to imitate analog processes of facial morphing that must always remain digital.[63] These technological improvements attempt to mask the processes underneath and help the user forget that quantization is always a reduction in data. Mori proposed that one day, robot construction would be such that robots and humans will be indistinguishable. Computer animation strives for that same goal. And while we ponder this eventuality in science fiction and philosophy, we are still left with the underdeveloped reality of the present: that our ability to make digital faces that resonate with us (for whatever reason) is incredibly limited.

How does one throw off the masks and become their own face, even when all faces are constrained by a program? Simply wearing the masks and enduring their chafing on the face is one valid response. Altering or breaking the code is another. Yet another requires the recognition that this is not, strictly speaking, a technological problem—that there are always faces and masks and spaces between them and different ways of throwing them off. Kara's bid for recognition paid off, her face successfully demanding an ethical response from her operator. However, she left the assembly line full of prerendered scripts for femininity and concealing a host of racial violences in her new role as the bright white ideal woman—not unlike many representations of empowered women that crop up in and around gaming culture. It is to these scripts that we turn next.

3

Gender, Power, and the Gamic Gaze

Re-viewing Portal *and* Bayonetta

Figure 3.1. *Dinosaur Comics*, October 6, 2006 (Ryan North, 2006). Image courtesy of Ryan North, www.qwantz.com.

The Persistence of the Gaze in Gaming

This chapter begins, as so many accounts of gender and gaming do, with Lara Croft. Though she was not the first action heroine in gaming, the star of *Tomb Raider* (1996) was an early focal point for the feminist critique of video games. An international media sensation, Croft was a digital iteration of the action heroines that emerged in 1990s cinema. Crude polygon resolution, which made it difficult to render human figures in photorealistic detail, meant that markers of the action hero/ine—sweaty hair, "bulging biceps and striated shoulders"[1]—were not feasible except in cartoon style, requiring exaggerated proportions and lighting details. *Tomb Raider*, which followed the rest of the industry in pursuing photorealism in conjunction with three-dimensional graphics, opted to represent Croft's femininity visually and her masculine power procedurally: she had famously large breasts, a small waist, and wide hips but also the ability to drag giant stone blocks, climb sheer cliffs, and blast dinosaurs into oblivion with dual-wielded pistols. The gamic camera in the original *Tomb Raider* remains in a voyeuristic position: a few feet behind Lara, with her buttocks featured in the frame, relentlessly pursuing as she moves in response to the gamer's control (see figure 3.2). Her physical design, too, appeals to a sexualizing gaze that undermines her credibility as an action hero exploring ancient ruins: short shorts, thigh-mounted pistol harnesses, ample bosom straining at a small tank top.

The breakaway transmedial success that *Tomb Raider* achieved, for better or for worse, turned Lara Croft into an icon for women in gaming and popular culture and, by extension, the first major focal point of feminist analysis of video games by fans and critics.[2] Unsurprisingly, early work critiqued Lara and the preponderance of sexy women in video games using the language of the male gaze, a concept developed by Laura Mulvey in her foundational essay "Visual Pleasure and Narrative Cinema."[3] The male gaze is the realization of heteronormative masculine power in Hollywood cinema, an effect of patriarchy that becomes

Figure 3.2. *Tomb Raider* (Core Design, 1996). Screenshot by author.

apparent in visual techniques that slow a woman in action and renders her body maximally available for the viewing pleasure or disciplinary desires of an assumed straight male audience. This way of looking prevents a woman from achieving full subjectivity in cinema, as it literally turns her into an object in the visual scene. Mulvey worked within a particular school of feminist theory organized around reformulating psychoanalytic perspectives on power and identity formation, and in the essay, she carefully lays out the psychic stakes that force the male gaze to do its work—namely, that the woman herself represents the terrifying lack of a penis and her threat must be neutralized by turning her into an image that will not remind the man of this fact.[4] Mulvey's take on the scopophilic encounter, perhaps minus the psychoanalysis, was useful for describing a prevalent orientation toward the feminine body that resonated with many women's experiences: sexual objectification, in which men are active gazers and women passive objects. In game studies and popular games criticism alike, most discussions of Lara Croft and other sexualized women ultimately look to Mulvey's male gaze to explain the character's representation on-screen. The male gaze was a controversial and contested concept even in its time,[5] but it has come to stand in for the more heterogeneous body of feminist criticism about the gaze that emerged alongside and after the piece. Indeed, when Jen Malkowski and TreaAndrea Russworm call for game studies to finally take up feminist criticism in a broad way, they do so under the banner of the "Laura Mulvey moment," placing the movement of feminist film studies (and, by extension, contemporary feminist game studies) under the sign of "Visual Pleasure and Narrative Cinema."[6]

The question of identification with the screen, of course, is much more nuanced in feminist and queer theory. Competing psychoanalytic perspectives emerged at the same time as "Visual Pleasure and Narrative Cinema," such as Constance Penley's "Feminism, Psychoanalysis, and Popular Culture," which argued for a more complex understanding of cross-gender libidinal identifications among consumers using the example of slash fanfiction.[7] Other versions of the cinematic gaze have been exhaustively explored, critiqued, and dismissed in the literature, from bell hooks's oppositional gaze that refuses identification with either subject or object of the camera to Carol Clover's insistence that film induces visual pleasure through identification with multiple subjects.[8]

Critics have exploded the cinematic gaze and its relation to identity politics to the point that Nicholas Mirzoeff in the introduction to *The Visual Culture Reader* characterizes the work of the field as operating with "a transverse look or glance—not a gaze, there have been enough gazes already."[9]

Engaging further with discourse about the gaze may seem like an anachronistic gesture at this moment, and my continued use of feminist film theory in the rest of this chapter might feel imprecise (if I put it generously) to specialists in the field. However, I am operating within a particular analytical space that holds multiple contradictory perspectives in tension with one another—a generative kind of theoretical trouble. On the one hand, there is the lofty register of psychoanalytic feminist film theory, whose historical depth and disciplinary specificity developed in response to the technologies and practices of cinema and was in place long before video games emerged, and that has trained generations of academics, filmmakers, and fans in certain modes of visual literacy. On the other hand, there is game studies, which has spent many decades attempting to differentiate itself from cinematic interlopers. On yet another hand (if you'll permit me some imprecision with this analogy as well), there is the popular reception of "Visual Pleasure and Narrative Cinema," which seems to inspire every subsequent generation that encounters it. Karen Boyle, in *Feminist Media Studies*' special issue on the fortieth anniversary of Mulvey's essay, describes the "excitement, relief, and joy" students inevitably express when she teaches the essay,[10] an experience that I and many of my colleagues also have witnessed. Despite its age, and despite the developments and conversations that have come after it, this particular essay continues to resonate in the study and understanding of popular culture.

Today, the vocabulary of the male gaze, largely removed from the rigorous psychoanalytic context that Mulvey constructed around it, is central to how mainstream audiences, the video game industry, and game studies itself understands and responds to feminist concerns in video games. In this form, it serves largely as shorthand for the way women are objectified for a presumably straight male viewer whose desire and power are channeled through the technologies of cinema. Important community resources like *Finally, a Feminism 101 Blog*, TV Tropes, and the Geek Feminism Wiki[11] all have entries dedicated to the male gaze, and they invariably credit Laura Mulvey with inventing the term even if they do not engage deeply with her theoretical framework. The popular webcomic *Dinosaur Comics*, featured in the epigraph, offers a typical definition: "The idea is that the camera is situated by and for men! Thus, we always see more of the woman's body than we do of the man's in film—the camera possesses the (heterosexual) male gaze, and thereby disenfranchises the woman by reducing her to the passive object of the gaze, while the male is elevated to the active gazer. It is a NOT UNCON-TROVERSIAL theory."[12] In more recent years, the widespread popularity of Anita Sarkeesian's "Tropes vs. Women in Video Games" video series, which went viral in the wake of a massive harassment campaign that preceded #GamerGate, signals the legibility of analyzing the representation of women based on the vocabulary of the male gaze. These high-profile conversations, in turn, inform how game designers understand and attempt to address feminist concerns in gaming.

This reason alone merits continued engagement with "the gaze" as matter to think with[13] whether or not I am able to preserve its original contextual and theoretical purity in my own appropriation of the much-appropriated term. I find the word *gaze* useful, additionally, in its colloquial meaning, because visuality does structure the relationship between user and apparatus in video games beyond character representation—though there are, as with cinema, many other cognitive and somatic connections as well. There are few words sufficient to describe the visual relationship of the gamer to the game, with "eyes . . . fixed on the screen with what is a potentially almost disturbing level of concentration,"[14] than that of a gaze, or even, as one critic wittily calls it, a "glaze."[15]

In the remainder of this chapter, you'll find a varied application and complication of classic feminist film theory with respect to the digital games of the present—an homage to the way work like Mulvey's continues to inform audiences' and gamers' reception of popular culture. As the *Dinosaur Comics* T. rex suggests, video game protagonists have a substantially different relationship to visuality than characters on a cinematic screen, and the current deployment of feminist theories of visuality to assess feminine bodies in video games do not sufficiently account for this difference, though even early scholarship, such as Helen Kennedy's "Lara Croft: Feminist Icon or Cyberbimbo?," began to probe it.[16]

Virtual bodies exist beyond the visual scene and have many functions other than that of eye candy or other spectacle. With the prevalence of games designed in the first-person perspective, for example, the avatar body is frequently invisible, haunting the screen with trace reminders such as hands or reflections. Even characters like Lara Croft, whose body is always available for viewing, exist in a visual field in which the camera reacts to the gamer's input, and sometimes their outright control, rather than to that of a director or cinematographer. Moreover, unlike the mythological avatar, who serves as a docile vessel for possession, there is much about the gamic avatar that constricts and directs the gamer's and camera's behavior. We need a more nuanced account of how video games complicate our understanding of the relation between feminine bodies and the gaze in order to move forward with a feminist game studies praxis that more aptly responds to gaming in its current state and recognizes new political possibilities within popular texts.

In order to explore how we might differently orient ourselves toward the gamic gaze, this chapter will consider two games chosen for both their cultural impact as well as the aesthetic, narrative, and technical devices that invite us to think about the gaze and the video game heroine's complicated relationship to formulations of femininity and visuality. In the first case, Valve Corporation's *Portal* (2007), I will unpack a seeming contradiction: the two central figures, both coded as feminine, uphold the traditional power dynamics of the white supremacist cisheteropatriarchal gaze despite the fact that women seem to hold all the power in the game's narrative universe. The game accomplishes this by splitting the feminine subject into warring halves: Chell, the first-person avatar body who cannot speak, and GLaDOS, a diffuse, seemingly bodiless artificial intelligence who has taken control of a science facility and killed off all the men. Players use Chell's power over the game's many cameras to reinstate order in this misandrist dystopian nightmare while glossing over her own status as a brown scientific test subject whose only function is to serve.

In the second case, the Platinum Games title *Bayonetta* (2009), I will demonstrate how the technological operations of video games, including their programmed cameras, can work against what we understand about the significance of representation and visuality to feminist politics. Bayonetta is a figure that easily fits within the trope of the hypersexual action heroine, but she disturbs this role with a queer femininity that reaches out through the game's technical apparatuses to implicate the gamer in its own pleasures while deftly avoiding the game camera that is programmed to prioritize battle over titillation in crowded visual scenes that resist easy viewing.

Chell is something of an inverse case to Bayonetta: though widely praised for her status as a woman in gaming that is not represented in sexualized terms, Chell's racial ambiguity and relationship with GLaDOS ultimately point to an antifeminist narrative contingent on a postracial, postfeminist present. Bayonetta, meanwhile, is widely condemned for being the same old sexpot in video games, although her queerness (anchored by the class benefits of posh British whiteness) offers her a latitude with femininity that enacts the radical potential of enticing, deflecting, and humiliating the male gaze. This chapter is a playful critique that aims to trouble received interpretations by inverting readings of *Portal* as "good" and *Bayonetta* as "bad" examples of the representation of women in video games. To that end, this analysis, like many others throughout this book, moves through registers of high theory, close reading, fan interpretation, and author intent. By bringing these two games and multiple critical modes together, I argue for an understanding of the gamic gaze that attends to more than what is looked at and who is looking, but to the procedural, historical, corporeal, and cultural contexts in which the looking is done. We must understand the power of visuality in video games, beginning with what we have learned about images from other disciplines, without losing sight of the multiple ways that computation and play help sculpt how we look at the screen—as well as how it looks back at us.

First Person: The Eyes of the Heroine

Valve Corporation's 2007 first-person puzzle platformer, *Portal*, puts the gamer in the position of a lone woman prisoner wielding a portal gun to navigate mazes in an abandoned science facility called the Enrichment Center. The "portals" in the game connect two places in Cartesian space, preserving the momentum of objects that pass through them: if the player places one portal on the floor and one on the wall, they can jump through the floor and emerge from the other portal in the wall.

Moving through a portal is a perspective-twisting displacement that dramatically changes the orientation of gravity and the visual field in relation to the avatar, and it is around this principle that the main gameplay revolves (see figure 3.3.)

Since *Portal*'s primary ludic goal is movement through space, it follows in the tradition of many other digital games in distributing its narrative information throughout the environment.[17] Narrative data are streamed into the game across many media channels that activate when the gamer achieves specific navigational goals: audio, image, text, space, and rarely, in-game cinematics that wrench control of the screen from the gamer, all provide crucial information about the game's world and story. At its best, *Portal* is one of the truly successful examples of merging gameplay goals (reach difficult places with a portal gun) with narrative ones (unravel the mystery of the protagonist and facility). Even when this system does not work as smoothly as desired, the game still allows the gamer to seek narrative without significantly interfering with play. Both play and narrative, however, are intimately intertwined through navigation and, by extension, the gaze itself.

In video games, navigation, combat, and puzzle solving are performed with the help of a virtual camera that renders the virtual world on a flat screen as if it were a film or television show.[18] Sometimes the

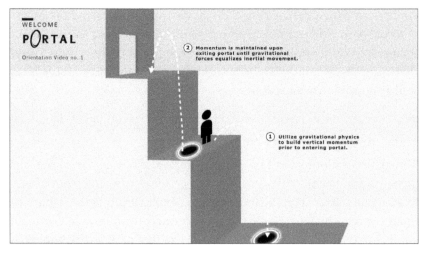

Figure 3.3. Diagram explaining how portals work. "Orientation Video No. 1—A Safe and Healthy Environment" in *Portal* (Valve Corporation, 2007). Screenshot by author.

camera is fixed in position to restrict the gamer's access to spatial information. Other times, it moves along with the player character. In other instances, the game camera functions as the player character's eyes from a position that sutures gamer to character through the gaze. Alexander Galloway traces the deviation of the first-person perspective in gaming from the cinematic subjective shot, in which the camera is meant to engage "the physiology of vision," including body and eye movements, "blinking eyelids, blurring, spots tears, and so on."[19] In the context of cinema, a visual medium that has developed without significant haptic components like game controllers, Galloway finds that the subjective shot is most often used as a means to express alienation in cinema, an analysis that follows earlier similar observations by theorists like Carol Clover and William Earl. However, Galloway argues that bringing the subjective shot into video games rehabilitates it as a gaze in which identification is not only possible but inevitable.[20] This is the essence of the first-person shooter (FPS): a subjective shot that encourages the gamer to assume the avatar's identity, and a gun in the foreground that gestures at their power in the world, evoking the phallus so central to psychoanalytic film theory. Although the coincidence of gaze with gun in the FPS genre literalizes what Carol Clover calls the "assaultive gaze,"[21] a penetrative gaze that we might associate with Mulvey's earlier formulation of the male gaze, Galloway argues that it is not the violent potentiality of the gun in video games but rather the "active, affective, mobile quality of the first-person perspective that is key for gaming."[22]

This is particularly true in *Portal*, which maintains a focus on nonviolent physics puzzles that frequently send the avatar flying through the air. The first-person perspective—the gamer's gaze—is integrally bound up in the execution of *Portal*'s major goals. Indeed, the portal gun is not a violent penetrator like the traditional FPS arsenal, but a science fiction device that dilates openings in space connecting two noncontiguous points together. Bonnie Ruberg analyzes the game's portals in terms of homoerotic orifices a la D. A. Miller's foundational queer reading of Hitchcock's *Rope*.[23] In this reading, portals provide a counterpoint to the phallic power of cinema and function as a symbolic bridge between media and the queer body.[24]

In terms of technical design, opening a portal literally places a new camera in the digital world. Each portal functions as an eye for its paired portal so that the gamer can see where in space they are approaching. These procedural cameras—the first-person view and the portal windows—are joined by motion-tracking security cameras that suggest an invisible watcher within the narrative of the game. However, the security cameras are merely aesthetic and do not offer their views to the gamer. *Portal's* tangled gazes participate in the story of a woman who stays out of the sexualizing spotlight commonly associated with the camera lens while also placing the power of surveillance in the hands of a feminine computer. These gazes interrupt and intersect each other both literally and figuratively, ultimately complicating what one might understand to be the power of the gaze over the Other. These gazes are specifically gendered feminine and are turned on one another in the marked absence of a masculine spectator, creating a thematic challenge to the predominant view of video game voyeurism as it is understood in the mainstream. However, *Portal* also fails to live up to the potentials of this subversion, instead falling back on the antifeminist trope of women destroying each other with an invisible man pulling the strings in the background.

The Feminized Acousmêtre

Fittingly for a game built around ruptures and non-Cartesian bridges in vision, *Portal* begins with an abrupt insertion into the game world. Without any sort of introduction, the gamer is thrust into the body of the avatar, the camera flaring against sudden harsh lighting, apparently waking up in a glass holding cell with a timer on the wall. After a few moments of unguided exploration that allows the gamer to learn how to move through the game world, a computerized feminine voice pipes through the air: "Hello, and again, welcome to the Aperture Science computer-aided Enrichment Center."

GLaDOS, now infamous in the gallery of video game villains, is the sole custodian of the Enrichment Center. She is alternately a guide and an antagonist to the gamer/avatar, a source of unhelpful suggestions and cheerful death threats. As her voice echoes through the chamber, white security cameras with red lenses track the avatar's movements through space and blurred windows high on the chamber walls suggest invisible observers behind the scenes. These traces of surveillance imply rather than confirm GLaDOS's presence in the facility, lending the game a paranoid mood that invites us to interrogate the game's many gazes. While the Foucauldian power dynamics implied by the panopticon are certainly at work here, the haunting intelligent presence of GLaDOS, whose voice guides the gamer with obvious knowledge of their movements, is more uncanny than regulatory. Michel Chion calls this type of unsettling disembodied voice the "acousmêtre," a special type of off-screen presence that emerged in early cinema. Unlike unsynchronized presences such as voice-overs or reading from a text, the acousmêtre is "the one who is not-yet seen, but remains liable to appear in the visual field at any moment."[25] This all-seeing, all-commenting presence lacks a body, preventing us from locating the source of its knowledge or power, and it haunts the physical space that its voice touches.

The capacity to see into and penetrate vast areas, in contrast to the strict directionality of cinematic vision, lends the acousmêtre a significant amount of power in a panoptic setting such as the Enrichment Center. While we may place her in a lineage of other murderous computers, especially the feminized MU/TH/UR mainframe of *Alien* (1979), GLaDOS's relationship with cameras and visuality makes her an obvious descendent of HAL 9000, the overseer and central brain of the *Discovery* in Stanley Kubrick's *2001: A Space Odyssey* (1968) and one of Chion's primary examples of the acousmêtre. Although GLaDOS has visible security cameras around the facility, the gamer can destroy most of them at will without affecting the computer's ability to monitor their activity. Like HAL, who surprises the *Discovery*'s crew (and the audience) by reading their lips when they are out of range of his microphone, GLaDOS is all-knowing, and her knowledge is based on the supernatural ability to gaze upon all, despite her explicit connection to rather mundane, completely canny technologies of sight: cameras. HAL's iconic lens-eye looms largest in the popular memory surrounding *2001*, and *Portal* invokes this all-seeing eye with its own red lens security cameras, as well as GLaDOS's personality cores—mechanical eyeballs that attach to her mainframe and represent different aspects of her temperament.

The relationship between vision and sound is crucial for both HAL and GLaDOS, who execute their will by the force of language but rely on sight to fuel their power. For Kubrick, cinematic meaning in *2001* is about visual experience independent of language—the panoramic vistas

and haunting sound-suck of outer space.[26] HAL's disturbance of this silence is significant: out of approximately forty minutes of dialogue in
the 160-minute-long film, the computer participates in almost half of
it. HAL's existence is rooted in relationships to mediated sound, from
his excessive presence in the audio field of the film to his death song,
"Daisy," the first song performed by the first speaking computer.[27] Like
HAL, GLaDOS is also one of only a few speaking characters in *Portal*[28]
occupying almost all acoustic space in the otherwise minimal sound-
scape of the game. GLaDOS is a withholding and deceptive intelligence.
She speaks only in exaggerated corporate euphemisms, and whenever
she does have clear and helpful things to say, the audio system conve-
niently glitches out and obscures her words.

While neither HAL nor GLaDOS have sex or gender in the form of a
biological body, their voices are recognizably masculine and feminine,
respectively, and this gendering extends to their behavior. GLaDOS
grounds her sadistic scientific curiosity in an obsession with cake—an
irrational object choice for a machine that cannot enjoy food but a fitting one for a feminized artificial intelligence who might have wandered
too far from the kitchen. Though details of her origins are inconsistent
in the original game and its supplementary texts, it is clear that scientists
activated GLaDOS "as one of the planned activities on Aperture's first
annual bring-your-daughter-to-work day,"[29] aligning her with affirmative action programs and bringing her gender into sharp relief vis-à-vis
her occupation as a scientist, a historically masculine field that has seen
an organized push for greater inclusion of women.

GLaDOS diverges as a gendered subject during the process of what
Chion calls "deacousmatization," the descent into impotence brought
on by locating the voice within a physical body. Critics Michael P. Nofz
and Phil Vendy suggest that HAL is a master of emotional performance,
particularly compared to the robotic humans occupying the *Discovery*,
and that his longevity in the public imagination is partially due to the
way he attempts to manipulate Dave into keeping him alive by appealing
to the ideals of forgiveness, teamwork, and sympathy.[30] His responses
are eminently logical, chosen carefully by a computer intelligence designed to read, respond to, and manipulate the behavior of an emotional
subject. Confronted with the rejection of his authority and with his own
mortality, HAL is rational to the last. GLaDOS, on the other hand, is

memorable for her erratic emotional performance. She maintains her clinical robotic demeanor until the gamer finally refuses her demand to participate in the sadistic Enrichment Center activities and escapes beyond the reach of the security cameras, at which point GLaDOS at last refers to herself in the first person, begins to lie uncontrollably to coax the gamer back out, and threatens them outright with death. Her statements beyond the daring escape in Chamber 19 (the last official level of the game) signal that GLaDOS's powers and field of vision do not extend beyond the test chambers and their surveillance systems, even if her voice still carries everywhere.

The entire quest through the Enrichment Center culminates in finding GLaDOS's physical body and destroying it. If, as the literature on voyeurism suggests, distance is an essential component of watching another, then closing that distance between the avatar's body and the acousmêtre cuts off her ability to see and, as a result, her source of power. Kaja Silverman, in discussing the disembodied feminine voice, describes this power source in a slightly different way: "To allow her to be heard without being seen would be even more dangerous, since it would disrupt the specular regime upon which mainstream cinema relies; it would put her beyond the control of the male gaze, and release her voice from the signifying obligations which that gaze sustains."[31] Deacousmatizing the feminine acousmêtre, then, also places her body within reach of the gamer's gaze and constrains her within a hegemonic visual regime that disempowers powerful feminine figures. If we put this in the terms of Mulvey's male gaze, the process of deacousmatization subjects the too-powerful woman to the gaze and turns her into an image that no longer threatens masculine authority.

An endlessly tall room houses the GLaDOS hardware, which is suspended from the ceiling and extends far beyond the gamer's range of vision. Four personality cores, her external independent eyeballs, cling like barnacles to her frame. In the game's developer commentary, Valve art director Jeremy Bennett describes her as "a huge mechanical device with a delicate robot figure dangling out of it," a design that was meant to capture her "raw power and femininity." In GLaDOS, the paradox of the all-powerful feminine figure is expressed as a literalization of the contradiction: giant and small, omnipotent and vulnerable, unfathomable yet always legible as feminine (see figure 3.4).

The "delicate robot figure" portion of GLaDOS sways ineffectually as she taunts the gamer/avatar for finding her. Artist and developer Steve Bowler, on his blog *Game-ism*, puts forward a theory that, far from an all-powerful computer nightmare run wild, GLaDOS is also a captive in the facility, which he illustrates by comparing a screenshot of GLaDOS with his own artwork of a woman bound, blindfolded, gagged and strung upside-down in a straitjacket (see figure 3.4).[32] Her powerlessness beyond the test chambers and particularly within her own body confirms this fannish fantasy: only when the gamer destroys her morality core, purportedly installed to suppress her murderous impulses, can GLaDOS respond to the attack on her mainframe. However, she can only react by indirect means such as neurotoxin emitters and a rocket-launching drone; her actual body cannot defend itself. The destruction of the morality core also activates the computer's third personality phase: speaking in low, sensual tones, she cycles through anger, sarcasm, sadness, and fear as the avatar pulls her apart, fully realizing the misogynist stereotype of the unstable hysteric. Once a cold and calculating scientist, the visualized acousmêtre has lost all power and can only stand by and talk while she is destroyed.

As the disembodied voice presiding over the Enrichment Center, GLaDOS's power and knowledge seem limitless, but when the action moves away from the networks with which her mind has contact, she becomes desperate, fumbling to regain control of her lost test subject. In the final confrontation, her body is useless, a dangling piece of

Figure 3.4. GLaDOS hardware. *Portal* (Valve Corporation, 2007). Screenshot by author.

Figure 3.5. GLaDOS in game next to Steve Bowler's artistic interpretation. *Portal* (Valve Corporation, 2007). Screenshot and image courtesy of Steve Bowler.

machinery ready to be picked apart and destroyed, and her mind fractures into multiple simultaneous affective states to call both weaponry and language to her defense. Unlike HAL's controlled panic, the frenzy of GLaDOS has no apparent strategy to deal with the aggression of the gamer/avatar that is directed toward her—no way to evade the gaze. And once this gaze is turned on her, unlike her rational masculine counterpart, GLaDOS cannot maintain control over her emotional response. The murder of GLaDOS is a desubjectification, the objectification of a woman in motion, who becomes trapped by the gamer's hostile gaze.

Chell's Bluest Eyes

To complicate this analysis further, it is necessary to question the cinematic terms that I have used to discuss *Portal* up to this point. The gamer, after all, is not merely watching the unmaking of GLaDOS; they are an active participant in the hunt for the voice, the unveiling of the acousmêtre, and the annihilation of feminine subjectivity. Their tool for committing this violence is the avatar Chell, an empty shell of a body with no will of her own that serves as the gamer's puppet in the game world. Silverman's argument that the disembodied feminine voice escapes the controlling power of the male gaze also underscores that it is as a body that the woman is most legible in culture. It is therefore simultaneously surprising (from the perspective of her function as a source of the controlling gaze) and unsurprising (from the perspective of the feminine as reducible to the body) that the avatar in *Portal* is a woman's body, made to bear gendered burdens that are complementary to those placed upon GLaDOS but complicated by the avatar's status as an incomplete subjectivity. Indeed, the avatar and GLaDOS might be seen to exist as two halves of the same whole: woman's mind and woman's body, perhaps ripped apart by the violent nature of a virtual world that requires empty bodies into which gamers insert themselves and absolute villains who deserve annihilation. In order to complicate the feminist politics of *Portal* further, I want to circle back to the beginning of the game, to the source of the rift and to what I recognize as GLaDOS's remainder: the spectral shell of the avatar—the gamer's point of insertion into the game world and their means to approach the symbolic threat of a woman's mind.

We have seen how the *Portal* gun functions as a gaze multiplier in the game, creating multiple cameras in gamespace through which the avatar can travel, throw objects, and extend their visual perception of their surroundings. Crucially, the portal gun is the gamer's only means for interacting with the world: even in the final confrontation with GLaDOS, the main puzzle is to place portals in such a way that the computer shoots rockets at herself. This weaponization of the gaze is not violent in the way that the machine guns and chainsaws of other first-person shooters are violent, but it does redirect the violence of a desubjectifying camera at the only true subject in the game. The gamer's gaze, focused through the portal gun, reduces GLaDOS to a pile of scrap metal, while it fails, except in very particular circumstances, to capture the body of the avatar herself.

Although the gamer's field of vision originates from the avatar's eyes, her body is completely invisible except through the lens of carefully arranged portals. Even in the first-person genre, the visual scene usually refers to the avatar's body through third-person cinematic scenes or even a hand displayed in the gamer's field of vision. However, the *Portal* avatar's arm only comes into view while enveloped by the Aperture

Science Handheld Portal Device. Her body is simply not visible by normal means. This particular restriction of vision has a curious effect for a character that has otherwise been granted the power of the gaze: she cannot look directly into the camera, only glance toward it from the side (see figure 3.5). The angles at which her body is available to view through the portals do not permit a full-frontal view. Laurie Taylor writes about the returned avatar gaze as an "uncanny, disruptive effect" that breaks the fourth wall and interrupts the identification of avatar with gamer. Drawing on Jacques Lacan, she traces out how video games take advantage of the ability to incorporate projected images into a sense of self but also make identification difficult by constantly shifting perspectives and by "removing the player from the field of the gaze" while simultaneously suggesting that they are within it.[33]

Indeed, the image here (figure 3.6) illustrates how looking back requires the avatar to break the physics of the game: the gamer's camera is pointed toward one portal (which appears blue in the game), yet Chell is looking away from it and into the other connected portal (which is orange, its border can be seen on the left side of the screen), even though her line of sight should follow the portal gun itself, if we believe the suggestion that the camera is coterminous with her eyes. In the context

Figure 3.6. Chell glancing at the camera. *Portal* (Valve Corporation, 2007). Screenshot by author.

of a game without cinematic interludes offering the avatar's body up for viewing, *Portal's* procedural mirror provides a unique example of crossed gazes. The gamer is introduced to these mirrors at the beginning of the game, directly following GLaDOS's introductory speech about the Enrichment Center. Upon concluding the countdown to the beginning of the test, a portal opens in the "Relaxation Vault" in which the avatar is detained, and as the gamer approaches it, they are able to view a wide angle of the avatar's body within the Relaxation Vault through the portal on the other side. In the game's developer commentary, Kimberly Swift explains that these introductory portals were set up in such a way that viewing the avatar's body would help the gamer orient themselves in the twisted spatial perspectives of the game, making these mirrors (unlike those explored by Taylor) integral to connecting with the avatar. Despite being a first-person game, *Portal* still relies on the third-person gaming convention of viewing the body at a distance to help gamer identify with avatar.

When subjected to the portal gaze, Chell is literally objectified (as the avatar-thing with which the gamer must identify), but not sexualized in the ways that one might expect of a woman who cannot look back. Outfitted in a full-coverage orange jumpsuit with a large Aperture Science logo on the back, she seems more like an inmate than a pinup model or a voluntary "test subject." Her appearance produces a sense of unease that plunges the gamer from the avataric realm of liminality straight into the uncanny valley, but the uncanniness of *Portal's* avatar runs deeper than the inadequate mimicking of human likeness that characterizes Masahiro Mori's theory. While she appears to be human within the limits of the digital uncanny valley, strange prosthetic devices protrude from her calves and force her to walk on her toes (the similarity to high-heeled shoes should not go unmentioned); these are explained to be heel springs that prevent injury from falling long distances, but they effectively project the avatar out of the realm of the human and into that of the cyborg. Her other physical characteristics lack clear markers that may be further used to classify her: she could belong to any number of racial or ethnic groups, or more likely, to some combination of them. This multiracial appearance can be read in an inclusive way—an attempt by the designers to create a character that reaches out across a broad spectrum of peoples in the spirit of multiculturalism. Her eyes, however, are quite unsettling.

Jennifer deWinter and Carly Kocurek document fan speculation on Chell's racial identity, which settled on Alésia Glidewell, the actress who served as the basis for the character's visual design. The *Portal* community embraced Chell as a multiracial figure because of Glidewell's Brazilian and Japanese ancestry, allowing women of color gamers to identify her as one of their own. Calling her "a flashpoint in player demand for more diverse representation in avatars and video game protagonists," deWinter and Kocurek point out that racial ambiguity itself is useful for designers to maximize the number of people that can identify with the avatar.[34]

However, this seemingly positive development in representation should give us pause. Chell is an ambiguous brown body who might potentially belong to a number of communities, but she is also a brown body who literally has no voice with which she can speak about her own history or desires. She is, instead, an object of desire for those gamers who have been denied representation in the media, a panacea that reaches out across a wide spectrum of race. If we believe, as I have argued elsewhere in this book, that racial logics operate in video games on levels much deeper than representation, then we must be skeptical of the surface value of racial and gender inclusivity in the case of *Portal* and identify what the racialized avatar actually does in this game. Chell's identity offers a solution for a wide swath of gamers concerned with representation. However, she is constructed according to a path-of-least-resistance model that maximizes market value while entailing little risk. Without a voice, without a history, there is little she can do to offend.

But her body can still speak for itself: like La Malinche's staring infant in Diego Rivera's mural *The Conquest, or The Arrival of Cortés*, Chell's unnervingly light eyes, a commonly fantasized index of multiraciality in the brown body, call attention to the buried traumas that predate her. Indeed, as a brown feminine body who is the focus of a scientific institution's efforts to keep her imprisoned and subject her body to experiments, it makes perverse symbolic sense that she cannot speak. Chell's eyes do the talking, glancing toward the camera in defiance of the game mechanics that control the rest of her body and calling forward the histories of women of color—mostly Black women like Henrietta Lacks, or the enslaved women who served as the original test subjects of gynecology—who have been forced into scientific experimentation in the name of the greater good.[35] *Portal*'s sequel sends Chell (and GLaDOS) into the depths of the Aperture Science facility to explore its origins in the mid-twentieth century, a whitewashed fantasy of scientific experimentation in which war heroes, Olympians, and eventually, poor volunteers, were the test subjects before GLaDOS enslaved the scientists themselves. In this narrative, it is white men, not Black and brown women, who are the historical victims of science. We are meant to believe that Chell is an anomaly in this regard.

Chell's ultralight eyes in an otherwise ambiguous brown body position whiteness as a marker of exoticization. This reverses the expectations of racial representation and produces anxiety in a postracial multicultural world order that refuses to recognize the continuing effects of race on material existence, generating what Soraya Murray calls an "aesthetics of ambivalence" that positions whiteness in crisis.[36] This fear of white masculine obsolescence permeates the game, particularly around the mystery of the missing scientists. Gendered anxiety thoroughly suffuses *Portal* through the haunting figure of the "Rat Man" who stands in for the lost masculine caretakers of the scientific facility and who has left evidence of his life in the facility in the forms of pinup calendars and paranoid verse on the walls. In *Portal 2* (2011), this narrative is driven even deeper (pun intended) through an exploration of GLaDOS's former life as Carolyn, the scientifically minded but ridiculed secretary of the lab's founder and CEO, Cave Johnson. The game files of *Portal 2* even include hidden recorded dialogue files that were never implemented in the game from what sounds like a rape scene, the moment in which Carolyn is forced into the GLaDOS construct by her dying boss. Once GLaDOS came alive, she became the castrating avenger who killed her enslavers and turned their experiments around on them, fulfilling the fantasy of the woman who rises to power and reverses the flow of gendered oppression once she arrives. The scientific laboratory, a hallowed bastion of masculine authority, turns into a horror house at the hands of a woman.

Earlier in this section, I briefly mentioned MU/TH/UR, Ellen Ripley's computer nemesis in *Alien*, as a precursor to GLaDOS. At the end of this reading, I find it prudent to return to her, because Ripley's continuous struggle throughout the *Alien* film franchise is one against reproduction, frequently understood as a defining feature of (cisgender) femininity.[37] In the 1980s, feminist film criticism of the *Alien* movies frequently lingered on the fact that Ripley, who should have been an empowering representation for women, was only ever battling other (albeit nonhuman) mothers rather than the masculine corporation that repeatedly put Ripley and her companions in danger in its attempts to enslave the xenomorph queen (and, specifically, the queen's reproductive capabilities) for science. *Portal* enacts a similar triangulation, pitting women of different racial backgrounds against each other in order to quell their revenge on the past crimes of white men. GLaDOS relentlessly pursues Chell with her all-seeing eye. Chell uses the gaze to trap GLaDOS within the signifying regime most suited to containing her power: visuality. Both of these women continuously hold each other in check with their gazes—the acousmatic gaze of GLaDOS or Chell's first-person camera—instead of turning this power on the white supremacist cisheteropatriarchal structures that put them there in the first place.

Third Person: The Body of the Hero(ine)

Many scholars have refuted Espen Aarseth's early assertion that Lara Croft's body is interchangeable for any other visual referent;[38] while a particular avatar body may not change the gameplay functions assigned to it, there is little doubt that Croft herself was an important factor in *Tomb Raider*'s success as a multimedia franchise. By bracketing Croft's physical body, however, Aarseth's approach misses both the external commercial and social apparatuses surrounding *Tomb Raider* as a franchise as well as the internal cultural meanings generated by Croft's feminine body in a particular procedural and narrative context. Feminist scholars in particular have picked up where this work leaves off, interrogating Croft's position as both sex symbol and mascot for feminine gamer communities. This tension between context and representation plays out in unique ways with Chell and GLaDOS, who subvert the expectations generated by visual inclusivity in their distinctly antifeminist crusade against each other in the game's goals and visual mechanics. There is no sexualized body on display in *Portal*, but the game nevertheless weaponizes the camera in a campaign to curtail feminine power.

When it debuted in 2009, Platinum Games' *Bayonetta* sparked a frenzy of debate among feminist gamers on the internet. Described variously as camp queen,[39] masculinist fantasy par excellence,[40] "love letter to femininity,"[41] and failed Lady Gaga,[42] the title character, Bayonetta, is situated at a divide in the community: What place does sexiness have in the cultural construct of the feminist heroine? The game features an unrealistically proportioned hypersexual witch who hunts down angels using magic powered by her hair, which also serves as her primary means of clothing. The more powerful the attack, the more hair is shifted from covering her body to destroying its target. Bayonetta brutally dispatches her heavenly foes to the bubbly sounds of Japanese pop music, interjecting bondage-themed special attacks among more traditional swordplay and shots from pistols in her platform heels, and her five-hundred-year-old European spellcasting maneuvers resemble contemporary exotic dance. On the surface, Bayonetta is the ideal candidate for thinking about the objectification of women in video games, yet while much popular critique holds Bayonetta up as an example of heteromasculine desire run wild, this femme fatale is not typical in her orientation toward heteronormative masculinity nor in her relationship with the visual apparatuses of the gaming machine.

The game follows Bayonetta's quest to reconstruct her memories after being resurrected in the twenty-first century, the last survivor of a war between her clan of women, the Umbra Witches, and the Ithavoll Sages (all men) that took place centuries ago during the historical witch hunts in early modern Europe. This narrative backdrop is a simplistic invocation of serious questions about gendered power, though the consistently campy execution might be read equally as parody of feminism or critique of patriarchy—and usually, it is a combination of the two. The game inverts the war between heaven and hell, placing Bayonetta and the gamer on the side of "evil" against a thinly veiled analogue of the Catholic Church. Most of the action takes place in the baroque environment of the fictional religious European city-state of Vigrid, and Handelesque choirs announce the arrival of angels (organized according to the celestial hierarchy first put forward in the fifth century by Pseudo-Dionysius the Areopagite) to do battle with Bayonetta. The game is segmented into "Chapters" and "Verses" rather than levels to add an additional biblical flair to the entire production. Set against the historical violences and prohibitions perpetrated against women and sexual minorities by chaste religious institutions, as well as the Catholic Church's ongoing position as a bastion of colonial, cisheteropatriarchal power, Bayonetta's sultriness has more purpose than the decontextualized sexiness of most heroines. In the words of games critic Chris Dahlen, "Her sex is a weapon,"[43] and it is aimed squarely at one of the world's most patriarchal, sexually prohibitive, and colonizing institutions.

Bayonetta's weaponized sexuality falls into the category of what micha cárdenas calls "femme disturbance," the propensity of femininity to disrupt phallic power structures through its own excess. Femme disturbance, rather than wholly reclaiming a feminine figure for progressive ends, instead disrupts simplistic notions of agency and resistance to open the way for recognizing how systems might be assailed from within.[44] Fictional figures are important in imagining new ways to confront oppressive regimes, and characters like Bayonetta are often looked over because they resemble too closely some of mainstream feminism's historically abjected subjects: the stripper, the sex worker, the slut. Unlike the invisible bodies of Chell and GLaDOS in *Portal*, Bayonetta is hypervisible, her body designed for a viewer's pleasure. Her hair-clothing appears as a skintight leather catsuit on her body, and she walks with a sassy swing in her hips. Her proportions are unrealistic, her body contorts in improbable ways, and her performance of sexiness sometimes seems un-self-aware, the perfect object for the voyeur (see figure 3.7).

The game's camera, in direct opposition to *Portal*'s, almost never assumes a subjective point of view, remaining fixed instead at a distance to view Bayonetta's body in the game. When looking at Bayonetta in traditional visual media like print and in-game cinematic sequences, one can find easy fodder for critique on the basis of the male gaze. Prior to the game's release, its marketing campaign came under fire for encouraging passersby in a Japanese subway station to undress a mural of Bayonetta by taking individual advertisement cards concealing her near-naked body.[45] Critics like Anita Sarkeesian rightly condemned this as a harassment training mechanism, particularly in the context of a subway system well known for sexual assault and harassment.[46] Developer commentary did not help matters much either. While lead character designer Mari Shimazaki is a woman, she and several other members of the team emphasized the role of director Hideki Kamiya in guiding the design of Bayonetta into his "ideal woman."[47] In fact, Kamiya's commentary in several interviews and developer blogs consistently emphasizes Bayonetta's sexiness. The most flagrant example of them all comes in modeler Kenichiro Yoshimura's blog, which detailed the techniques he used to bring the characters from Shimazaki's sketches into three-dimensional avatars. His biggest challenge? "I really wanted to get Bayonetta's backside perfect. I guess I am into that sort of thing . . ."[48] The consistent and exaggerated emphasis on sexiness feels like part of the marketing strategy, a cynical and sexist ploy to maximize the game's visibility.

This is, admittedly, a difficult context in which to perform a reparative analysis of *Bayonetta*. However, the visual enticement of misogynist consumers is only one side of Bayonetta's story, and there is a rich history of fan and academic critique that reads against author intentions in order to uncover different dimensions of a text's ideology. Like *Portal*, there is more to *Bayonetta* than meets the eye. The game is preoccupied with and skeptical of both the cinematic eye and the male gaze, whatever the original intentions of the creators during the design process. Bayonetta's relationship to visuality is complicated, both narratively and procedurally. She has the ability to make herself invisible at will by crossing into Purgatorio, a parallel plane of reality in which witches and angels can meet to do battle but into which normal humans cannot see. Human characters in the game world will still react to Bayonetta's destruction of

Figure 3.7. Bayonetta struts toward the camera. *Bayonetta* (Platinum Games, 2009). Screenshot by author.

physical objects and will act startled when she runs by, but they cannot see or touch her. During one cinematic sequence, an investigative journalist named Luka attempts to take a picture of Bayonetta with his camera only to discover that she cannot be captured on film (see figure 3.8). She uses invisibility to her advantage particularly against this relentless pursuer, running circles around him and painting his face with lipstick while he attempts to ascertain her position.

Heteromasculine desire in the game's cutscenes is mediated through the figure of Luka, whose fantasies about Bayonetta are enacted by the cinematic gaze and coincide with his inability to "really" see the world around him. In Chapter 5, for example, Bayonetta launches herself at Luka unexpectedly. They fly through the air. Time slows down. Luka's hand slides across her buttocks. Bayonetta clutches his face to her bosom. They land, Luka on bottom and Bayonetta steadying herself with a sexy flourish, as the platform on which they had been standing gets destroyed by a falling pillar. Bayonetta leaps off of him without another word to battle the incoming foes that he can't even see. In this way, Luka's fantasy of a willing embrace is shattered when it turns out Bayonetta was saving him from a danger he was unable to perceive. Similarly, in Chapter 14, Bayonetta watches for danger as Luka pilots a helicopter.

Figure 3.8. Luka attempts to take a picture of Bayonetta. *Bayonetta* (Platinum Games, 2009). Screenshot by author.

When she commands him to look, his response is a breathless, "Oh, I'm looking . . ." as another fantasy slow-motion sequence focuses on water dripping down Bayonetta's breasts.

Then they get blown apart by missiles.

Both scenes (and several others like it) parody Luka's inability to see what he calls "the reality of things." William Huber, in his blog about gendered power in *Bayonetta*, suggests that Luka is a stand-in for the masculine gamer—though Huber's basis for this claim rests largely on his skepticism of Bayonetta's function as a point of identification in the game world rather than an object purely for viewing.[49] Luka refers to characters from unrelated video games as ex-girlfriends, lending credibility to Huber's reading while also playing to a fannish desire for "Easter eggs" by connecting Luka to a metatextual world to which only gamers have access. If he does function as a gamer-surrogate in some ways, however (for masculine viewers rather than feminine ones, who from this critical perspective presumably would have no trouble identifying with a woman avatar), his status as the punch line to numerous jokes about vision also implicates the masculine gamer himself within this critique.

From the beginning, the narrative codes heterosexual union as deviant and dangerous: Bayonetta is the product of a witch mother and a sage father, a violation of the gendered clans' separation that plunges the world into war. So many critiques of Bayonetta focus on her relationship with men on and offscreen, including with the director Kamiya, to the exclusion of the other feminine characters around her: Jeanne, the sister-witch who is her primary antagonist until near the game's end, and Cereza, a child who wanders into the line of fire and accompanies Bayonetta through most of her journey. Father Balder, who is the Lumen Sage at the head of Ithavoll as well as Bayonetta's father, brings the further charge of pedophilia and incest when he seeks to unite his body with Cereza, whom he reveals to be Bayonetta's childhood self, by luring the girl into his lap. Cereza's role can be read as a means to constrain Bayonetta to the familiar role of mother and caretaker. However, the revelation of the girl's true identity toward the end of the game shifts the meaning of their relationship: protecting the little girl orients Bayonetta toward radical self-care rather than reproductive futurity. Her growing affection for Cereza is actually directed inward, her combat skills put toward self-actualization.

While Bayonetta does eventually require assistance to survive the end game, it comes not in the expected form of Luka but in Jeanne, the rival Umbra Witch with whom she is much more evenly matched intellectually, sexually, and in terms of actual power. Their girl-power relationship—and indeed, the entire conceit of a separatist clan of powerful warrior women—is the stuff of 1970s lesbian feminist fantasies. They maintain a healthy adversarial respect for one another throughout the early stages of the game, which develops into recognition and deep affection as they recall their history together: childhood friends who grew up and fought alongside one another in the war. The game is bookended by a repeated animation, reskinned to reflect a change in costume after five hundred years, which has them twirl in the air and match up back-to-back, descending as Bayonetta shouts, "Just stay close to me!" Though there is never an explicit sexual encounter between the two, neither is there one with Luka, whom Bayonetta taunts and punishes in much the same way as she does the angels in the game. Indeed, the "Torture" attacks that are often identified as part of the game's BDSM aesthetic are influenced not by sexual practice but by instruments of torture like iron maidens and guillotines, invoking the historical witch hunts in Europe more than sex dungeons. The one notable exception is the bondage horse, an actual piece of fetish furniture, which she uses against the only feminine-bodied angel in the game to bring her to an explosive orgasm.

Bayonetta engages queer narrative and aesthetics just as much as she actively refuses heteronormative gestures in the game, but her relationship to queerness exists in more than these surface signifiers. While the cinematic scenes in the game metaphorically ridicule Luka's gazing male eyes, they also by extension call into question the reality of the events the camera can show the spectator. The game's stylized cutscenes come in two varieties: those fully animated by a computer and storyboard sequences in which still images and partially frozen movement take the place of full motion animation. These latter scenes are framed with film sprocket holes, as if the cinematic eye has been overtaken by the procedural camera of game animation, not only relegating cinema to a pastness of narrative visuality but also undermining its reliability to capture the full details of a narrative event. What replaces it is a type of machinic vision unique to video games.

The Gamic Gaze and *Bayonetta*'s Sexual Analogues

I previously outlined Galloway's discussion of gamic vision as it evolved and remains distinct from the cinematic subjective shot, expanding the ability of the first-person point of view to encourage rather than thwart the spectator's identification with the camera's subject. Implicit within gamic vision is the machine-eye view—a subjective shot from the perspective of the rendering engine responsible for tracking and drawing the portions of gamespace visible to the gamer in real time. Where a film critic might look to the creative decisions of the director behind the camera, a gamic camera may or may not have a human subject framing the shots.[50] Because of the way that a player feels in control of the visual scene, many contemporary commercial games like *Bayonetta* require a gamic camera to automate the framing process as the gamer navigates through the 3D virtual world. *Bayonetta*'s real-time camera primarily functions to keep the avatar in the middle of the screen and is locked at a distance that prioritizes a wider radius for ease in negotiating the game's combat sequences, which are fast-paced, crowded with moving elements, and often feature enemy combatants that are orders of magnitude larger than Bayonetta herself (see figure 3.9). While some gamic camera systems allow the user to control both the angle and zoom of the shot, this is not a feature of *Bayonetta*'s scopic regime. This lack of control has been a source of complaint by fans on message boards both in regard to personal combat preference and sexual frustration over the inability to view the avatar up close. Indeed, the only way to zoom in on Bayonetta's body during play is to manipulate the system in a way that resembles sexual assault of both avatar and camera: the gamer must position Bayonetta in a corner and rotate the camera so that it becomes pinned between avatar and wall and is forced closer to her. Here, the enticement of voyeurism clashes with technological restriction. Watching Bayonetta becomes quite complicated during gameplay, and the gamic camera has much to do with this. Twitchy combo-driven combat mechanics ensure that Bayonetta as an avatar is usually a blur. The camera only slows to witness her most powerful (though not necessarily most sexual) attacks, and the photo-finish freeze-frames that end a sequence of battles (eliciting much commentary about her status as an

object for the camera) often obscure Bayonetta's figure behind an explosion of bloody body parts.

What is visible is a complicated matter in video games that is bound
up in software procedures like the constant calculation of visual output
based on user input or game rules such as the "fog of war" that determine what the gamer is allowed to see based on their previous actions
and earned abilities in the game. In *Bayonetta*, an exploit known as the
"camera trick" exposes the strange ways in which procedures interact
with visuality in the game: if the gamer activates a special power known
as "Witch Time" during play and has the gamic camera positioned such
that the enemies on-screen are not visible, they will not attack Bayonetta
even if they had been actively hostile before triggering the event. This is
a procedural accident, not an intentional design. These types of interactions, wherein user control over the gaze works on more than simply
the visual scene of the game, indicates that in gaming, the gaze can be
permeable and recursive. Indeed, just like in pornography or horror, it is
in the visual scene that gamers receive the information that transforms
the medium into what Carol Clover and Linda Williams call a "body
genre,"[51] a type of film that elicits strong reactions from the viewer's
body. In the case of a game, however, the loop is closed, with the bodily

Figure 3.9. Bayonetta (center, barely visible on-screen) fights the gigantic Temperantia.
Bayonetta (Platinum Games, 2009). Screenshot by author.

response feeding back into and transforming what happens on the screen via a peripheral device like a game controller. The question of the body in film spectatorship has been taken up extensively by film critics, and I am not suggesting that cinema does not engage the body in meaningful ways. However, my contention here is that the kinesthetic nature of the interface and the virtual rendering of space in gaming are qualitatively different than that achieved by cinema or other visual arts. This, in turn, has consequences for the gendered power dynamics of video games.

One difference is that the gamer's body physically interfaces with the game in ways that those of cinematic spectators do not. When it comes to sexualized content, this can create quite different bodily responses than those elicited by such content in film. Brenda Romero's history of sex in video games cites an interview with Atari founder Nolan Bushnell that suggests that developers considered the sexual implications of gaming hardware as far back as the arcade joystick.[52] In fact, an early Atari arcade cabinet called Gotcha sought to offer a nonphallic gaming option with an unsuccessful experimental control shaped like two breasts. Current mainstream game consoles do not employ peripherals designed exclusively for sex (although the teledildonics industry is thriving in this niche for the home computer market) but rather create moments that I call sexual analogues in which controller functions mimic sexual activity.

Certain weapons, for example, allow Bayonetta to create and mount a pole around which she twirls, dealing significant damage to the unfortunate audience of this spectacle; the gamer must perform this action by twirling the analog stick on the controller. The game's sexual analogues get really interesting during the "Torture" attacks that require swift, repetitive single-button presses in order to max out the power of the attack. This mechanic is by far the most common in the game, and its sexual implications aren't fully illuminated until a boss battle, when the attack is given the label of "Climax." This sexual analogue, unlike those in other games that mimic the rocking back and forth of penetration (as in Santa Monica Studio's *God of War* series) or *Simon*-like button-pressing sequences that code heterosexual coupling as a complicated but routine sequence of moves (as in Quantic Dream's *Heavy Rain*), the "Climax" finishers in *Bayonetta* invoke clitoral masturbation, particularly when one considers the common gamer strategy of placing the controller in their own lap and pressing with the index finger rather than the thumb in order to maximize button-pressing speed.[53] If we take the metaphoric potential of the game's sexual analogues seriously, the gamer's pleasure as registered by the body is characterized not by the twisting, phallic columns of hair summoning demons on-screen or suggestive combat moves of the avatar but by the simulation of clitoral stimulation on the controller. *Bayonetta*, as a soft-core production, certainly induces masturbatory pleasure as its critics claim, but it forces the tactile enactment of that pleasure into a clitoral structure.[54]

However, this gesture is merely disruptive rather than necessarily progressive in nature, working against the prevalence of phallic structures in video game culture, in soft-core practice, and in cinema. It pushes back, but from within a binary gender system in which phallus and clitoris are metonyms of cisgendered bodies. *Bayonetta*'s plot and gameplay take this one step further by leading the gamer to destroy a men-only Vatican analogue by systematically dismembering its giant, glittery, white angelic guardians.

From a scopic regime that entices the consumer oriented toward the exploitation of the male gaze, *Bayonetta* ultimately enlists the gamer in a project that deprivileges and ridicules phallic scopophilia, dismembers the structures of religio-corporate masculinity, literally and figuratively castrates its central figures, and channels masturbatory pleasure at the game's climaxes into a clitoral form. Here, Clover's comments about the dual sadistic and masochistic nature of the gaze are particularly salient: just as horror films use sadism as the sleight of hand to entice audiences into an ultimately masochistic experience, so too does *Bayonetta*. Tanner Higgin's primary complaint—that *Bayonetta* ultimately fails to "make men uncomfortable" about their potential desire for her body[55]—neglects to take into account the game's thinly veiled (and numerous) references to castration, which range in transparency from sequential bodily dismemberment, to bloody tentacle-severing, to casually shooting the penis off of a cherub statue.

Clover argues that horror films subvert what she calls "our ultimate gender story," that "sadistic violence is what finally distinguishes male from female," and that masochism has no place in hegemonic straight masculinity.[56] Her description of the critical response to the violent rape-revenge film *I Spit on Your Grave* (1978) is worth quoting at length:

This film provides, for many long stretches of its hour-and-a-half narration, as pure a feminine-masochistic jolt as the movies have to offer. No such possibility is even hinted at in the reviews that led to its condemnation and censorship, however. On the contrary, the film was characterized, in tones of outrage and in the name of feminism, as the ultimate incitement to male sadism, a "vile film for vicarious sex criminals," a "sleazy exploitation movie" that "makes rapists of us all." But there is something off here: something too shrill and totalizing in the claim of misogyny, something dishonest in the critical rewritings and outright misrepresentations of the plot required to sustain that claim, something suspicious about the refusal to entertain even in passing the possibility of involvement with the victim's part, something perverse about the unwillingness to engage with the manifestly feminist dimensions of the script.[57]

What happens in *Bayonetta*'s reception is an echo of this same reaction—a milder version in response to what one might call a milder text playing out decades later. Feminist critics condemn the way the game seems to offer her body up to the male gaze without interrogating the ways in which she demonstrably avoids it and turns it on itself. Chris Dahlen documents the shame and embarrassment professed by straight men playing the game, echoed in academic blogs by figures like Tanner Higgin and William Huber; for these men, she is a grotesque representation of what they are supposed to find attractive, an object to possess rather than to serve as a point of entry into the game world. Those who write in Bayonetta's defense mark her as a point of identification only for women (and, significantly, queer) gamers.[58]

Here again, we see the repetition of a failure to believe in a masculine identification with a feminine character, despite the game's other appeals to the so-called hard-core and presumed masculine gamer audience. *Bayonetta* is a brutally difficult game that focuses on skill and familiarity rather than luck: it is important to master the combat combos and special moves, because basic attacks are not adequate to survive the waves upon waves of angels that the gamer must face. Though it is a single-player experience, it maintains a highly competitive essence, with each Verse of each Chapter graded according to the gamer's offensive and defensive performance and reliance on supplementary items; those seeking a challenge are enticed to return and perfect their score by an in-game reward (unlocking a new avatar) for gaining the highest score on each Chapter, and those who perform poorly are mocked on the scoreboard. Performing well earns praise from Bayonetta herself, who coos "Baaaad boy!" from the speakers. There are also numerous hidden challenge rooms that reward thorough exploration and virtuosic combat skills. All of these gamic attributes, which seem to appeal to the masculine core video game demographic that values challenge and mastery of technology, nevertheless encourage critics to believe that Bayonetta's body is on offer only as eye candy rather than as an extension of the gamer's own subjectivity into the game world.

This failure to believe in transgender gamer identifications thoroughly infuses the industry's public statements and gamers' own self-assessments. The discourse of the "target demographic" of straight white adolescent boys—covered by researchers like Adrienne Shaw, who notes that it permeates popular and academic conversations alike[59]—is one of the foundational mythologies upon which video games are designed. It is the reason given for the preponderance of bald white space marines and the continued objectification of feminine bodies: you must give the market what it wants. On an individual level, researchers like Nicholas Yee have found that "male"-identified gamers playing "female"-bodied avatars often explain their behavior as driven either by voyeurism—the desire to watch a woman rather than a man's body on-screen—or by strategy—the "advantage" given to them by being perceived as women by other players.[60] When critics and academics alike take for granted that the power fantasies supplied by video games are accessible to all players and yet, except in rare cases, fail to explore the queer and transgender fantasies that attend feminine avatars in games that court masculine audiences, this seems to point to a repetition of the disavowal that Clover identified decades ago. This is also a repetition of Helen Kennedy's early critique about the reception of Lara Croft: "any kind of identification with Lara is disavowed through the production of stories and art that tends to want to securely fix Lara as an object of sexual desire and fantasy."[61]

It seems no surprise, in light of Clover's work, that the particular woman around which this controversy revolved does significant, unreserved violence not simply to men but to masculinity. However, the deeper issue here—that her essence somehow cannot be contained by the camera—gets at the heart of how game studies tries to articulate its object against other media forms like film: if something like a gaze operates in gaming, it is more than a visual field. It is, rather, a matrix of recursive vectors of desire among the elements of a gamic system: human, hardware, software, rules, narrative, and representation. What mediates Bayonetta, then, is not the penetrative cinematic camera described by Laura Mulvey and against which gamers judge her fitness as a feminist icon, but rather a recursive gamic system that kinesthetically entangles the body of the gamer via technological peripherals and the demands of play. Bayonetta's aggressively feminine, queer sexuality reaches beyond the screen to implicate the gamer in its own pleasures, disturbing the narratives we tell about what it means to be a gamer, or a woman, or a slut, or a hero in contemporary times.

Re-viewing the Visual Politics of (White) Feminism

Bayonetta offers a substantively different relationship between gamer and gaze than Portal. Where Portal weaponizes the gaze in order to discipline feminine subjectivity run wild, Bayonetta locks the gaze on its always-moving central figure as she castrates her way up the chain of patriarchy. And yet even this interpretation is only a partial victory: there is so much more to be said about both of these games. I will leave this analysis off, however, with a gesture at work yet to be done: namely, around accounting for the proliferating vectors of race that complicate seemingly straightforward questions of gender in "feminist" games. Bayonetta's whiteness, exaggerated by her posh British accent, gives her the ability to enact violence against patriarchy, and perhaps a power over the gaze, in a way quite unique to white feminists. This is a power that GLaDOS/Caroline possesses and Chell explicitly does not (indeed, her main function is as a puppet for patriarchy). GLaDOS and Bayonetta as rape-revengers offer a fantasy version of feminism that is empowering in its imagination of the violent end of patriarchy, but this is also the fantasy feminism that lies at the heart of misogynist backlash: the fear of a matriarchy just as brutal and oppressive as its masculine counterpart—a violent white supremacist matriarchy that women of color have long warned about.[62]

And so we return to the First Lady of gaming, whatever the suspect historical circumstances under which she ascended to that position. Soraya Murray observes that Lara Croft's whiteness operates to position her both as a "pure" damsel in distress and also as a powerful colonial subject in the context of a savage land. Croft enacts an embattled version of whiteness, a whiteness that "strategically mobilizes itself as a form of otherness" as it fights for survival and seeks to civilize its surroundings, reflecting the anxieties of a white supremacy straining to maintain its power in the wake of racial power shifts (both real and fantasized) during the Obama era.[63] Significantly, Murray also notes that Lara was a character who was whitened in the production process, her surname transformed from the brown Cruz to the posh British Croft.[64] We should add to this transformation her gender swap as well: she was originally designed as a man, akin to Indiana Jones.

Whatever the reason for the identity shifts, a white woman became the successor to Indiana Jones and his legacies of racial violence. Though she began her life as a buxom exaggeration of femininity, Lara Croft has since grown up. The 2013 reboot of the *Tomb Raider* franchise features a more realistically proportioned and appropriately dressed budding archaeologist who becomes shipwrecked on an island and endures a series of physical trials that eventually result in her ascension to the role of the hero—including the rescue of a damsel in distress. The developer chose to demonstrate the game to the public before its release with a preview sequence that critics decried as a potential rape scene: Lara, hands bound behind her back, is pinned against a building by a large man who leans his face in close to her neck and runs a hand down her hip. While the scene in the game plays out as a life-or-death struggle rather than a sexual assault, this eroticized encounter is, significantly, the first time that Lara kills another human being. Murray argues that white femininity in *Tomb Raider* "vacillates between the visual representation of a vulnerable female figure and the urgent drive to protect that playable figure from harm,"[65] subsuming Lara into familiar visual territory. These whispers of the rape-revenge cycle place her tangentially into the lineage of avenging women in cinema, setting the stage for the development of an excessively violent persona. When her life and the lives of her (predominantly nonwhite) crew are at stake, Lara commands an arsenal of weapons as impressive as any Hollywood commando and can wield a pickax in brutal execution moves uncharacteristic of her previous incarnations.

These deeds do not go unanswered, however, and the game's set-piece moments revolve around excessive trauma to Lara's body. Many of these moments are mediated through "quick-time events," in which the gamer must successfully complete a timed sequence of button presses or lose the game. Quick-time events offer developers the option to animate and script game events without accounting for unpredictability in user input; because there are fewer possible outcomes to these events, they often provide more elaborate experiences in terms of narrative and animation. *Tomb Raider's* extensive use of quick-time events in comparison to similar action titles means that there is an impressive bank of unique graphically rendered deaths for her to experience. Even more than this, the developers went to great lengths to animate unique deaths for Lara during live play, a notable creative decision within the complicated economy of resources that constitute a digital game. These deaths seem gratuitous in their variety and attention to detail: Lara is impaled through the jaw and skull on a long pole, crushed by rocks, strangled, strung upside-down and bled out, electrocuted, simultaneously penetrated by multiple arrows, and more. While spectacularized violence is not unique in video games, such physical vulnerability in the hero is more common in survival horror games, a genre quite different from gritty action titles like *Tomb Raider*.[66] Even Bayonetta, despite the fantastic brutality of her action title and the fact that she could die during gameplay, never endured so much as a scratch to her body during cinematic action, nor does she experience the kinds of prolonged physical suffering that Lara Croft does in her latest adventures.[67] This is certainly a reminder, perhaps even a warning, about the frailty of a woman's body, but it is also more ambivalent, to borrow Murray's terminology. Through what various entities have called "The Passion of the Croft,"[68] Lara also ascends to the status of the divine, her wounds paying entry for something of a patriarchal canonization. After enduring countless cycles of death and resurrection, Croft becomes conqueror of the island's demonic Japanese queen and savior of its savage inhabitants.

We must read these racial structures into the dynamics of the gamic gaze. Like many contemporary games, the visual field of *Tomb Raider* is minimalistic, the better to leave undisturbed the gamer's sense of immersion by excluding excessive nondiegetic information. Instead of a health bar, for example, damage done to Lara's body manifests as blood spatters on the screen, obscuring the gamer's gaze in a way that suggests a merging of avatar eye with camera lens. The third-person camera of *Tomb Raider* takes on the physiological aspects of the first-person camera as described by Galloway. This technique amplifies the gamer's connection to Lara, despite the placement of the camera at a distance from her body. In one notable sequence, Lara is parachuting through treetops, with the gamer acting to help her dodge obstacles along the way. After a successful landing, she trips and slides through a gate before being dumped into the alleyways of a shantytown that constitutes the game's next stage. Color drains from the screen and the image distorts with the pain of the impact, the controller pulsing and Lara whimpering with every step as the gamer guides her limping body around—bringing to mind how the body genre focuses on not only the excess sensations of corporeality but also the "inarticulate cries" that accompany them.[69] This pain prevents Lara from performing physical feats like scrambling up ledges, a gameplay incentive that points the gamer in the direction of medical supplies on a nearby helicopter.

This sequence in the game is exemplary of the gamic gaze: a visual field that gives voyeuristic access to the virtual world, which is then complicated by a recursive set of multisensory input and output that serves to invoke a sense of copresence (and commiseration) with the avatar. The gamic gaze does not depend on a first-person point of view to offer a subjective perspective, nor does it remain fixed in a single direction. While the visual is predominant among the data streams and transmits spatial and corporeal information, it is bolstered by audio and tactile information channels that are then returned by the gamer in a forward-looking, anticipatory loop that engages digital and physical bodies. Lara may never look back at the gamer with her eyes, but she does exist as more than an object separate unto herself. Like Bayonetta, Lara's body reaches back through the gamer's gaze upon her and imposes its own demands on their behavior. Like GLaDOS and Chell, she is simultaneously subject to and attendant over the gaze, and most importantly, she shares these positions with the gamer as well. But like Indiana Jones, Lara is both kick-ass avenger and brutal colonizer whose main gameplay functions are to map, pillage, and secure the wild island of Yamatai from its restless natives and supernatural queen.

In such a visual regime, gendered power negotiations are, as we have explored in each of these games, more troubled than they might seem at first glance. Let us complicate how we understand the power, and powerlessness, of (different kinds of) women in the media, the role of technology and game mechanics in producing politics, and the ways we conceive of visuality in computational media.

4

Does Anyone Really Identify with FemShep?

Troubling Identity (and) Politics in Mass Effect

Rather than claiming that digital identity politics references
a new form of socio-politically engaged identity production,
I suggest that I = Another names the dominant tendency
within the digital image regarding questions of identity and,
further, that this tendency taps into (but also complicates
an assessment of) the differential form as a component of
early twenty-first-century social movements under capitalist
production.

—Kara Keeling, "I = Another: Digital Identity Politics"

Here's a fun provocation: FemShep, the playful nickname given to the
female version of *Mass Effect*'s customizable hero, doesn't actually exist.
This would come as a surprise to many folks, including actor Jennifer
Hale, the writers who scripted dialogue with her paramours, the artists who sculpted a feminine face and body for the character, and the
fans who rallied around her as a much-needed example of a woman
action hero in video games.

FemShep's nonexistence would come as the biggest surprise to the
folks who were able to play out their lesbian fantasies in her epic space
opera romance. After all, BioWare's reputation as a queer-friendly
developer (or pervert-friendly one, according to some guests on Fox
News[1]) was thanks in no small part to FemShep's sapphic dalliances,
particularly since the male version of the character had no same-sex romance options until the final game in the original trilogy.[2] It was a common complaint, in fact, that queer representation in *Mass Effect* favored
women, even after a romanceable gay man was introduced to the series.
In gaming diversity calculus, FemShep represents the ability to incorporate not only gender and racial difference, which are easily implemented

as surface characteristics on an avatar, but sexual orientation as well, which involves more complicated narrative and procedural entanglements. FemShep is *diversity* personified for the *Mass Effect* series, anchored by her lock on queerness in the trilogy. However, I and many others contend that what we interpret as a queer woman in *Mass Effect* is no woman at all, but a consensual hallucination that the character is not simply a man whose superficial components have been swapped out for "women's" ones.

The latent transphobia of this statement emerges not only because video games more often than not enforce a binary gender (male or female) choice in avatar but also because digital character design begins with the essentialist, quantized approach to bodies (usually starting with a white man's body) discussed in chapter 2. While it is possible for some gamers to find liberatory trans potential in this arrangement, my reading proceeds from a deep skepticism that any women—trans, cis, nonbinary, and more—are accommodated at all in this arrangement. In the words of critic Carlen Lavigne, FemShep's diversity is "less a political statement or act of inclusiveness than an accident of code."[3] For Gabriela Richard, the experience of FemShep is "playing as a woman as a woman as if a man," where the feminine markers appended to the avatar are not enough to hide the fact that her experiences make more sense in a man's story.[4] Anita Sarkeesian calls this formulation "Ms. Male Character."[5] This hallucination is possible thanks to the modularity of digital media, the masking abilities of computer animation, and crucially, the very desire for a playable action hero, here embodied in FemShep, that can satisfy different personal fantasies of diversity.

Before I lose my FemShep readers to a justified fit of indignation, let me explain, first, that I understand FemShep's centrality to a queer feminist history of gaming and, according to any standards by which we should judge these things, FemShep is indeed a real thing (perhaps even a real character) in the world. By making a case that FemShep doesn't exist, I want to shift attention away from how characters like FemShep stand as icons of identity politics, singular units of representation on which audiences, academics, and creators may hang their aspirations and disappointments. No individual can bear the burden of such scrutiny, and decades of women of color feminism have instructed us to move beyond the singular when reaching for political effectiveness. We

don't need more Lara Crofts or Chells or Bayonettas to imagine new political formations in gaming, because we largely know how to read and
what to do with these types of figures—and FemShep herself has been
the subject of much analysis and hand-wringing.[6] Instead, I would like
to understand FemShep in terms of the gaps and holes that structure
her existence as a customizable character, because these are the fissures
into which gamers suture their own investments and begin to "identify
with" the character. I use this phrase in a casual way to indicate the multiple ways that gamers forge connections with avatars. As the title of this
chapter suggests, I am indebted to the work of scholars like Adrienne
Shaw, Nick Yee,[7] and others who have extensively explored the complicated ways that players do and don't identify with game avatars. I myself oscillate between different modes with different avatars; however,
like many other fans of *Mass Effect*, my relationship with Commander
Shepard has been particularly personal over the years.

The original *Mass Effect* video game trilogy, released between 2007
and 2012, is a space opera spanning the five-year battle of Commander
Shepard, one of the galactic special agents known as Spectres, against
an ancient group of machines called the Reapers who emerge every
fifty thousand years to wipe intelligent life out of the galaxy and make
way for new organic species to evolve. Shepard must bring together the
loosely allied interspecies galactic community, overcoming political and
cultural differences along the way, in order to prevail in a struggle that
has never been won. It is an original IP developed by Canadian studio
BioWare, a company well known for its deep and lengthy role-playing
experiences in franchises like *Dragon Age*, *Star Wars: The Old Republic*,
and *Neverwinter Nights*. BioWare cut its teeth on the genre by applying
the *Dungeons & Dragons* rules and narrative universe to a computer
game to create the massively successful *Baldur's Gate* in 1998. Since that
time, the company has developed a reputation for quality writing, massive stories, and an emphasis on characters and conversations that puts
building relationships on an equal footing with violent action.

To summarize *Mass Effect*'s three games in two sentences is a reductive gesture that erases the labor and time that goes into creating and
completing the entire story. The three main games have at least sixty
hours of primary gameplay, with dozens more hours of optional story
and mission content. As with any good role-playing game, the gamer

can customize the gender and physical appearance, within certain limits, of their character, and as with any good drama, *Mass Effect* has plot twists and needless exposition, triumphs and betrayals. The cast of characters required to sustain such a vast narrative is significant: Commander Shepard has nearly twenty significant companions rotating over the course of the series. The player, as Shepard, develops relationships with these individuals and more over time. The pixel people populating *Mass Effect* are startlingly compelling, their stories disarmingly authentic: always intimate, sometimes romantic, occasionally tragic. *Mass Effect* also offers players the opportunity to live out erotic fantasies with straight, gay, and interspecies romance options tailored to either of the choices of gender for Shepard.

To approach such a text as a critic is a daunting task. There is the standard concern of time investment: with a minimum of sixty hours for a single, incomplete playthrough, thoroughness and familiarity with the material comes at a high temporal price. There is the unfathomable multiplicity of content: two morality poles, hundreds of conversation trees, important plot points determined by different gamer actions. I have been aided in no small part by meticulous fans on YouTube who have documented their own journeys with Commander Shepard (chief among them, FluffyNinjaLlama, whose archive of *Mass Effect* romances is both impressive and thorough), but my analysis will necessarily seem fragmented in comparison to the vastness of the text with which it grapples. More difficult than all of this, however, is the affective burden of personal investment, which surpasses engagement with characters in other media: to put it bluntly, one might fall in love with Mr. Darcy on the page, but one does not have the opportunity to engage him in flirtatious banter and carefully decide on the conversational responses that might lure him in.[8] BioWare games present a particular challenge for critical distance if for no other reason than the sheer difficulty of maintaining psychic separation from a character whose body and world one must inhabit for close to hundreds of hours at a time—a diluted version of the holodeck that *Star Trek* imagined for our future. In my own work, I find Henry Jenkins's designation of the "aca-fan," a position that self-consciously negotiates between emotional attachment to and critical distance from a pop cultural object, to have particular potency here. My personal attachment to FemShep may not come with a confusion of identities, but it does come with a series of emotional entanglements that may peek through my analysis at different times. And yet, it is only through this personal attachment to the idea of my FemShep, a kickass genderqueer butch action hero with a complicated polyamorous love life and fierce dedication to preserving as many sentient lives as she could, that I was able to appreciate all the ways that she existed in spite of, rather than thanks to, BioWare's careful design. My playthroughs of the *Mass Effect* trilogy were full of jarring disconnects that drew attention to the ways my FemShep was different from what the technical and narrative systems of the games had in mind.

This chapter synthesizes the book's goal of troubling common strategies of representational analysis by weaving them into a broader view of the gamic system while also imagining new forms of politics that can emerge when we focus our attention on the elsewhere of an object of identification: in this case, the places where FemShep fails to cohere as a character. FemShep as a presence activates familiar scripts of identity politics and representational critiques, even as they have been changed over the years through savvy game studies analysis. FemShep as an absence, on the other hand, can trouble the way we think about identity politics in video games by reminding us of the political potential of difference in and of itself.

Modular Bodies, Parallel Romance: Deriving FemShep from BroShep

Games like *Mass Effect* advertise the array of narrative and customization options available to the gamer, but these possibilities create real challenges for artistic and technical design teams, who must fully develop the content for each potential scenario and ensure that the game fits a particular budget of time, money, and storage. These challenges are not trivial, though the extent to which developers understand their resulting decisions as political is unclear. As a technical object, Commander Shepard is nominally customizable. *Mass Effect*'s character customization system operates with slider bars that offer discrete, rather than fluid, differences in the targeted parts of the face: the gamer is offered a menu of objects to assemble into a unique face rather than a procedural mesh to tweak. Compared to other systems, including those of other games such as the FaceGen-based *Fallout 3* (2008) system explored in chapter 2, the options for facial manipulation in *Mass Effect* are more limited; one cannot, for example, exaggerate facial features using sliders to the same degree in *Mass Effect* as in *Fallout 3*. Faces in this game retain a higher degree of statistical probability than others, to use the vocabulary of the FaceGen designers. It is possible to give FemShep scars and less stereotypically feminine facial features, but on the whole, Shepard's face is difficult to render gender ambiguous. Gender expression, therefore, is limited to an array of hairstyles that are exclusive to the gamer's choice of Shepard's sex.[9] Race is similarly flattened out to a matter of style, with a discrete set of skin colors and facial features available to create convincing but limited racial diversity in Commander Shepard.

Mass Effect fans celebrate the flexibility of the facial customization interface despite, or perhaps because of, its limitations (there is pleasure, after all, in wrestling with the interface). Faces of Gaming, an online collection and showcase of avatars from a variety of video games, began its life as the *Mass Effect 2* Face Database, a collaborative homage to the customizable face of Commander Shepard. Site members upload snapshots of their own renditions of Commander Shepard, along with an explanation of the inspiration behind the face and creation codes that visitors can plug into their system to re-create them. Users create Shepards based on themselves, significant others, other video game characters, their own impression of what Commander Shepard might look like based on the character's voice, and so on. The site also has a large selection of celebrity-inspired Commander Shepard faces. Site users rate and comment on the faces in the database, establishing a hierarchy of proficiency with the limited tools available, and they share creation codes to encourage facial creation that does not resort to modding the software. At the time of this writing, there are more than 4,500 Commander Shepard faces uploaded to the database, an increase of 2,000 since I first began this project after the *Mass Effect* trilogy had been completed.

Women action heroes have been pivotal in the development of feminist film theory over the decades, yet Commander Shepard offers the rare opportunity to study an action hero that exists as both a man and a woman. Yvonne Tasker coined the term *musculinity* to discuss the emergence of 1980s and '90s woman action heroes who challenged the dominant gendered paradigm of the popular Hollywood genre by appropriating muscles as a signifier of masculine power.[10] Sigourney Weaver, Linda Hamilton, Grace Jones—these action stars disrupted the binary of soft women and hard men in Hollywood, initiating an era of feminine heroics based in brutish physicality and bulging biceps. FemShep does not appropriate the muscles of her male counterpart; while he is large and visibly strong, her frame is slight and her limbs are notably slender. Nevertheless, she can execute the same muscular approaches to social interaction as BroShep (the fannish designation for the male version of Shepard),[11] headbutting armored aliens, carrying fallen comrades over her shoulders, and starting bar brawls. A scene early in *Mass Effect 3* pits Commander Shepard against Lieutenant James Vega in a sparring match, their two contrasting bodies providing a jarring demonstration of the aesthetics and affects of musculinity.

Vega is a massive marine bruiser who executes thirty pull-ups as Shepard initiates the conversation. His personal space in the cargo bay has all but disappeared under dumbbells, just as his neck has receded into his bulging traps. Instead of agreeing to talk more, Vega asks Shepard to "dance" with him, initiating a quick-time event in which the two box each other and discuss Vega's suppressed anxieties about a past disastrous mission. This tough-guy therapy, depending on the gamer's choices and performance, sees both Shepard and Vega calmly and quietly trade bloody noses and appreciative grunts in between hard-hitting armchair psychology sound bites. As with all other cutscenes in the game, the conversations play out nearly identically for both FemShep and BroShep, and despite the vast difference in size, weight, and muscularity between the two, FemShep can neatly best Vega in hand-to-hand combat by throwing him over her shoulder and onto the ground, establishing her musculinity credentials without needing the actual muscles (see figure 4.1).

One explanation for this interaction is that *Mass Effect* exists in a fantasy universe in which both male and female bodies are granted unrealistic physical abilities compared to what bodies can do in real life. Another is the postfeminist fantasy that women have achieved political parity with men in this universe, which has become inscribed in their bodies' equal ability but normative physical appearance—one should be able to be both beautiful and strong, after all. However, the most likely explanation is much simpler: at the level of technology, the bodies of

FemShep and BroShep are intimately linked by body movements despite having quite different aesthetic designs. Modularity, which Lev Manovich identifies as one of the defining aspects of new media,[12] allows designers to switch out particular properties of software objects without changing their other characteristics. This allows customization to work in video games. The software can simply substitute one face for another without relying on extra data for information on how that face will move, for example. Characters are layers of data: skeletons, animation, skin, face, armor, accessories. Many of these features in *Mass Effect* are customizable to a degree.

Bodies and animations, however, are not. BioWare's recycled animations span race, species, and narrative universes. One can find examples of identical conversation animations that occur in both the science fiction context of *Mass Effect* and the medieval fantasy world of *Dragon Age*, as if the movement of a body depends only on its physical construction rather than the cultural practices and norms that surround it.[13] Unlike platforms like *Second Life*, in which users can load different animations into their avatars so that they can move in ways unique to the rest of the virtual world, *Mass Effect* uses the same animation data from FemShep to FemShep. It also uses the same animation data from BroShep to FemShep, resulting in incongruities such as the Vega brawl or the stereotypically masculine poses FemShep assumes while wearing

Figure 4.1. FemShep boxes Vega. *Mass Effect 3* (BioWare, 2012). Screenshot by author.

a dress, which lead her to expose herself to the camera.[14] There are queer and transgender potentials in this decoupling of masculine behavior from a man's body, but the effect is more likely a technical accident than a progressive social move.

Such gender-bending technological coincidences are not unprecedented in video games, and they rarely emerge from a desire to implement queerness in a game. Lionhead Studio's *Fable II* (2008), for example, was the first in the series to allow the gamer to choose a man or woman (both named Sparrow) for their avatar, making little distinction between the two except in initial physical appearance. Clothing, hairstyles, equipment, and even facial hair can be changed at any point in the game and worn by either avatar, opening up queer and transgender fashion possibilities for otherwise normatively gendered bodies. Sparrow's body changes and develops according to the player's actions: certain foods will make them gain and lose weight, alcohol will make them drunk, and their behavioral and moral choices become written on the body in the form of halos or horns, for example. The game also causes Sparrow to become increasingly muscular as they improve their strength statistics, resulting in a hulking physique that received negative

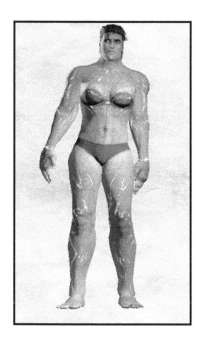

Figure 4.2. FemSparrow avatar with all statistics maximized. *Fable II* (Lionhead Studios, 2008). Screenshot by author.

attention from fans who wanted their FemSparrow avatars to be both strong and normatively attractive (see figure 4.2).

The queer spectacle enabled by *Fable II* masks a more limited technical infrastructure of gender and sexuality, as most such games do. While Sparrow's Amazonian female form might be appropriate to portray certain genderqueer individuals or body-building enthusiasts, procedural quirks suggest that gender flexibility in the game is less an attempt to represent queerness than an incomplete implementation of femininity within a normative masculine framework. For example, sexual activity in the game is structured around the biological penis: though same-sex encounters are an option, only condoms allow players to choose protected sex, and only when a "male" avatar is involved. Having protected or unprotected sex, among other in-game consequences like contracting a sexually transmitted infection, can affect the Pure–Corrupt meter of the game's morality system, which influences character appearance. By suggesting that women cannot have protected sex with other women and that intercourse is the primary sexual activity of heterosexual couples, the safe sex mechanic in the game ultimately centers cisgender men's bodies in sexual activity.

This is also borne out by the dialogue performed by the gamer's romantic and sexual partners. *Lesbian Gamers*, a blog once dedicated to lesbian issues in gaming, included *Fable II* on its Lesbian Uncanny Valley chart, which used Masahiro Mori's theory of realism and affect in robots to demonstrate unsettling, unrealistic representations of lesbians in popular culture. The chart observes that "your *Fable 2* wife calls you handsome," but might also have cited the moment when a feminine partner gushes about Sparrow's muscles during sex.[15] Much like Commander Shepard's unmuscular masculinity, Sparrow's bodily changes and sexual encounters speak to a small portion of queer and transgender sexual desires while on the whole pointing to femininity as only an add-on feature in the game, secondary to and indeed derivative of masculinity. Sparrow's performance of masculinity from within a woman's body is quite different from other transgender and genderqueer masculinities that destabilize and often seek to challenge heteronormative cisgender masculinity.[16]

The homogeneity of bodies in *Mass Effect* runs deeper than just the main characters. Masculine and feminine bodies across the *Mass Effect* universe are seemingly identical. Even nonhuman characters have the same measurements as the one-of-a-kind hero of the galaxy, a fact that is jarringly illustrated in the original game, in which all three possible lovemaking scenes are animated in nearly the same way[17] but occupied by different bodies depending on the character pairing. From an economic perspective, creating a multitude of body shapes that must be animated in order to have a world populated by diverse characters is a drain on resources that has little apparent benefit. Managing system resources is a vital part of the game design process, but the result here is an entire galaxy in which nearly all men and all women have identical bodies—bodies that imply a certain gender, race, and cultural heritage common to all (see figure 4.3). The white male Commander Shepard designed as the game's default avatar and marketing mascot serves as the index for all other characters in the game. In the context of a game that not only emphasizes user customization but turns on a narrative of multispecies, multinational cooperation, the sameness of body and movement, far from being a mere technical inconvenience, strikes a multiculturalist, postidentity chord that places white masculinity at the center of subjectivity all over again.

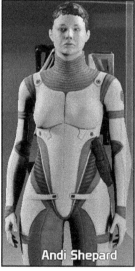

Figure 4.3. Identical women's bodies. *Mass Effect* (BioWare, 2007). Screenshots by author.

Just as FemShep's gestural vocabulary originates in a white man's body, her verbal script remains mostly unaltered from BroShep's version as well. Jennifer Hale's vocal performance as FemShep is a major factor in the character's popularity, and this parallel script provides handy evidence for fans warring over whether Hale or her counterpart, Mark Meer, offers the most compelling performance as Commander Shepard. The parallel scripts can also illuminate the messy seams generated by the assumptions and oversights of gender customization. Similar to *Fable II*, the easiest place to find these seams are in romantic and sexual relationships, as if the most important material impacts of sex and gender are on choice of romantic partner. Because almost all potential partners in each game are exclusive to a specific sex of Shepard, their romance story lines are written specifically for that instance of the character and have unique dialogue and animation content for each Shepard.

There is one parallel romance that exists for FemShep and BroShep in the first *Mass Effect*: the courtship of Dr. Liara T'Soni, an archaeologist of the Asari species, who was the only "lesbian" romance option in the game and therefore served as the vector for queer desire early in the series.[18] Described at various points as either monogendered or allfemale, the Asari are phenotypically feminine, their bodies resembling (indeed, identical to) the bodies of human women in the game. They can reproduce with any gender of any sentient species and are known throughout the galaxy as diplomats and entertainers. There is little deviation between the FemShep and BroShep scripts for the romance with Liara, which positions Commander Shepard as an experienced soldier (and lover) pursuing the naïve, reticent academic. The modular animations expose not only how FemShep becomes BroShep in the Liara lovemaking scenes but also that normative gender performance is fundamental to the way the game thinks about sexuality. The animations have clearly marked masculine and feminine positions, with Shepard's position determined entirely by their partner. The interchangeable lovemaking scene in the first game illustrates this quite well. *Mass Effect 2* features a cuddling scene that changes FemShep's position based on a masculine or feminine partner. While her combat and professional behaviors are unchanged from her masculine counterpart (who remains legibly masculine in all of his romance and sex scenes), FemShep is either masculine or feminine in romantic situations according to which partner the gamer chooses.[19]

BroShep almost had a parallel gay romance in the first game as well, but it was never fully developed. The first fan mods to enable a gay relationship for BroShep in *Mass Effect* uncovered recorded but unused dialogue for him to flirt with Kaidan Alenko, the straight love interest for FemShep. However, early versions of the mod were not able to adequately alter the game's animations, so the playable versions of the mod used the only animation available for a Kaidan romance, with Kaidan in the masculine position and FemShep's body abruptly substituted for BroShep's. Though Kaidan's parallel romance was never finished for inclusion in the final version of the first game, he did emerge as a love interest for BroShep in *Mass Effect 3*, where many of the conversations and animations were parallel to the FemShep romance (although they had some significant divergences because of the narrative framework necessary to account for the different times in which the relationships began). Crucially, although the love scene with Kaidan did utilize the same animation in both the BroShep and FemShep versions, it is Kaidan, not BroShep, who occupies the "feminine" animation used by FemShep in the straight version of the scene.

As with Sparrow, the existing BroShep template means that relationships play out with FemShep performing as a reskinned straight man rather than a masculine-of-center queer woman, no matter the superficial similarities that might exist in behavior between the two. It is important to maintain these distinctions, because conflating heterosexuality with gendered queer arrangements such as butch/femme, which the Liara/FemShep relationship seems to portray,[20] erases the important political and ontological differences of nonnormative gender and moves backward from decades of queer and transgender studies on precisely this topic.[21] Given the centrality of lesbian FemShep to the character's iconicity and function as an arbiter of difference in the series, that her sexual and gender identity largely derive from an original man is devastating indeed. Customizable gender and sexuality, rather than opening up possibilities for queer expression, funnel that expression into binary gender performances that strongly suggest an original masculine character onto which was added feminine attributes during the only moments in which such distinctions "really" matter.

Two of the biggest script differences between the Shepards emerge in the first game while courting Liara, and they reveal a curious conflation of interspecies relationships with homosexuality. At one point in the courtship conversations, Shepard has the option to ask Liara if she's sure about their relationship. BroShep questions her about species preference, while the FemShep question is about gender. Similarly, the optional love triangle that takes place in the game revolves around those respective issues: Liara's masculine rival is concerned that FemShep is a lesbian, while her feminine rival can't understand why BroShep would want someone of a different species. While conflating species with race is common in science fiction genres because it allows the exploration and exploitation of racist tropes without disrupting the fantasy of a united humanity, *Mass Effect* offloads gender onto species as well. The Asari occupy the feminine position in the galaxy, and most of the other major species that the gamer encounters are coded masculine. This has a narrative justification, such as the short-lived, scientific Salarians, who are reported to have a 90 percent male population, or the warlike Krogans, whose reproductive difficulties mean females are precious commodities that are rarely let off the homeworld. The games rarely, even into the final episode of the trilogy, included female members of galactic society.

Separating gendered differences by species helps essentialize the cultural traits that we associate with certain types of bodies. The queer potentials of the Asari's unique reproductive characteristics are undermined when their society is simultaneously represented as the promiscuous peacemakers of the galaxy. At 106 years old, Liara is still cast as an inexperienced young lady, with the explanation that Asari life cycles are vastly different from those of humans. Her reluctance to cast off her virginity is also explained as a species tendency: Liara claims that despite rumors concerning Asari sexual habits (as well as the seeming abundance of Asari sex workers across the galaxy), many of her kind are actually quite careful about partner selection due to the deep and lasting bonds formed during their psychic sexual activity. This transparent appeal to the fantasy of a wholesome yet sexually appealing young woman for the hero to conquer is emblematic of the ways in which BioWare has used species to stand in for gender. In fact, the only discernably masculine Asari encountered in the game, Matriarch Aethyta, presumably comes by her rougher edges thanks to her Krogan father.[22]

Condensing stereotypically feminine traits and stereotypically feminine bodies around an alien nucleus decenters humanity's gender troubles from the equation and offers one way for *Mass Effect* to portray a post-feminist fantasy of gender parity in humans while still taking advantage of conservative sexual fantasies and affirming the commonsense sexism accompanying the belief that women are *inherently* anything.

These narrative phenomena, however, have complicated relationships to design and technology: while it is a mere truism among fans that female alien models in the original game were left out due to technical constraints (in line with Gordon Van Dyke's comments about *Battlefield Bad Company*),[23] *Mass Effect* artists have in fact expressed anxiety about the labor involved in creating female bodies for the game. In a video interview with *Game Informer Magazine*, *Mass Effect 3*'s art director, Derek Watts, explained how Turian species design was functionally limited by the human skeletons underpinning the rigging of the game's characters, and then moved on to the question of gender: "And they're all males in the game. We usually try and avoid the females, 'cause . . . what do you do with a female Turian? Do you give her breasts, what do you do? Do you do lipstick on her? There's actually some of the concept artists [who] will draw lipstick on the male one and go, 'Hey, it's done!' And we're like 'No! No, can you take this serious?'"[24] Lead character artist Rodrigue Pralier, during an interview focused on the sculpting technology used in character modeling, suggests that female characters "in general" are more difficult to design because "we all have a different idea of what a beautiful woman looks like."[25] Jonathan Cooper, lead animator on *Mass Effect* and *Mass Effect 2*, has commented in interviews that adding women to a game is a matter of a few days' work and shortcuts that might "compromise" quality but offer the "more important" outcome that "you can actually play as who you want to play as."[26] Though his comments specifically addressed claims by Ubisoft employee Alex Amancio that adding a playable woman to *Assassin's Creed: Unity* would "double" the workload,[27] Cooper specifies that using mostly the same animations across the board and altering only a few to add character to an avatar only works if the male avatar provides the basis for these movements—otherwise, the result is, in his estimation, too effeminate.[28] These examples are somewhat wide-ranging, but they all add up to reveal a core belief in women as the second, ornamental sex. Moreover, the intimate entanglement of technology and aesthetics enables designers to conflate cultural biases with technological determinism, concealing the fact that it is precisely the investment in the white masculine body as digital Adam, so to speak, that creates extra labor and anxiety in sculpting digital Eve.

My deployment of anachronistic clichés here is meant to draw attention to the asynchronicity of mainstream gaming culture with academic and activist conversations, which we explored in the first chapter to think through how fan discourse addresses the immediate intellectual and political needs of its own community. In this case, developers that are considered progressive in the industry fail to apply a deep approach to meaningful inclusion, instead swapping surface signifiers in order to reap a maximum appearance of diversity (which theoretically comes with increased market share) at the lowest cost. Their explanations for failure also defer to the logic of the market and to what many perceive as the inflexible structures of technological design: it takes too much effort, economically speaking of course, to create a woman from scratch. FemShep's lacy lingerie (which matches that of all other women in the game and echoes their body-sameness as well) gives the lie to this engineered inclusivity: a tough macho exterior underwritten by the simpering style and mannerisms of a romantic leading lady. This could be really queer, and FemShep is often upheld as an example of a complicated action heroine in gaming who can kick ass and cuddle in equal measure. It could also simply be an accident, the result of a bizarre calculus designed to simulate a more diverse range of character identities:

```
CreateShep()
{
    str gender;
    animation = default;
    script = default;
    body = default;
    voice = default;
    chooseherogender(gender);
    if (gender == "female")
    {
        body = woman;
```

```
    voice = Hale;
    undergarments = lacy;
  }
    if (partner == "woman") fucklikeaman();
    else fucklikeawoman();
}
```

This pseudocode is tongue-in-cheek, of course, but it lines up with the way other critics talk about gender and sexuality in so-called queer games: gay buttons[29] and flags[30] and other remnants of the programming that lies beneath. Certain switches are flipped to create the illusion of FemShep, flattening distinctions between sex, gender, and sexuality and rendering any nuance meaningless. It is difficult not to come to the admittedly old-school conclusion that FemShep is, more literally than the cinematic action heroes against whom this charge is usually leveled, a "figurative man" in the shape of a woman. The transphobic undertones of this critique are important to note, though I would like to be clear that all of this reflects the inflexible frameworks of computation rather than the actual nature of gender identity. To call someone "really" a man or "really" a woman in this context is to reflect on the ways that certain bodies are boxed into menu choices in the system and how such boxes influence the way designers think about these individuals.

I = FemShep, and Difference That Makes a Difference

The switches that enable these changes nevertheless are important to those of us who manipulate them, even if they give us the shallowest means to access what makes us different from the norm. Commander Shepard is not a fictional entity like Ellen Ripley, whose appearance, actions, relationships, and sexual and romantic proclivities are firmly written in a set of canonical texts that are equally accessible to all those who seek them out. Instead, the character consists of fixed lines of dialogue (spoken by different actors according to gender) and a generally uniform plot arc, as well as many important characteristics that are left open for customization: the player decides the gender, appearance, family history, combat skills, sexual and romantic activities, and moral character (including genocidal tendencies) of their version of

Commander Shepard. Indeed, the work required to cohere an identifiable "FemShep" from the variety of aesthetic, narrative, and gameplay choices available glosses over the very important fact that she is a figure who looks, behaves, and loves differently in every playthrough. She emerges as a character in her own right only through the extensive fan labor that brought her to life, from the online blogs and communities that orbit around her to the widespread fan campaign to put her in the game's official marketing materials. And yet she is also not the empty and silent avatar that we see in games like *Elder Scrolls* or *Fable*, which makes her more useful as a political rallying point than figures like the former's Dragonborn or the latter's Sparrow. It is the tension between these two poles of representation, which BioWare cofounder Ray Muzyka characterizes as "first-person" and "third-person" characters,[31] that turn Commander Shepard into a particularly compelling figure.

FemShep's very existence, forged into a single imagined entity by those who are, in various capacities, the driving force that makes one FemShep different from any other FemShep, points to a paradoxical process of identification very specific to video games that can help us imagine new ways of enacting identity politics. Although there are many documented and competing theories about identification in video games,[32] I am interested in an approach that understands identification in terms of the ways users take on the mantle of another's identity, locating themselves not in the fixed structure of a character's personality but rather in the flexible points of customization that allow different versions of that character to exist.

This resembles what Kara Keeling formulates as *I = Another*, a process of identification that takes advantage of digital media's destabilization of the index to generate a coalitional politics that centers unity in difference. Working through queer of color critique, Keeling posits that the development of identity politics beginning in the 1960s and 1970s eroded the index over time and that the emergence of digital technologies helps bring that erosion to the foreground.[33] Here, the "index" is both the referent of representation as well as the "I" of identification itself: "Rather than heralding the triumph of identity as a self-evident equation of the index with its seemingly proper referent (I=I), the emergence of identity politics as a logic of collective identification and action strikes a blow to the very confidence with which 'I' achieves its coherence."[34] This is exemplified by the transition of feminist identity away from a unified concept of "woman" toward an intersectional politics that recognizes how that unified concept of "woman" erases the experiences of the most vulnerable members that might lay claim to that identity. As the index recedes from dominance, it allows a politics in which "difference functions in and as the index."[35] It is this notion of difference as the index, difference as the core of an identity rather than its accessory, that informs my reading of Commander Shepard.

In the case of a customizable narrative-based game avatar like Fem-Shep, the index (the central referent of either the character itself or the I of the player-avatar relation) is destabilized by customization options that allow a variety of individuals to take on, and alter, her identity. There is no FemShep because we cannot locate the essence of FemShep in her sameness across platforms, which would privilege her representational and programmatic entanglement with the BroShep template. We must, therefore, locate her in the gaps that create the differences between every FemShep that exists.

When I opened this chapter, I facetiously declared FemShep "diversity personified" in the *Mass Effect* trilogy for the way that she incorporates multiple forms of difference into her customization framework. This aligns her with what myself and others have recognized as the neoliberal tendency to offer diversity as a set of menu choices for the purposes of inducting broader populations of consumers into a privileged club.[36] I = Another, however, offers us a way to reclaim difference from the neoliberal funnel of diversity politics. The differences of avatar customization are not inherently politicized, but gamer activism around FemShep points to the ways that they can be. We see the seeds of this in the way that FemShep provides a space for marginalized gamers to build community with one another. For example, the *Border House*, a blog for intersectional feminist video game critique that was active from 2009 to 2015, featured a "My Commander Shepard" series where different contributors—all of whom were women, queer, and/or people of color—shared their versions of the character. All writers showcased FemSheps who were women of color.

Fan production also points us to the ways that unity in difference functions for FemShep. FemShep.com is an online community dedicated to the celebration of the character in all her multiplicity. An homage to a woman that "forever changed the way we look at games,"[37] FemShep .com was one of many fan interventions on BioWare's policy of only using BroShep as the official face of the *Mass Effect* series. Formerly a Ning social network site, the 2019 version of the website hosted galleries of individual FemSheps, a forum to discuss *Mass Effect* and other BioWare games, a chat room, and a role-playing community that allowed participants to continue the story of FemShep with friends. One of the projects to come out of FemShep.com is Sage's "The Many Faces of FemShep," a fan video retelling of the events of *Mass Effect 2* from the perspective of the individual FemSheps submitted through the FemShep .com and BioWare Social Network communities.

Released in 2011, "The Many Faces of FemShep" takes the viewer through the story of *Mass Effect 2* while seamlessly transitioning different FemSheps in and out of the footage. Jennifer Hale's vocal performance and the movements provided by character animation bind the different bodies and faces of the FemSheps together, demonstrating the paradox of a single character united because of the breadth of her multiplicity. *Mass Effect 2* begins with the death of Commander Shepard and their resurrection by a secretive paramilitary organization. "The Many Faces of FemShep" first introduces FemShep as a series of different women morphing into one another during a wake-up animation, after which a voice-over explains the resurrection process: "Our orders were clear: make Commander Shepard who she was before the explosion—the same mind, the same morals, the same personality. If we alter her identity in any way, if she's somehow not the woman she used to be, the Lazarus Project will have failed." In the context of the game, this recording, which Shepard discovers in the introductory mission after coming back from the dead, serves to connect the player to the uniqueness of their particular Commander Shepard by referring back to the decisions made in the previous game of the series, many of which are imported at the beginning of *Mass Effect 2* and influence the new narrative in different ways. By juxtaposing the voice-over against the many faces of FemShep, Sage draws attention to the contradictions of this narrative technique while simultaneously suggesting that there is a unifying thread linking the minds, morals, and personalities of all possible FemSheps.

At the same time that it relishes in this unity, the video forgoes narrative coherence to celebrate the mutually exclusive choices that different FemSheps make: she kills a companion who is later seen fighting at her side, takes a number of different lovers in the single night before her final mission (an impossibility in the game's programming), and specializes in a startling variety of combat and weapon skills. FemShep is a sniping engineer, a shotgun-wielding biotic, and a machine-gunning soldier all in one, a highly improbable occurrence in a single playthrough. She is Black and brown and white, straight and gay and potentially bisexual. She also performs both Paragon and Renegade actions (the two moral poles of the *Mass Effect* series), which Sage emphasizes by tinting certain scenes blue and red, respectively.[38] Viewers watching for their particular choices will be satisfied at some point during the video, even if the FemShep who performs them looks nothing like the one from their own playthrough. The result is a veritable unity in difference, where all FemSheps come together by virtue of their conflicting characteristics.

The video turns political by closing with a critique of BioWare's policy of never using FemShep as its *Mass Effect* spokesperson: in the final shot, FemShep leans in a doorway with a *Game Informer Magazine* cover featuring BroShep on the wall (digitally inserted into footage from the game), her voice-over (pulled from in-game audio) proclaiming, "I'm just here to get the job done. Let someone else be on the poster." With this final gesture, Sage became a voice in the growing fan conversation to pressure BioWare into recognizing FemShep as a real character worthy of becoming a public face of the series instead of a customization option invisible to anyone who won't choose her. The controversy over FemShep's exclusion from marketing materials is part of a larger conversation about the right of women to take up space in gamer culture, and FemShep's potential to facilitate a community grounded in difference is beautifully metaphorized during the ending credits sequence of "The Many Faces of FemShep," which acknowledges the individual FemSheps and their creators for contributing her likenesses to the video by featuring each one in turn. As the sequence comes to a close, the FemShep images multiply into an increasingly numerous grid, shrinking them beyond individual recognition while preserving their accumulated presence. This matrix of faces, which reflects a range of gender and racial identities, emphasizes that there is an intimacy accompanying the sheer volume of FemSheps incorporated into the story (see figure 4.4). FemShep is cast here as a multitude, an overwhelming array of individuals who not only retain their own names and identities but are connected to real users whose fannish affinity ensures that each and every one is part of a larger affective network. The final face in the sequence is Default Jane, BioWare's original preconstituted avatar, who lingers on the screen as the music crescendos dramatically before she becomes one of many, implicating even anonymous FemSheps within this matrix.

"The Many Faces of FemShep" ties users to avatars to other users through the gaps in the character that facilitate her difference. If I = FemShep, and all these other users = FemShep as well, transitivity dictates that I could = other users. The potential for feminist community with this particular action hero is quite potent. However, there are limitations to this model. Although "The Many Faces of FemShep" primarily celebrates the diversity of FemShep, it also highlights the technological quirks that undermine her existence as a character in her own right. Sage just as easily could have transitioned BroShep bodies into the scene and achieved a similar result. As I have discussed, this is true of *Mass Effect* more broadly, which treats gender and sexuality as if only

Figure 4.4. Grid of FemSheps. "The Many Faces of FemShep" (Sage, 2011). Screenshot by author.

superficial physical characteristics make one a woman, or a man, or a gay person, or a straight one. Digital technologies, tied to the discrete quantities that inform their logic, cling to difference as a set of isolated equivalences that may be swapped out for one another rather than a system of traits that are more fluid and less manageable. This flattens difference into modular categories, requiring individual differences to coexist independently without troubling the others.

In the previous section, I briefly outlined *Mass Effect*'s curious conflation of gender, race, and species, as if major categories of difference have collapsed together all over the galaxy, even as humanity maintains a superficial type of postfeminist, postracial diversity. FemShep's function as unity in difference for *Mass Effect* fans certainly results in a diverse array of FemSheps that span contemporary formulations of race, as we have seen in "My Commander Shepard" and "The Many Faces of FemShep." However, the difference that occupies almost all the space in public discourse around Commander Shepard centers on gender and sexuality, as if race has no bearing on this particular conversation. The origins of I = Another in queer women of color feminism, specifically the "house of difference" theorized by queer Black feminist Audre Lorde, requires the recognition that no gender or sexual identity exists without being inflected by the realities of race, class, ability, and other forms of difference, yet FemShep, and the unity that emerges around her, seems made to obscure everything else.

And yet, for all its postracial ideology, the *Mass Effect* narrative universe is completely wrapped up in racial politics of a type that explicitly implicate FemShep in its nuances. Christopher Patterson reads the narrative arc of the *Mass Effect* trilogy in terms of a neoliberal reckoning in which the gamer, role-playing as Shepard, performs as a "multiculturalist umpire" to reconcile groups triangulated by legacies of colonial violence under a militaristic new world order. Humanity occupies an ostensibly neutral but highly self-interested position in a galaxy fraught with racial tensions that have been subsumed, in classic science fiction style, under the sign of species. Crucially, only the player, performing through the human Shepard, possesses the agency and power to make and break alliances, heal old wounds, and reinforce established power hierarchies all over again, placing them in a position analogous to Western, specifically US, peace brokers in postcolonial states.[39]

Eva Zekany notes that the central conflict with the Reapers, a race of sentient machines who emerge to wipe out organic life every fifty thousand years, provides a radical other against which the species of the galaxy can understand their own comparatively trivial differences,[40] and the narrative subsequently takes on uncomfortable overtones of racial purity. For example, in *Mass Effect 2*, Shepard primarily operates on behalf of a group aiming to secure human supremacy in the galaxy. The Reapers themselves offer a fate more horrifying than death: incorporation into the Reaper collective via physical transformation or mind control. Indeed, one of the most popular fan theories circulated to resolve disappointment in the *Mass Effect 3* ending involves deconstructing the "good" ending of synthesis between organic and synthetic life as proof that Shepard has been compromised by Reaper indoctrination. This preoccupation with racial purity has continued in *Mass Effect: Andromeda*, a sequel taking place beyond the boundaries of Shepard's story, in which Milky Way colonists find themselves in a new galaxy battling a foe that genetically modifies them to become part of its own species.

For Patterson, the racial conflicts of *Mass Effect* become more complicated through the player's choices and the voice actors' performances, which provide multiple possible contexts for resolving (or instigating) conflict. However, it is the very choice of FemShep that enables more radical potential in *Mass Effect*, as this "shifts the game's attitude from one of multiculturalist umpire toward one of multiracial coalition by focusing on remaining structures of patriarchal power and reproductive control,"[41] something that the identity of BroShep cannot draw out by virtue of his identity as a member of the dominant class. Patterson mostly refers to the ability of femininity to draw attention to these power dynamics by association, but he also cites a minor difference in the conversation between FemShep and the female Krogan leader Eve that ends with an acknowledgment of gender solidarity. This shift helps focus attention on the ways that gendered power is inextricable from the history of colonial and racial oppression facing the different species in galactic society. By Patterson's own admission, however, only a unique set of choices and an attentive player may create the conditions that make these connections explicit. FemShep is a conduit for such an understanding, but she does not guarantee that any given player will connect the dots. What she does provide, regardless of player input, is a vocal performance that situates crucial moments of decision-making in a more dynamic affective register than the monotone soldier voice of BroShep.[42]

Whether coalition builder or multiculturalist umpire, each FemShep becomes defined through the player's choices in the game world, though certain elements of her personality anchor all these differences within a set of fixed characteristics. The oscillation between player and Fem-Shep produces a character whose sameness is generated in moments of inaction and spectatorship but whose differences emerge through performative actions. But the game does more than simply provide the opportunity to make choices: it requires the player's performance. Fem-Shep, and the game itself, collapses without input from the player. Difference, therefore, is not merely an option to pursue but a conscious series of choices and a requirement for advancement. In *Mass Effect*, these choices are driven by the structure of a hero's journey and constrained by the acceptable range of difference dictated by the game's design. This is not the unity in difference of multiracial coalition. This unity in difference is driven by an I, the heroic player merged with heroic avatar, who is primarily accountable to their own decisions, feelings of empowerment, and sense of agency. This is the multiculturalist umpire in action, forcing unity through individual action. In order to rescue difference from this model, we must call into question the centrality of the individual in our narratives of progress.

No More Heroes: Achieving Coalition in the House of Difference

Audre Lorde's notion of the house of difference, on which Keeling's I = Another is based, is a place where communities can converge around their distance from hegemonic forms of power in order to collectively support one another.[43] However, it does not offer the easy comforts of unity in sameness. It is a place of vulnerability and instability, an uncomfortable and some might say troubled place where individuals must confront the reality that difference itself cannot, and perhaps should not, be overcome. Unity in difference is an ethos of coalition, not assimilation. We might interpret it as a space in which the I of identification learns to take a back seat and sublimate itself to the I's of Another. These arrangements are necessarily precarious and difficult to maintain, if for no other reason than that they require individuals to remain most vulnerable to those with whom they may share very little in common but with whom they are in community. This is an important way to distinguish diversity from difference: diversity politics seek harmony in spite of difference rather than a unified struggle through and with difference.

Now that we have reached this point, I will up the ante on my original provocation and state plainly that FemShep should not exist, because if she did actually exist, she would represent not the convergence of incommensurable differences in tactical coalition but rather the top-down disciplining of difference for the sake of a greater good. In *Mass Effect*, this plays out narratively as the sidelining of marginalized struggle in the name of eliminating the radical Otherness represented by the Reapers. This is Patterson's multiculturalist umpire, helping everyone compromise in order to fall in line under the umpire's (empire's?) authority. Technological and ludic structures reinforce this grand narrative, because they organize difference in ways that reduce its complexity for easy management. This is true of all the game's customization, conversation, and combat systems, all of which enable (or compel) the expression of difference but constrain it into a set of convenient choices. This was vividly illustrated once fans united in their differential FemSheps for political action and successfully demanded BioWare's inclusion of FemShep in the *Mass Effect 3* marketing materials. The implementation of this victory was a notorious setback for feminist gamers who had worked so hard for recognition: for FemShep to finally exist in the public sphere, BioWare implemented a voting mechanism whereby anyone could decide her appearance. This was widely criticized as a gesture that placed FemShep in the position of other women whose appearances were up for scrutiny by a predominantly masculine public.[44] However, it also further tamed the differences of FemShep into a set of faces determined by the corporate logics of diversity politics, and the FemShep who was finally chosen by the majority was a normatively feminine, attractive white woman with red hair.

The language of diversity is central both to feminist gamer politics and to the industry's attempts to address its own shortcomings. There are demonstrable problems with the representational practices of the industry, and many developers' responses to calls for inclusion, as we have seen with FemShep, tend to preserve the underlying structures of heteronormativity and patriarchy while simply swapping out surface signifiers. Diversity has a history of being easily co-opted by institutions to extend the life-span of hegemony—or at the very least, of directing change in the most convenient ways possible. The critical record on this score is quite extensive. Jasbir Puar, for example, demonstrates how the assimilation of queer identities into the productive nation-state requires participation in the creation of the new, more threatening figure of the Orientalized terrorist.[45] In *Freedom with Violence*, Chandan Reddy traces a long history of government policies designed to advance minority rights in the US that are invariably yoked to legislation and cultural movements extending the state's violent influence over other minority populations both at home and around the world. Once taken up by institutions, affirmative action policies that were developed mostly in response to racial inequalities in education and hiring practices seemed only to begin closing a gap between white men and white women.[46] Advocating for and achieving diversity may present an initial challenge to oppressive institutional structures, but those structures can easily recover and even benefit from these changes.

Roderick Ferguson captures the problem best in his compelling account of the mid-twentieth-century proliferation of minority identities and their subsequent absorption and utilization by the state, capital, and the university: "[The] conventional account of radicalisms that transgress and hegemonies that recoil mobilizes the sixties to produce a repressive hypothesis that locates hegemonic power only within the work of repression. But capital's investment in social movements compels us to rebut this repressive hypothesis because it cannot help us appreciate the role that minority difference played in the transformation of power."[47] Given the ease with which corporations monetize difference, it is no surprise that video games are waking to their untapped market. While it is a common refrain now that women in particular make up at least half of the gaming population, there is evidence to suggest that this has always been the case, and it is only as technology allows for cheap and easy imitations of diversity that attempts to include women and people of color in a broad way are being implemented. Yet it is this monetizing tendency that makes appeals for inclusion on the basis of consumer spending power such a risky proposition in terms of social justice. In the best-case scenario, it makes inclusion contingent on economically favorable conditions: resources will always be an acceptable (if disingenuous) excuse for lack of representation. At its worst, the incorporation of difference can enlist new populations in the perpetuation of oppressive systems.

Even if FemShep were a complicated, empowered individual woman designed in her own right, rather than a reskinned man, she may not exhibit the best characteristics of a progressive champion. Lisa Coulthard, in her analysis of violent action heroines in genre cinema, suggests that even while they might disrupt the gendered binary on which the "figurative man" critique insists, these women still operate within an exceptionalist model of capitalist individualism and cannot therefore be useful to a feminist politics of "solidarity, collectivity, or political action."[48] FemShep, as a heroine of late capitalism, would more than likely seek to lead us out of the house of difference to smash the radical Other.

This problem can be attributed to the conservative nature of mainstream media and the simple fact that glorious triumph appeals to every individual, but let us dwell for a moment on agency—specifically, the ways in which agentic fantasies of control have been taken up in marketing efforts for mainstream gaming. Video games, with user-driven action sequences and an emphasis on fun and winning, provide excellent power fantasies for any gamer. The language of power exists in slogans everywhere from hardware manufacturers (Nintendo: "Now You're Playing with Power") to games publishers (EA Games: "Challenge Everything") to retail stores (GameStop: "Power to the Players"). On the back of the *Mass Effect 3* N7 Collector's Edition packaging, BioWare makes a lofty promise: "Groundbreaking interactive storytelling drives the heart-pounding action in which each decision you make could have devastating and deadly consequences." While I have discussed how these promises are rarely accurate, that they persist even in contemporary advertising and gaming culture speaks to the powerful sway the fantasy of agency has over industry and fan expectations.

In 2012, fan response to the ending of *Mass Effect 3* proved the extent to which the fantasy of agency over narrative can be a motivating factor in playing a video game. Complaints about the highly anticipated ending of the trilogy were wide-ranging but crystallized around the accusation that BioWare failed to implement the decisions of over a hundred hours of gameplay in meaningful ways. Instead, at the game's original conclusion, gamers make a single decision that initiates one of three short endings—all of which seem to end, thanks to sparse narrative detail, in the destruction of the entire galaxy. In addition to offering far less than the proliferating possibilities promised by the continuous stream of choices made throughout the three entries in the *Mass Effect* series, the ending failed to cohere thematically to the game's nuanced conflict between organic and synthetic life, and the lack of a happy ending effectively eviscerated the power fantasy of Commander Shepard.[49] Angry fans wrote blog posts, signed petitions, and raised money in the hopes of changing the final few minutes of the narrative. One fan even filed a false advertising complaint with the Federal Trade Commission, claiming that the ending did not live up to the "advertising campaign and PR interviews" BioWare ran in advance of the game's release.[50] A month after the game debuted, Electronic Arts (EA), the publisher responsible for bringing *Mass Effect 3* to the masses, was voted *Consumerist* magazine's "Worst Company in America" for 2012. EA's chief operating officer, Peter Moore, attributed this honor, in part, to the *Mass Effect 3* ending.[51]

Games critic Sparky Clarkson characterized the outcry as a matter of wounded pride: BioWare did not respect the power that the gamer had over the narrative universe it had created, and Clarkson read most of the reactions, including the extensive close readings fans produced to make sense of the contradictions, as a matter of taking control back from BioWare. Many other commentators shared this sentiment, whether they felt personally injured by the game's end or felt that the individuals complaining were entitled brats.[52] Ray Muzyka, cofounder of BioWare, admitted, "Mass Effect 3 concludes a trilogy with so much player control and ownership of the story that it was hard for us to predict the range of emotions players would feel when they finished playing through it."[53]

Returning to Coulthard's comments about the individualistic war hero of late capitalism, it is difficult not to see the narrative conflicts of Commander Shepard reaching out into *Mass Effect* fandom and mingling with the power fantasies promised by the video game industry. The revision of *Mass Effect 3* in response to audience criticism is not an unprecedented move in the games industry or in other media, but BioWare is particularly receptive to and communicative with its fans: even when they do not make corrections based on fan input, they do often engage the community in public conversation and defend practices like the inclusion of gay and lesbian romance options to their critics. The *Mass Effect* fandom enjoys a privileged position to the series' canon compared to many other fandoms, yet at least some of the reaction to the ending of the third game reveals a troubled relationship between gamers and corporate behemoths. The Retake *Mass Effect 3* movement, for example, which raised eighty thousand dollars in fan donations through *Penny Arcade*'s crowdfunding Child's Play donation service before being shut down by the organization, spawned a smaller and short-lived group called Retake Gaming to "provide gamers with a voice against the oppression of large gaming companies" after BioWare changed the endings.[54] The language of identity politics seeps in here, and it's far from the only place: organizations like the Video Game Voters Network, Game Politics, and the Entertainment Consumers Association indicate both a crystallization of "gamer" into a coherent identity and, moreover, a fear of being taken advantage of or persecuted because of this identity.

While it is important to recognize the difference between perceived oppression of consumer desires by content creators and actual oppression enacted by institutions on those without an equal degree of power, the former discourse clearly draws from the latter and inherits much of its historical baggage. Recent feminist critique characterizes the discourse around agency as one that locks critics into the conceptual domain of neoliberal subjectivity, even and especially when it is cast as a requirement for resistance. Kimberly Hutchings places contemporary conceptions of agency within a genealogy dating back to the development of revolutionary subjectivity during the eighteenth century, arguing that the revolutionary subject on which our notion of autonomous agency relies was a product of rather than a precursor to actual revolution. She writes at length, "Marxist and liberal revolutionary narratives conflated revolutionary agency with normative ideals of autonomy institutionalised in the Revolution in the form of the republican nation-state and the rights of man. These normative ideals of autonomy were clearly closely bound up with Enlightenment rationalism and romanticism and with Western capitalist modernity. And self-identification with these ideals has, as feminism is well aware, led as much to conditions of oppression and violence as to conditions of equality and peace."[55]

Hutchings's analysis emerges in the context of feminist scholars questioning whether any woman can, should, or must become an autonomous agent as we understand it in order to enact the goals of feminism. Their critique comes largely from postcolonial and women of color feminist schools of thought that challenge white feminism's demands for a particular kind of subject that can demonstrate a particular type of resistance to patriarchal regimes: one prominent example of this is Saba Mahmood's study of veiled Muslim women in Egypt who do not fit the Western model of feminist agency and yet made significant contributions to projects of resistance.[56] Hutchings and others contend that the agency-coercion split in feminist discourse impoverishes the possibilities for imagining a feminist future, yoking it instead to notions of "freedom" that are contingent on participation in economic and institutional structures that continually reproduce oppressive conditions. This split between agency and coercion also intersects with feminist debates about sex work and popular culture. For example, Rosalind Gill and Ngaire Donaghue argue that the language of agency can function as a way to shut down critique of postfeminist positions that valorize traditional gender roles: by this logic, there can be no oppression or marginalization when a woman chooses to conform.[57]

There is a similar mechanism at work in gaming culture, in which the fetishization of user choice, from avatar expression to control over a narrative, is seen as the ultimate extension of social justice in the industry. It is clear that the identitarian fantasies enabled by increased avatar choices, for example, fit neatly within neoliberal regimes of representation and implementation of diversity politics that prioritize the individual consumer's power. Choosing from among a constrained set of options is still a way to exert one's control over the system. This seems to proliferate diversity and enhance a developer's reputation while actually deferring their responsibility to create meaningfully diverse representations. This is also a fragile arrangement: the conflict over the *Mass Effect 3* ending demonstrates what happens when a critical mass of gamers feels that the agency they had been promised has been abruptly exposed as the illusion it always was—when the envelope is ruptured.

Emphasizing multiplicity and coalition avoids the individualist trap of agentic thinking as a prerequisite for political action, a structure that is so easy to replicate in video games. Hutchings points to Elizabeth Grosz and Mahmood as models for a feminist politics of becoming rather than being, one that is characterized by the "affirmation of plurality . . . in the register of humility."[58] When put together with mainstream gaming, already set up as a continual negotiation with a technological, textual, and identity system that emerges from hegemonic practices, these theories may enact the kind of diversity work as phenomenological practice that Sara Ahmed identifies in *On Being Included*. For gamers, I = Another is the troubled meeting of individual with interface that often devolves into a struggle for control with the system but can, given the right system and the right user, open up into a symbiosis with radical potential.

In order to heed the call to complicate the distinction between agency and coercion (or control and freedom, as expressed by Wendy Chun,[59] or "the unnecessary binarism of free will and determinism," according to Judith Butler[60]), I return to FemShep's fraught avatarial position: the woman created from the man, occupied by the player. Ultimately, Commander Shepard fails as an embodiment of difference. The closure of the trilogy reveals the limitations of customization options and collapses the illusion of possibility into a constrained set of choices that hew closely to the game's middle road, just as the vote for an official FemShep locked down some of her characteristics to a crowdsourced lowest common denominator. It is impossible to separate this disappointment into a failure of technology or human imagination, because both mutually constitute each other in the process of designing a game. On one level, the struggle for FemShep is a consumer struggle for representation, and BioWare's response a containment strategy to expand (or maintain) their hold on a niche market. And yet in this failure, and in the fan activism that has emerged around her, FemShep contains lessons for moving games and gamer culture toward justice.

Each player discovers the truth about choice in *Mass Effect* in different ways: struggling with an avatar interface that centers whiteness, thinness, able bodies, and binary gender; cringing through queer sex scenes generated from heterosexual encounters; making life-or-death choices for colonized people; remaining in the closet until the developers give the option to come out. When these moments of friction intersect with someone's identity, it is hard not to feel the sting of disappointment. For those who experience marginalization regularly in their lives, this disappointment resonates with other personal and collective histories of trauma. Kai Green and Treva Ellison, writing to encourage white queers to confront anti-Blackness in their conversations and activism around queer liberation, point out that the house of difference is "not a singular place, but . . . a geography of injury and interdependence, one of pain and possibility."[61] It is a place to come together and share experiences of marginalization, to forge community that respects the uniqueness of experience, and to strategize for the greater good. For some, FemShep is that place.

Throughout this chapter, I have argued for an understanding of FemShep not as a character in her own right (the singular hero who saved the galaxy) but as a hegemonic structure (an avatar centered in white masculinity) riddled with holes and inconsistencies through which fans have achieved solidarity—not, crucially, by ascending to the status of the hero themselves but by inhabiting her contradictions, learning from them, and leveraging them to speak back to the policies demonstrating that she (and they) are less than in gamer culture. She offers imperfect possibilities for a range of differences, a makeshift shelter for the marginalized that nevertheless falls short of what she needs to be. And ultimately, though I find much to fault in the deployment of FemShep, she is an inextricable component of my own and other gamers' experiences with identity and politics in video games.

Critique is an important and vital part of achieving justice, and I want to close with the suggestion that it is better for developers to keep trying and failing at these efforts rather than not risk failing at all—as long as they keep failing in good faith. Keeling herself warns that the deployment of I = Another is inherently dangerous, that it risks falling into "a politics of appropriation and essentialism" and that effective implementation requires an awareness and acknowledgment of its own riskiness.[62] This collapse is precisely why FemShep fumbles as an implementation of diversity politics. BioWare chose to appropriate her difference and turn it into sameness for the sake of marketing: in the spirit of democracy, they pursued the desire of the majority rather than risk of alienating their "core" demographic with a policy that would highlight the diversity that she actually represented for many gamers. But FemShep is not the end of the story of action heroines in video games, and further efforts to create avatars, characters, and game systems that prioritize difference and coalition over the singular hero will continue.

Culture, like games, develops in iterative patterns, with incremental improvements and setbacks. The important part is to keep learning, keep developing, keep striving to improve. Whether justice will ever win over money in mass culture video games is still an open question, but the continued activism of fans and critics will at least ensure that creators have endless opportunities to learn.

Conclusion

Playing the Long Game

The angers between women will not kill us if we can articulate them with precision, if we listen to the content of what is said with at least as much intensity as we defend ourselves against the manner of saying. When we turn from anger we turn from insight, saying we will accept only the designs already known, deadly and safely familiar. I have tried to learn my anger's usefulness to me, as well as its limitations.
—Audre Lorde, "The Uses of Anger"

Do not get lost in a sea of despair. Be hopeful, be optimistic. Our struggle is not the struggle of a day, a week, a month, or a year, it is the struggle of a lifetime. Never, ever be afraid to make some noise and get in good trouble, necessary trouble. #goodtrouble
—US representative John Lewis, @repjohnlewis

Reclaiming the Agon

In the Wachowskis' film *The Matrix* (1999), Morpheus offers Neo the choice between the red pill and the blue pill after explaining to him the ugly truth of his existence: far from being a more or less free individual in late-twentieth-century society, Neo is a human battery pack enslaved by machines, his physical body held prisoner in a liquid cell while a simulation program distracts his mind. Taking the red pill will wake his body up and enlist him in the real-world fight against the machines, while taking the blue pill will return him to the simulation with no memory of what he has learned about the world. This scene dramatizes a question at least as old as Plato's allegory of the cave: is it preferable to remain in blissful ignorance of the chains that bind us or to pursue the constant struggle of engaging with the world in all of its complexities? When I was in college, *The Matrix* was still cool enough to help twentysomethings think about ideology, but as a gamer, I found it particularly compelling in how it explored the superpowers I always felt like I had when jacking into a virtual world. It is perhaps no coincidence that the Wachowskis themselves identify as gamers. The film's flashy martial arts fight scenes helped articulate another truth I (ironically) never realized video games had taught me: obviously, ideology was for fighting against—with your fists.

I mentioned in the introduction to this book that the metaphor of the red pill has been taken up recently by certain misogynist elements of internet culture to represent an awakening from the purportedly hegemonic ideology of feminism, which has led them to wage their own fight to liberate men from their long-standing oppression. I also flipped the script on this appropriation, suggesting instead that their red pill is, in fact, blue—a way to regress to a state of gendered relations prior to the challenges presented to hegemonic masculinity by feminism. I find questions of ease and difficulty in political relations particularly compelling not out of any Protestant sense that hard work is a virtue, but because gamers have always created purpose and fun for themselves by pursuing unnecessary obstacles. In fact, gamers cultivate systemic thinking in such a way that they are frequently attuned to questions of power, exploitation, and fairness without necessarily thinking of them in identitarian or even political terms. The gamer's pursuit of difficulty and conflict is, I argue, incredibly useful for political change, if currently underutilized or oriented in a regressive direction.

In exploring the potentials and limitations of video games and game studies for queer (and) women of color feminist political possibilities, I have emphasized how trouble in the form of community conflict, technological histories, human-interface interactions, and representational practices continually force gamers to negotiate power and identity both inside and outside of the envelope of play. Gamers' frictional encounters with the forces that structure the gamic system, from rules and mechanics to interfaces and other players, are not unlike the performative frictions that Judith Butler outlined in *Gender Trouble*. Certainly, they offer us another set of relations to test out and expand our understanding of power and identification in the age of networked media. To do this, I have drawn upon scholars of new media, digital humanities, and queer and women of color feminist theories.

In the final chapter of *Gamer Trouble*, "Does Anyone Really Identify with FemShep?" I explored the possibility of radical community in gaming through Kara Keeling's formulation of I = Another, which itself is built on Audre Lorde's house of difference as described in her biomythography *Zami: A New Spelling of My Name*. In perhaps her most famous essay, "The Master's Tools Will Never Dismantle the Master's House," Lorde further develops her account of difference as that which energizes meaningful political change: "Advocating for the mere tolerance of difference between women is the grossest reformism. For difference must not be merely tolerated, but seen as a fund of necessary polarities between which our creativity can spark like a dialectic. Only then does the necessity for interdependency become unthreatening. Only within that interdependency of different strengths, acknowledged and equal, can the power to seek new ways to actively 'be' in the world generate, as well as the courage and sustenance to act where there are no charters." Flattening difference, or subsuming it under the sign of "diversity" that seeks unity in sameness halts the generative friction that produces power for the marginalized, as I argued in the chapter. Without a bit of trouble, political relations stall out and harden into immovable, easily sortable categories that are ripe for exploitation. Lorde seeks coalition driven by the friction of difference rather than the ease of diversity, insisting that a failure to recognize the inevitable conflict that such differences cause will never get anyone free.

In game studies, one of our primary means for understanding conflict is the *agon*, proposed by Roger Caillois as the mode of play that is "like a combat in which equality of chances is artificially created, in order that adversaries should confront each other under ideal conditions, susceptible of giving precise and incontestable value to the winner's triumph."[1] Stephanie Boluk and Patrick LeMieux, reading through McKenzie Wark, position the agon as a quintessential capitalist form: "*Agon* lies at the heart of the most ancient games and, not coincidentally, at the heart of capital."[2] By requiring that everything submits to quantified comparison in the interest of declaring a victor, the agon becomes something of a villain in the story of gaming culture told by leftist game studies, rendering all forms of competition according to the zero-sum logic of capitalism. Indeed, I myself have argued in parts of this book (such as in my characterization of the ludologist's quest to defend game studies from outsiders) that the pursuit of certain types of conflict necessarily ends in oppressive forms of domination.

However, this interpretation is only one dimension of what the agon—and by extension, gaming—could mean for political possibility. Caillois himself identifies the take-no-prisoners version of the agon as a corruption, perhaps more accurately an eruption, of the natural instinct of competition into the "real" world. Unbounded by what he calls the "civilizing" forces that keep play constricted within rules and limits (in other words, the game, but also things like laws and social norms), the human proclivity to compete can result in all manner of violence and exploitation.[3] Caillois understands complex societies in part by how they negotiate between agon (understood as merit) and *alea* ("chance," understood as heredity) in formal and informal ways, including the use of games like national lotteries to manage the expectations of those who are too poor, too unskilled, or too unlucky to ascend a purported meritocracy.[4] According to this model, competition is a desirable element of the social order that is only dangerous when allowed to proliferate unchecked.

Other theorizations of the agon align it more closely with the kind of generative political turbulence envisioned by Lorde. So-called agonistic politics—pioneered by political theorists like William Connolly, Bonnie Honig, and Chantal Mouffe[5]—centers conflict in political life without imagining its end in a utopian stillness free of disagreement. According to these theorists, disagreement is not merely inevitable but crucial for pluralistic societies to function, and liberal political projects that seek harmony will never account for those inevitably left outside of a new social order except by relegating them to the status of aberration and ultimately suppressing or eliminating them. In this vision of politics, there is a crucial distinction drawn between agonism, in which adversaries compete on a field of mutual respect and interdependence, and antagonism, in which enemies attempt to eradicate or supersede one another. In this scheme, the "fatal either/or" that Wark associates with the agon[6] falls under antagonistic relations, where collective identity is forged, as Keeling describes it, at the expense of another.[7] Rather than pursuing a peace grounded in subjugation or "mere tolerance," agonism is a political process that is honest about the incommensurable differences between various factions and identities that nevertheless recognize the value in multiple perspectives.

By placing Lorde in conversation with these political theorists, I don't wish to overwrite her contributions with voices that may resonate more strongly with the center of academic discourse. Indeed, I regard Caillois's work, and game studies' subsequent veneration of it, with great suspicion thanks to his deep investment in racializing his invented typography of gameplay to uphold white supremacist standards of civilization.[8] Lorde can be a corrective to his work as well, and I want to highlight how she anticipates some of the political problems of today that are outlined by both Caillois as well as the proponents of agonistic politics. For example, Lorde has her own version of the difference between agonism and antagonism:

> For it is not the anger of Black women which is dripping down over this globe like a diseased liquid. It is not my anger that launches rockets, spends over sixty thousand dollars a second on missiles and other agents of war and death, slaughters children in cities, stockpiles nerve gas and chemical bombs, sodomizes our daughters and our earth. It is not the anger of Black women which corrodes into blind, dehumanizing power, bent upon the annihilation of us all unless we meet it with what we have, our power to examine and to redefine the terms upon which we will live and work; our power to envision and to reconstruct, anger by painful anger, stone upon heavy stone, a future of pollinating difference and the earth to support our choices.[9]

We may not initially read anger as an agonistic emotion, but Lorde classifies it here as a survival mechanism for Black women, quite akin to Caillois's competitive "law of nature,"[10] which, when not kept in check, leads to the wanton destruction and "ruthless warfare"[11] like Lorde describes above. And while Caillois maintains a colonial investment in the civilizing power of rules and social norms, perhaps leading us to question the usefulness even of the righteous anger of the Black feminist, feminist affect scholars like Sara Ahmed and Barbara Tomlinson, whom I discussed at length in chapter 1, expose how hegemony perpetuates itself, in part, by selectively and hypocritically disciplining the anger of the marginalized, reducing their efficacy at the scene of contest. What Lorde describes in the end of this selection is precisely the agonistic struggle of the marginalized, who are constrained by the rules of an unequal society.

For Caillois, one key problem with agon outside of the envelope of play is the simple fact that competition rarely happens on equal terms. This truth is fundamental to identity knowledges and theorists of social justice as well. The drive to win becomes instead a mechanism for domination. Agonism becomes antagonism. Here, the distinction between agonism and antagonism, which marks the difference between adversary and enemy (those who engage in inclusive struggles vs. those who engage in exclusive ones), is particularly useful to determine how and when one should invest one's energy in a given conflict. Online harassment campaigns are antagonistic, premised on patently asymmetrical terms of engagement and designed to dominate and expel individuals from a social group. So too are encounters staged around the rejection of white supremacist speakers on campus, whose eliminationist rhetoric undermines the spirit of agonistic exchange and thus cannot contribute to a politics organized around plurality. On the other hand, debates about whether figures like Bayonetta and Chell are empowering or sexist should be carried out in the spirit of agonism, allowing the clash of conflicting but nonexclusive perspectives to generate new insights and new ways of talking about media and power, a fulfillment of Lorde's vision of feminist agonism, in which feminists meet in solidarity but without the expectation that relationships will be easy or even peaceful.

Ludology versus narratology could have been an invigorating moment of agonistic debate for the discipline, if only it had not been staged in terms of scarcity and colonization. In Lorde's example, the encounters between angry Black feminists and guilty white ones can never move toward justice if they only seek peace. Resolution, when predicated on the absence of complaint, often serves to erase needs rather than meet them. In Mouffe's words, "Too much emphasis on consensus, together with an aversion towards confrontations, leads to apathy and to a disaffection with political participation,"[12] a disaffection that she points out can itself lead to violent nationalism and a proliferation of antagonistic encounters when the exasperated seek another outlet. This is an apt way to describe the political situation of today: simultaneously apathetic and passionate, characterized by highly divided attitudes that can bear neither compromise nor the friction of continued disagreement. Even if we cannot heal each other's wounds, we ought to try to identify appropriate ways to move forward, in trouble, together. Lorde and the agonists agree: liberal (and neoliberal) narratives of progress, attitudes toward the costs of disagreement, and demands for civility get in the way of pursuing justice.

So too does basking in victory. Honig remarks that "once any conception of politics and identity or agency begins to sediment, its usefulness as a lever of critique is diminished and its generative power becomes a force of constraint," a condition that Mouffe characterizes in terms of constantly shifting hegemonies. Agonism is not useful simply to keep ideas moving and reflexes sharp. It is crucial because power is crafty and will constantly assume new forms, so we must pursue the type of agility Rita Raley identifies in tactical media practices and politics "for the next five minutes."[13] In the history of feminism, the continued struggles of Black, brown, third-world, trans, and lesbian feminists against the mainstream white concept of "woman" that privileges a small subset of the group illustrates this quite well, as do more recent struggles in the queer community around white cisgender gays and lesbians who have been embraced by straight society and use their newfound status to reinforce hegemonic boundaries (which have expanded to include homonormative queers) instead of further eroding white supremacist cisheteropatriarchy. As US representative and Civil Rights leader John Lewis's rallying call in the epigraph suggests, the pursuit of what he has long called "good trouble" is, necessarily, a long haul.

I don't mean any of this as an endorsement of simple pluralism, a fantasy wherein all voices (even those who seek the domination of others) are heard equally, nor as a way to endorse increasingly pugilistic modes of engagement—we have far too much of that today. However, there are alternate ways to approach conflict that do not return us to white supremacist cisheteropatriarchy, as Honig suggests by reading a queered woman as the source of her *virtù* politics (shifting its root from *vir*, "man," to *virago*[14]—a heroic woman often perceived as mannish and uncontrollable) and, later, in her rereading of Antigone as a figure for solidarity.[15] Lorde's elaboration of the uses and limitations of anger performs a similar kind of differentiation and similarly suggests that it is an avoidance of conflict on the part of the privileged that allows structural inequalities like racism to proliferate.

What I am doing is advocating for a reclamation of the agonistic (rather than antagonistic) spirit of the gamer, that spirit which is invigorated not by decisive victory but by struggle in the context of a fair distribution of power. In order to reclaim this spirit, we must be able to face hard truths and hard problems without the expectation that they will be amicably resolved, to legitimate nonpeaceful resolutions to old and deep problems, and to differentiate between conflict and violence, contest and conquest. Crucially, all of this requires a frank and honest assessment of power differentials and places the burden on those with more power and privilege to level the playing field in whatever ways possible, including by making themselves uncomfortable, uneasy, and open to making mistakes. This is where many quests for justice end: our inner heroes abhor weakness and disadvantage and are loathe to take risks that leave us exposed to ridicule or social penalties. However, if we tap into the inner gamer who embraces constraint, failure, and fair(er) contest, we may yet find the courage to try.

In Pursuit of Good Trouble

As a graduate student, I took a seminar in the feminist studies department called "Feminism and Colorblindness across the Disciplines." It was coordinated across campuses around the US and was designed to help us understand how scholarly disciplines, including feminist studies, facilitate postracial perspectives that conceal or elide the material effects of race on our lives and scholarship. One of the assignments I completed for the class was to write a pledge of allegiance to and a declaration of independence from my discipline. I was technically in an English department at the time, but I had been doing game studies research and writing since my undergraduate days and was fortunate to have advisors who encouraged my identification with the field. That exercise, which I completed just as I was beginning the research that eventually became this book, has informed the way I approach my relationship to the many disciplines with which my work is in conversation, but it has especially informed the way that I think about myself as a game studies scholar.

Throughout *Gamer Trouble*, I have explicitly interrogated some disciplinary practices and tried to model other ones, including stitching together a bibliography across the disciplines that is well suited to approach games from a queer (and) woman of color feminist critical perspective. While I am by no means the first author to do such work, I offer *Gamer Trouble* as a platform that explicitly names and advocates for such changes in the troubled discipline that we call game studies, in the hopes that it will amplify the calls of my predecessors, offer others a leg up on their own projects, or even induct newcomers into the community with better scholarly practices centered on video games than many of us had access to as students.

As anyone who has expressed an opinion in public can imagine, I am terrified about what will happen when this book hits the proverbial (and actual) shelves. I have my own history with trouble: as a rabble-rousing graduate student in the so-called #transformDH Collective, I have been pushing up against (and receiving pushback for) disciplinary walls (in that particular case, of the digital humanities) through much of my career. These conversations are always messy and uncomfortable, and frequently, simply initiating them is scary. Sometimes, they require folks to rethink how they have become accustomed to doing their jobs over the years. This is not easy to ask of anyone. We in #transformDH were lucky: although we received public criticism from senior scholars in the digital humanities, we had enough feminist, queer, and ethnic studies mentors who had prepared the way and were willing to back us up that most of us have been able to continue our work in satisfying ways.[16] I personally also benefitted from my white-passing name and complexion and probably from my masculine presentation as well.

As we have seen over and over again, this is not the norm for most folks who cause trouble in their communities. In chapter 1, "Of Dickwolves and Killjoys," I explored the ways that both fans and academics become embroiled in conflict when they express unpopular, frequently feminist, opinions, and how academia is no shield from vitriol, especially for vulnerable members of the community. Graduate students like Emma Vossen and junior faculty like Shira Chess, Kishonna Gray, and Adrienne Shaw can easily become targets of harassment campaigns as well.[17] The harassment can even come from one's professional colleagues: at the 2017 Foundations of Digital Games conference, junior faculty and award-winning game designer Gillian Smith was singled out for her feminist critiques about the keynote presentation, which featured graduate student researchers remotely kissing their supervisor through the proxy use of robots. The keynote speaker, Adrian Cheok, proceeded to berate her on Twitter until long after the initial event.[18]

Such behavior, of course, is not limited to game studies. Barbara Tomlinson was writing about the field of musicology in her study of Tough Babies in academia who suppress feminist critiques using various bullying rhetorical strategies.[19] There are the high-intensity battles over the Boycott, Divestment, and Sanctions movement against Israel, which often involve heated social media exchanges and steep professional penalties. There is also the particular case of Dorothy Kim, a woman of color in a junior faculty position, whose calls for white faculty in medieval studies to use their classrooms to confront how white supremacists use medieval tropes in their organizing prompted passionate pushback in the community, including by Rachel Fulton Brown, a tenured professor who alerted Milo Yiannopolous to Kim's work and set off a harassment campaign against her.[20] Even when the costs are high, individuals keep pursuing the good trouble that comes with the quest for justice.

But what, if anything, does any of this trouble have to do with video games?

In part, the connection comes from the pervasive association of online harassment campaigns with #GamerGate, which emerged explicitly from conflicts within the gaming community. Some critics have made demographic connections between #GamerGate and the toxic groups that constitute the alt-right and other right-wing movements,[21] which suggests that gamers (an identitarian designation that denotes specific people) are the ones responsible for the political turmoil of the ludic century. However, I prefer Katherine Cross's reading of #GamerGate as a manifestation of the gamification of activism because it allows us to think about these incidents in terms of the behaviors and affects structured by gaming rather the people who compose the movement per se. What Carolyn Gallaher has recognized as a wider "war on the ivory tower" by right-wing groups[22] uses many of the tactics that, although they have been applied in many previous instances like Dickwolves and *Fat Princess*, became widely acknowledged through #GamerGate and explained by both Cross and some proponents of #GamerGate themselves as gamer strategies for dealing with trouble. In her epigraph, Cross quotes an anonymous proponent of #GamerGate describing their approach to the conflict: "You are going up against gamers. People who are programmed to win, to grind and slog for months for a prize, who can put up with the most horrendous insults being thrown at them."[23]

While we are primarily accustomed to recognizing the grind of games on the level of ludic goals, I have also argued for recognizing the work that gamers put into negotiating the interfaces of gaming and identifying (or not) with the representations on-screen. This work was initiated in chapter 2, "Making a Face," which looked at the troubled history of facial measurements and how their centuries-old connections to techniques of racism and sexism gain new relevance in the context of computer animation and avatar facial customization. When these technologies are built from the ground up on such problematic foundations, it is no surprise that many users experience such interfaces as frictional and oppressive. Chapter 3, "Gender, Power, and the Gamic Gaze," continued this work by interrogating some of the critical foundations of feminist critique in game studies in an attempt to complicate the conversations we have about representations of women in video games. While ludologists flippantly dismiss the value of thinking about the curves of digital women's bodies, I dig deeper to place them in a more complete context of the conflicting circuits of power that flow through technology, play, and visuality. This chapter also included some playful interrogation of the dreaded feminist film theory that has structured feminist game studies in the form of Laura Mulvey.

My work throughout this book has been to weave these many levels of conflict together to help us consider that the violent hate speech of trolls playing games with politics is inextricable from the dehumanizing logic undergirding computation; that the optimization strategies of gameplay are inextricable from the representational practices marginalizing people of color, women, and queers in entertainment media; that the exclusion of certain bodies from industry and academia is inextricable from the way we talk about the troubles that structure them. By exposing these relationships and proposing new connections to theorists outside of game studies proper, I have pursued good trouble in the form of a disciplinary remix that has been feared, desired, and performed continuously over the decades.

Cultivating Gamer Trouble

What happens when we look to gamer trouble and affirm the importance of conflict and disagreement for political change? For one thing, we can identify how harassment campaigns, the pursuit of unfettered capitalism in the form of exploitative labor practices, and the cultural valuation of a winner-takes-all meritocracy constitute what Caillois would call "perversions" of the agon rather than an actual politics structured by agonism. These modes of competition are more akin to what agonistic theorists identify as antagonism, the us versus them relation between enemies, rather than the relation between adversaries that provides structure to political communities and helps us determine who should and should not be given a platform to speak. We could further identify the mechanics of play internal to the envelope between gamer and interface, from technology to representation, as part of an agonistic relationship that has a reciprocal transformative impact on all components of the system. Finally, we could embrace disciplinary disagreements and multiple interpretations—in short, criticism—as part of the reward, even joy, of playing, reading about, and writing about games, if we can approach such disagreements in agonistic terms.

As I look to the future of games and gamers and game studies, I don't see us putting down our controllers in the name of wokeness, refusing to play problematic games or ceding the territory of online culture to toxic masculinity, any time soon. There will, of course, continue to be an expansion of video game aesthetics by a vanguard of independent developers, but the lure of the popular will never wane, and developers' interest in cultivating new markets means that "diversity" is perhaps irreversibly on the rise. All of this means that there will be many more battles, largely of an antagonistic nature, to come. However, if we can learn to cultivate the trust, balance, and mutual investment required of agonistic struggle (beginning, of course, by addressing the very legitimate grievances and safeguarding the presence of the most vulnerable among us), we can begin to balance the mechanics of gaming culture such that our arguments can play out in a more equitable field.

Perhaps in the ludic century, our task is not simply to learn how to game "the" system (which is itself composed of many different systems) but to understand how the forces of hegemony shape any particular system so that we can game it in ways that move toward justice. There are many ways to game a system, as we've seen throughout this book. Sometimes that means working within and bending the rules, even within our own minds, and sometimes it means manipulating and breaking them. Sometimes, the answer is to throw out the rules entirely and invent a new game. Let's tap into the gamer's unique affinity for tuning in to questions of power, balance, and exploitation and the game's unique ability to shape flows of attention, affect, and power and see what else we can do.

The most important thing is to stay with the trouble rather than to steer clear of political questions for fear of doing it wrong. According to Donna Haraway, this "requires learning to be truly present, not as a vanishing pivot between awful or edenic pasts and apocalyptic or salvific futures, but as mortal critters entwined in myriad unfinished configurations of places, times, matters, meanings."[24] Recognizing our entanglement with the unfinished eases the demands of neoliberal capital, which pressures us into productivity and winning while not quite allowing us to quit or permanently fail at what we do. There is no other world in which to live, to love, and to play. We are all we've got.

Gamers love trouble—perhaps a little too much at times. But gaming the system can cut in multiple directions. For every troll grinding out sock puppet accounts to multiply hateful voices on the internet, there are those, like #GamerGate target Zoë Quinn, who recognize that the gamer's skills can be applied in many directions. Under consistent, violent threats of harassment by hordes of antagonists, Quinn takes a defiant position: "I'm better at games than they are."[25]

Shall we play a game?

ACKNOWLEDGMENTS

It is impossible to make good trouble without accomplices. My initial thanks go to the readers and editorial staff at NYU Press, including Dolma Ombadykow and Eric Zinner, for shepherding me through a process that has forged *Gamer Trouble* into its very best self. I have done what I could with your careful advice, and I assume all responsibility for what this book inevitably lacks.

This project would never have come to fruition without a number of institutional sponsors. The University of California, Santa Barbara, Humanities Special Fellowship and the Mellon/ACLS Dissertation Completion Fellowship supported me while in graduate school. The postdoctoral fellowship that enabled me to prepare the book for submission was provided by the IMMERSe Network, funded by the Social Sciences and Humanities Research Council of Canada, as well as the Interdisciplinary Frontiers of the Humanities and the Arts grant of the University of California, Davis, Office of Research. Georgetown University generously provided summer funding that enabled the revision and resubmission of the manuscript, as well as assistance with research, bibliography, and media gathering, which was expertly and efficiently provided by Bridget Sellers.

My professional colleagues across institutions have been tremendously helpful with their support and feedback. At Georgetown, my colleagues in the Department of English have cheered me every step of my journey as a member of the faculty, including at my most memorable job talk, which was supposed to be one of the most harrowing experiences of my career. Instead, it set the stage for a beautiful and supportive relationship. Thank you in particular to Caetlin Benson-Allott, Marcia Chatelain, Nathan Hensley, Brian Hochman, Dana Luciano, Ricardo Ortiz, Seth Perlow, and Christine So for making Georgetown feel like home. At UC Davis, I am grateful for the faculty and students of the Department of English and the ModLab, who provided a space of intellectual and technical innovation that helped me transition from grad student to professional; in particular: Gina Bloom, Stephanie Boluk, Seeta Chaganti, Ranjodh Singh Dhaliwal, Kris Fallon, Maryam Griffin, Caren Kaplan, Patrick LeMieux, and Colin Milburn. And of course, the project was only possible thanks to a rigorous and careful start at UC Santa Barbara, where classmates and mentors from the Departments of English, Feminist Studies, and Film and Media Studies helped me launch my little boat: Charlotte Becker, Laurica Brown, Jeremy Douglass, Megan Fernandes, Carol Hong, Chelsea Jones, Kim Knight, George Lipsitz, Mireille Miller-Young, Teddy Pozo, Elizabeth Rahilly, Lindsay Thomas, Carly Thomsen, and Barbara Tomlinson. Bishnupriya Ghosh, Alan Liu, Lisa Nakamura, and Rita Raley ensured that *Gamer Trouble* got off to a strong start, and I hope I have done them justice since.

Over my career, I have also had the support of rad queer feminists and antiracist scholar-artist-activists who have pushed my work (and my politics) in ways that I couldn't have achieved on my own. I am grateful for the camaraderie and rigor of the #transformDH Collective, who gave me my first taste of professional trouble, and to friends and colleagues across the disciplines who do this work and continue to inspire me: Moya Bailey, Fiona Barnett, micha cárdenas, Kishonna Gray, Tolonda Henderson, George Hoagland, Jessica Marie Johnson, Elizabeth Losh, Jen Malkowski, Veronica Paredes, Whitney Pow, Margaret Rhee, Trea Russworm, Jacque Wernimont, and Ann Wu. I also include in this group the creators who generously engaged with me about their work and gave their blessing for its inclusion in this book: Steve Bowler, Melissa McEwan, Ryan North, Sage, and Courtney Stanton.

I am grateful for The Best Writing Group: Alex Agloro, Josef Nguyen, Bo Ruberg, and Adrienne Shaw. Your ability to dispense critique, support, and love in equal measure keeps me going.

Finally, there are those who are there for my day-to-day struggles and give me the strength and inspiration to make good trouble. The regal womyn and men of Alpha Lambda Zeta Fraternity, Incorporated, especially my bois ChivALrous, Debonair, Ecstatic, Enthroned, Icey, Koncise, Magnificent, Premiere, StimuLuz, and Undisputed. My distant friends: Anne Cong-Huyen, Adwoa Gyimah-Brempong, Evan Lauteria, Casey Moore, Jacqui Mullings, Steven Pokornowski, and Andrea Santoro Monagle. My DC family: Nirvana Green, Dee Loeffler, Alexis

Lothian, Michelle Ohnona, Erica Shirley, Lily Wong, and Yan Zheng. My siblings: Amy, Joseph, and EL. My bio parents: Tami and José. My stepparents: Deborah, Jeanne, and John. My grandmother Loretta and abuelita Margarita. My grandfather John. My inlaws: Seema and Sneh. My family in Florida and across the South. Mi familia en Guadalajara y Zacatecas. My hearts: Shyama and Yakshi, without whom my life would never be as fierce, as interesting, or as filled with love.

Thanks to you all (and many more not listed here), I have written a book that is worth a fraction of everything you gave me. I will never be able to repay the rest, to you or to the world, but I promise never to stop trying.

NOTES

INTRODUCTION

1 See Bergstrom, Fisher, and Jenson, "Disavowing 'That Guy.'"

2 Kocurek, *Coin-Operated Americans*, 146.

3 See Golding and van Deventer, *Game Changers*.

4 This claim is widely circulated in news media and explored in books like Megan Condis's *Gaming Masculinity* and Angela Nagle's *Kill All Normies*. Kishonna Gray, Jen Jenson, Anita Sarkeesian, and Emma Vossen have also participated in roundtables and interviews on the topic. See CBC Radio, "Dangerous Game." Milo Yiannopoulos, the infamous media provocateur, was a figurehead for both #GamerGate and the alt-right, and Steve Bannon, one of Trump's former campaign and White House advisors, expressly credits #GamerGate as one of the funnels for young people toward alt-right politics. See Green, *Devil's Bargain*, 147.

5 In addition to investigations into harassment claims as a result of #GamerGate and similar movements, which frequently fail to result in legal consequences, gamers are also increasingly associated with the practice of *swatting*, or calling law enforcement to someone's residence with false claims of an in-progress emergency. On December 28, 2017, police shot and killed Andrew Finch at his Wichita, Kansas, home after Tyler Barriss mistakenly swatted Finch's house on behalf of Casey Viner, who was attempting to retaliate against Shane Gaskill over a $1.50 *Call of Duty* bet.

6 Porpentine, *How to Speak Atlantean*, "heart core."

7 This claim goes as far back as 1982. See Kinder, *Playing with Power*, 88.

8 ESA, "US Video Game Industry Revenue."

9 ESA, "Essential Facts."

10 See Brookey, *Hollywood Gamers*.

11 Greenfield, *Mind and Media*, 179.

12 McGonigal, *Reality Is Broken*.

13 Zimmerman, "Manifesto for a Ludic Century."

14 Murray, *Hamlet on the Holodeck*, 144.

15 Paul, *Toxic Meritocracy of Video Games*.

16 Dyer-Witheford and de Peuter, *Games of Empire*, xv (emphasis in original), xix.

17 Wark, *Gamer Theory*, 24.

18 Shaw, "On Not Becoming Gamers."

19 Alexander, "Gamers."

20 Ahmed, *On Being Included*, 182.

21 Entertainment Consumers Association, "About the ECA."

22 See Salter and Blodgett, *Toxic Geek Masculinity*, for more on the rise of toxic geek masculinity in response to the mainstreaming of geek identity, which follows a similar pattern.

23 Bogost, "Videogames Are a Mess."

24 See Wiegman, *Object Lessons*, 1n1, for her genealogy of this term.

25 Haraway, *Staying with the Trouble*.

26 Butler, *Gender Trouble*.

27 Truth, "Ain't I a Woman?"; Lorde, "Master's Tools"; Crenshaw, "Mapping the Margins."

28 In fact, Sara Ahmed cites Black feminist Ama Ata Aidoo's novel *Our Sister Killjoy* as an origin point for theorizing the killjoy. Ahmed, *Promise of Happiness*, 68.

29 Fraser, "Social Justice."

30 Malkowski and Russworm, *Gaming Representation*, 1.

31 Zimmerman, "Jerked Around."

32 Murray, *Hamlet on the Holodeck*, 98.

33 Ash, *Interface Envelope*, 88.

34 Boluk and LeMieux, *Metagaming*, 9.

35 This illusion is at the core of Stephanie Boluk and Patrick LeMieux's argument that video games are not actually games at all but rather tools for making metagames. While I find this a worthy provocation, I will not engage with it here.

36 Boluk and LeMieux, *Metagaming*, 281.

37 Ibid.

38 Salen Tekinbaş and Zimmerman, *Rules of Play*, 77.

39 Suits, *Grasshopper*, 45.

40 Wark, *Gamer Theory*, para. 97.

41 See, for example, the conversations about queer failure in games in Ruberg and Shaw, *Queer Game Studies*.

42 Suits, *Grasshopper*, 60; see also Consalvo, *Cheating*.

43 Murray, *Hamlet on the Holodeck*, xii.

44 Aarseth, "Narrative Theory of Games," 130.

45 Vossen, "On the Cultural Inaccessibility."

46 Vist, "Actually, It's about Aca-Fandom"

47 Aarseth, "Computer Game Studies, Year One."

48 Murray, "Last Word."

49 Zimmerman, "Jerked Around."

50 On this topic, see, for example, the 2016 conference Gaming Metrics: Innovation and Surveillance in Academic Misconduct at UC Davis, which thought through faculty responses to the prevalence of metrics in evaluation.

51 Ahmed, *Living a Feminist Life*, 148.

52 Gray, "#CiteHerWork."

53 Consalvo, "Confronting Toxic Gamer Culture."

54 Russworm, "Call to Action."

55 Ahmed, *Living a Feminist Life*, 149.

56 I won't attempt to create a comprehensive list, but recent book collections include Ruberg and Shaw's *Queer Game Studies*; Jennifer Malkowski and TreaAndrea Russworm's *Gaming Representation*; Kishonna L. Gray, Gerald Voorhees, and Emma Vossen's *Feminism in Play*; Nicholas Taylor and Voorhees's *Masculinities in Play*; and Todd Harper, Meghan Blythe Adams, and Taylor's *Queerness in Play*. Special issues include Nina Huntemann's "Feminist Game Studies" issue of *Ada* and Ruberg and Amanda Phillips's "Queerness and Video Games" issue of *Game Studies*. Monographs include Shira Chess's *Ready Player Two*; Gray's *Race, Gender, and Deviance in Xbox Live*; Soraya Murray's *On Video Games*; Ruberg's *Video Games Have Always Been Queer*; and Shaw's *Gaming at the Edge*. Then of course, there is the rise of queer indie game developers like Anna Anthropy, Mattie Brice, merritt kopas, Dietrich Squinkifer, Porpentine, and more, all of whom are prolific designers and theorists.

57 Shaw, "Are We There Yet?"

58 Hemmings, *Why Stories Matter*.

59 Ahmed, *On Being Included*, 178.

60 Janet Murray did eventually go on the record with her suspicions that the response to her work in *Hamlet on the Holodeck* was in part influenced by gender. See Murray, *Hamlet on the Holodeck*, 190. As of this writing, Emma Vossen's work on the hostility of game studies toward women and nonbinary scholars is still in dissertation form, but it represents a vital voice in this conversation as well. Shira Chess and Adrienne Shaw allude to the sidelining of feminist critique in "We Are All Fishes Now," and Sal Humphreys makes similar gestures in "On Being a Feminist in Games Studies."

CHAPTER 1. OF DICKWOLVES AND KILLJOYS

1 Salter and Blodgett, "Hypermasculinity & Dickwolves."

2 Phillips, *This Is Why*, 10.

3 Crawford, *Video Gamers*; Heineman, "Public Memory and Gamer Identity"; Nguyen, "Performing as Video Game Players."

4 Cote, "Writing 'Gamers'"; Shaw, "On Not Becoming Gamers."

5 Chess, *Ready Player Two*; Condis, "No Homosexuals in *Star Wars*?"; Nakamura, "Queer Female of Color"; Salter and Blodgett, "Hypermasculinity & Dickwolves."

6 See Gray, *Race, Gender, and Deviance*; and Nakamura, "It's a N****r!," for more on identity-based harassment during gameplay.

7 You would be right to think I am alluding to, but not stopping to become mired in, a discussion of the shifting histories of hermeneutics as they influence scholarly and sacred communities. For this particular discussion, I feel it is sufficient to point toward the etymology of *hermeneutics*, which originates in the interpretation of sacred texts, to emphasize the fervor with which interpretive communities (as Stanley Fish calls them) guard the importance of their differing truths. Other

scholars, such as Brian McKernan in his "The Meaning of a Game: Stereotypes, Video Game Commentary, and Color-Blind Racism," have drawn on Pierre Bourdieu's notion of cultural fields to explore similar phenomena.

8 Braithwaite, "It's about Ethics?"

9 See Lynch, "Final Word on #notyourshield," for the history and methods of #NotYourShield. On Twitter, Black feminists exposed a similar scheme, unrelated to the gamer community, that attempted to discredit feminists: the #EndFathersDay movement. Shafiqah Hudson began a movement to uncover and expose these fraudulent accounts with the counter-hashtag #YourSlipIsShowing. See Hampton, "Black Feminists Saw Alt-Right Coming."

10 Lynch, "Final Word on #notyourshield."

11 Lorde, "Uses of Anger."

12 Harris was speaking specifically of the reaction of white folks to affirmative action. I use his phrasing here for the apt way it captures the essence of political backlash of this type but not to imply an equivalence in racist and sexist backlash. Many white women who identify as feminists benefited from affirmative action policies at the expense of Black women and men.

13 Massanari and Chess, "Attack of Social Justice Warrior," 529.

14 Kocurek, *Coin-Operated Americans*.

15 Brathwaite, *Sex in Video Games*, 35.

16 McKernan, "Morality of Play."

17 Kenyota, "Thinking of the Children," 789.

18 McKernan reports that every single *New York Times* article about the Columbine massacre ties video games into the story ("Morality of Play," 317). Harris in particular was known to create levels for *Doom*, some of which were rumored to resemble the high school. In the wake of the tragedy, families of the victims sued twenty-five entertainment companies for liability. Their case was dismissed in 2002. See National Coalition against Censorship, "Timeline of Video Game Controversies." Gregory Kenyota notes in his "Thinking of the Children" that Columbine also touched off another round of congressional hearings about video game violence.

19 For a detailed account of the discovery of, confusion over, and fallout from "Hot Coffee," see Brathwaite, *Sex in Video Games*, chap. 4.

20 Calvert and Richards, "Precedent be Damned."

21 See National Coalition against Censorship, "Timeline of Video Game Controversies," for a more extended account of video game controversies.

22 Krahulik, "Child's Play."

23 The "murder simulator" was a frequent talking point of Jack Thompson, the attorney who was characterized as a crusader for the censorship of video games because of his fiery rhetoric when seeking to remove the regulation and enforcement of video game ratings from the ESRB, an industry-controlled entity. At the time of this writing, his website includes excerpts and links to transcripts of his various television appearances, which document not only his extensive use of the

phrase but also his consistent claims about the links between violence and video games generally. For the collection, see Thompson, "Transcripts."

24 CSPAN, *Video Game Violence*.
25 In the 1993 hearings, for example, witness Parker Page said that there was not yet sufficient research about causality but then added that the few studies that had been done suggested a link between video games and short-term aggression in children. Following him, Eugene Provenzo, author of *Video Kids: Making Sense of Nintendo*, makes the sweeping statement that "video games are overwhelmingly violent, sexist, and racist." CSPAN, *Video Game Violence*.
26 Buckley, "Open Letter to Jack Thompson."
27 Salter and Blodgett, "Hypermasculinity & Dickwolves."
28 Tassi, "Can We Forgive Hillary Clinton?"
29 See Brathwaite, *Sex in Video Games*; and Wysocki and Lauteria, *Rated M for Mature*, for extensive coverage of adult sexual content in video games.
30 Stang, "Big Daddies and Broken Men"; Gallagher, "Minecrafting Masculinities."
31 Yiannopoulos, "Who Said It?"
32 Cross, "The Nightmare Is Over," 179.
33 Krahulik, "Dickwolves."
34 Krahulik, "Star Wars."
35 Holkins and Krahulik, "Sixth Slave."
36 "Pratfall of *Penny Arcade*."
37 Tomlinson, *Feminism and Affect*, 3.
38 Tomlinson arrives at this nomenclature from Theodor W. Adorno by way of Thomas Dumm. See ibid., 88.
39 Ibid., 90 (emphasis in original).
40 Ibid., 3.
41 Ibid., 106 (emphasis in original).
42 Holkins and Krahulik, "Breaking It Down."
43 His comments have since been deleted but are described in "Pratfall of *Penny Arcade*."
44 Holkins and Krahulik, "Breaking It Down."
45 Krahulik, "Tragedy Is."
46 "Pratfall of *Penny Arcade*."
47 Ahmed, *Promise of Happiness*, 59.
48 Ibid., 66.
49 Dibbell, "Rape in Cyberspace."
50 Herring, Scheckler, and Barab, "Searching for Safety Online," 374.
51 Filipovic, "Blogging While Female."
52 Kendall, "Harassment Game."
53 Mantilla, *Gendertrolling*. While this chapter focuses on harassment in blogging spaces, there is a separate body of literature addressing how women and people of color experience harassment during gaming sessions. See, for example, Cote, "I Can Defend Myself"; and Gray, *Race, Gender, and Deviance*, for more.

54 McEwan, "Commenting Policy."

55 McEwan, "I Write Letters."

56 McEwan, "*Fat Princess* Update."

57 McEwan, "*Fat Princess* Greatest Hits."

58 McEwan, "*Penny Arcade* Open Thread."

59 McEwan, "*Penny Arcade* Open Thread II."

60 Stanton, "Here Is a Shirt."

61 Stanton, "Why I'm Not Speaking at PAX East."

62 Stanton, "Fuck This Noise."

63 "Pratfall of *Penny Arcade*."

64 Stanton, "Here Is a Project."

65 Ibid.

66 Krahulik, "Okay That's Enough."

67 Holkins, "On the Matter of Dickwolves."

68 Hernandez, "*Penny Arcade* Artist."

69 Salter and Blodgett, "Hypermasculinity & Dickwolves."

70 McEwan, "*Fat Princess* Update."

71 There are conflicting accounts of the term's origins, but it emerged in feminist circles in the 1970s. Key defining texts include *Rape: The First Sourcebook for Women*, edited by Noreen Connell and Cassandra Wilson, and *Rape Culture*, the 1975 documentary by Margaret Lazarus. There is a steady stream of feminist scholarship engaging with rape culture through the 1990s, including Dianne Herman's 1984 "The Rape Culture," which explicitly refers to the way that US culture brings together violence and sex. A Google Books Ngram view of the phrase *rape culture* shows it reaching a peak in 1997, then tapering off through 2008. The 2010s saw another increase in publications referring to rape culture, particularly through the analysis of social media practices, such as in Carrie A. Rentschler's "Rape Culture and the Feminist Politics of Social Media" and Tanya Horeck's "#AskThicke: 'Blurred Lines,' Rape Culture, and the Feminist Hashtag Takeover."

72 Nakamura, "It's a N****r!"

73 Voorhees, "Criticism and Control."

74 Aarseth, "Computer Game Studies, Year One."

75 See Moberly, "Pre-emptive Strikes"; Phillips, "Negg(at)ing the Game Studies Subject"; Voorhees, "Criticism and Control"; and Vossen, "On the Cultural Inaccessibility," for more on the rhetoric of colonization in early game studies scholarship.

76 Eskelinen, "Gaming Situation."

77 Murray, "Last Word."

78 Harrigan and Wardrip-Fruin, *First Person*.

79 See Emma Vossen's work on the ludology versus narratology debate and the gendered nature of discourse in game studies. See Shaw, "Are We There Yet?," for an alternative genealogy of game studies that centers the contributions of women.

80 Greenfield, *Mind and Media*; Kinder, *Playing with Power*; Laurel, *Computers as Theatre*; Loftus and Loftus, *Mind at Play*; Murray, *Hamlet on the Holodeck*; Ryan, *Narrative as Virtual Reality*.

81 Aarseth, "Narrative Theory of Games," 130.

82 Aarseth, "Genre Trouble," 48.

83 Murray, *Hamlet on the Holodeck*, 190.

84 Leonard, "Not a Hater."

85 Leonard, "Young, Black (& Brown)," 255.

86 Everett and Watkins, "Power of Play."

87 Taylor, "From Stompin' Mushrooms," 115.

88 The fictionalized cities in the game have obvious US counterparts that are recreated with some fidelity: Liberty City / New York City, Las Venturas / Las Vegas, Los Santos / Los Angeles, San Fierro / San Francisco, and Vice City / Miami.

89 Jenkins, *Fans, Bloggers, and Gamers*, 199.

90 Ibid., 202.

91 Ibid., 206.

92 Ibid., 203.

93 Ibid., 207.

94 While this collection contributes a majority of the examples in this section, as a whole it represents the writings of seventeen different game studies academics.

95 Hemmings, *Why Stories Matter*, 21.

96 Leonard, "Young, Black (& Brown)."

97 *MAC*, 2.

98 Ibid., 14.

99 Ibid., 41.

100 *GS*, no page.

101 *MAC*, 32.

102 Ibid., 37.

103 Ibid., 129.

104 *GAC*, 265.

105 *MAC*, 206.

106 Ibid., 207.

107 It often takes the form of depoliticizing vocabulary that has been developed for antioppressive scholarship. For example, *subversive play* refers not to practices that undermine hegemony but to the formal action of playing a game in a way not intended by the designer. The analogy here is clear but perhaps undertheorized. In another example, *ideological critique* comes to mean "testing the limitations of a set of rules" in the game (*MAC*, 129)

108 See Sara Ahmed's study of diversity work in academic institutions, *On Being Included*, for compelling arguments about how gender and race critique are positioned as "over" as part of an investment in a white supremacist cisheteropatriarchy.

109 *GAC*, 144.

110 *MAC*, 179.

111 Ibid., 130.

112 *MAC*, 108.

113 Ibid., 240.

114 Gray, *Race, Gender, and Deviance*, 24.

115 See also Dyer-Witheford and de Peuter, *Games of Empire*; and DeVane and Squire, "Meaning of Race."

116 *MAC*, 77.

117 Ibid., 104.

118 One paper presented at the Digital Games Research Association (DiGRA) does attempt to reconcile critical race theory with philosophical conceptualizations of humor, but as a single-author piece falling outside of the collaborative scholarship process, it is beyond the scope of the critique I am making here. Nevertheless, its main argument is less to complicate the understanding of *GTA*'s racial humor than to undermine critical perspectives on race with ones on humor.

119 *MAC*, 144.

120 Ibid., 159.

121 Pulido, "Rethinking Environmental Racism," 26.

122 *MAC*, 143–44.

123 Ibid., 143.

124 In addition to examples from earlier in this section, another chapter in the *MAC* collection cites the nineties gangster rap of *San Andreas* as a mechanism to create a meaningful sense of place in the virtual world.

125 Ferguson, *Reorder of Things*; Ahmed, *On Being Included*.

126 I was struck, for example, by Sal Humphrey's account in "On Being a Feminist," which alluded in very general ways to unequal treatment without providing specific examples.

127 Humphreys, "On Being a Feminist," 7.

128 Chess and Shaw, "Conspiracy of Fishes," 213.

129 Chess and Shaw, "We Are All Fishes Now."

130 See Humphreys, "On Being a Feminist," for more on the ways feminist critique in particular becomes siloed in the discipline.

131 Chess and Shaw, "We Are All Fishes Now," 27.

CHAPTER 2. MAKING A FACE

1 Zimmerman, "Narrative, Interactivity, Play, and Games."

2 This does not include visual-effects animation, which does conform to photorealism in order to blend in with live action.

3 See, for example, Stuart, "Photorealism"; Raab, "How Video Game Makers"; and Heaven "ButtonMasher."

4 Gaboury, "Hidden Surface Problems."

5 Ibid., 57.

6 Grossman, *High Tech Trash*; Gabrys, *Digital Rubbish*; Maxwell and Miller, *Greening the Media*.

7 See, for example, China Labor Watch, "Analyzing Labor Conditions"; Dyer-Witheford, *Cyber-Proletariat*; and Maxwell, *Routledge Companion*, for an array of scholarship about labor issues in the tech industry.

8 Der Derian, *Virtuous War*; Crogan, *Gameplay Mode*.

9 Wernimont, *Numbered Lives*.

10 Harrell, *Phantasmal Media*, 29.

11 Cooper, "Quantic Dream's 'Kay' Demo."

12 Halberstam, "Automating Gender," 443.

13 cárdenas, *Transreal*.

14 Parke, "Computer Generated Animation of Faces."

15 Neither of these demos is hosted by the parent companies anymore, although they are referenced in forums and news articles. See Pixologic's interview with William Lambeth; and StunningAnimation, "Image Metrics How-To Video" for the Samburu warrior. See MCV, "VIDEO: Black Kennedy" for the Kennedy speech. See Reed and Phillips, "Additive Race," for an extensive discussion of how racialized bodies ground the realism of motion-capture performance.

16 Reed and Phillips, "Additive Race," 131.

17 Hoelzl and Marie, *Softimage*.

18 Graham, "Lavater's Physiognomy in England," 562.

19 Erle, "Face to Face."

20 Cowling, *Artist as Anthropologist*; Levitine, "Influence of Lavater"; Stemmler, "Physiognomical Portraits."

21 Pearl, *About Faces*, 6.

22 Ibid., 14.

23 Miller, "Anatomy of Scientific Racism," 127.

24 Darwin, *Expression of the Emotions*, 16.

25 Lavater, *Essays on Physiognomy*, xxii–xxiii.

26 Gray, *About Face*, 108.

27 McPherson, *Reconstructing Dixie*, 25.

28 Browne, *Dark Matters*; Magnet, *When Biometrics Fail*.

29 Blas, "Fag Face."

30 Harvey, "CV Dazzle."

31 Manovich, *Language of New Media*, 188.

32 Parke, "Computer Generated Animation of Faces," 451.

33 Ingebretsen, "40 Year Old 3D."

34 Platt and Badler, "Animating Facial Expressions."

35 ImageMetrics, "Sculpting the Face."

36 Patricia Beckmann-Wells and Scott Wells explain this decision as a way to foreground migratory flows rather than race specifically as a reason for regional facial variation, and they use the five categories determined by the United Nations for their geographical classifications. Beckmann-Wells and Wells, *Face It*.

37 Parke and Waters, *Computer Facial Animation*.

38 Forensic anthropologists are able identify a skeleton's assigned birth sex with a high degree of accuracy when multiple factors are taken into account, though researchers agree that the pelvis yields much more useful information than the skull. One study demonstrates only 70 percent accuracy based on skull analysis compared to 100 percent based on the pelvis (Đurić, Rakočević, Đonića, "Reliability of Sex Determination"). Determining race based on skeletal evidence is a much more complicated and controversial procedure.

39 Beckmann-Wells and Wells, *Face It*, 10.

40 Manovich, *Language of New Media*, 195–96.

41 Williams, "Performance-Driven Facial Animation," 242. Lance Williams himself performed the animation that was then mapped onto the digitized face of Annette White, a Black woman and personal friend of his, enacting a high-tech Blackface performance that, because of its status as a proof-of-concept demonstration and not performance per se, escapes association with this lineage. I include these details here because of this chapter's secondary, ongoing interrogation of the role of performing bodies of women and people of color with relation to technology.

42 Full performance capture is rapidly becoming the industry standard, with more recent releases such as Quantic Dream's *Beyond: Two Souls* (2013) featuring Hollywood actors in full digital form. A game's promotional media will often now include documentary footage of motion capture in action.

43 Quantic Dream, "Making of 'Kara.'"

44 Totillo, "Why Modern Video Game Armies."

45 Farokhmanesh, "Ubisoft Abandoned Women Assassins"; Brown, "Blizzard Explains Why."

46 Colour Separation, the 1997 digital project by the Jamaican-British collective Mongrel, aptly illustrates the dynamics that occur between slick digital interfaces and painful, messy inter/faces. One part of the project is a gallery of composited images, each of which consist of a mask made out of an image of a face stitched to the face of an individual of a different race. Mongrel made faces specifically for this application: merging the faces of over one hundred people, they created eight composite images that represented "un-glamourous stereotypes of black/yellow/brown/white men and women" in order to mask them on top of one another and suture them with grisly stitches that literalize Gloria Anzaldúa's metaphor of the interface. In the installation portion of the project, users click on the faces, which causes a digital spitball to appear on the image as a voice tells a story of racial violence. See Mongrel, "Colour Separation," now archived on the Wayback Machine, for full details of the project. See Chun, *Control and Freedom*; Gonzalez, "Face and Public"; and Hansen, *New Philosophy*, for commentary on this project, which can be enriched by an Anzaldúan reading to attend to its queer dimensions.

47 Researcher Nicholas Yee, whose Daedalus Project features survey responses from over forty thousand players of massively multiplayer online (MMO) games, has documented character creation motivations that range from physical

attractiveness to usefulness in a group setting. MIT professor Fox Harrell has discussed his attempts to create avatars that reflect different aspects of his identity. Fans on blogs like the *Border House* routinely create game protagonists that challenge the straight white male so often central to heroic adventure stories, even when the identity of the protagonists they create doesn't match their own.

48 Huber, "*Kingdom Hearts* Game Play Visualizations"; Huber, "Ludological Dynamics of *Fatal Frame II.*"

49 Unsurprisingly, and relevant to the topics covered in this chapter, the "Monster Factory" creations are humorous largely because of their deviation from normative perceptions of beauty and the human face, which results in visual gags that are frequently sexist, transphobic, racist, and ableist.

50 See, for example, intplee, "Good Looking Gal."

51 "*Fallout 3*'s Curious System of Race."

52 Lamarre, *Anime Machine*, xx.

53 Ketchum, "FaceGen," 199.

54 Andrew Beatty, quoted in ibid., 188–89.

55 Ketchum, "FaceGen," 191.

56 Ibid., 192.

57 Ibid., 197.

58 Lauteria, "Ga(y)mer Theory." See also Sihvonen, *Players Unleashed!*

59 FaceGen manual, quoted in Ketchum, "FaceGen," 189.

60 Nakamura, *Cybertypes.*

61 LadyMilla, "Creating a Custom Race," 3.

62 GECK, "Race."

63 For example, more recent interfaces in *The Sims* series and *Fallout 4* (2015) allow gamers to stretch and pull the body like putty, in addition to adjusting the sliders. They still, however, maintain their strict quantized scales, as evidenced by modder attempts to hack their interfaces.

CHAPTER 3. GENDER, POWER, AND THE GAMIC GAZE

1 Brown, *Dangerous Curves*, 32.

2 This is true, in particular, of humanistic game studies critique. Lara Croft studies have overshadowed a richer history of women in video games that includes, for example, Samus Aran of Nintendo's *Metroid* series and Chun-Li of the Capcom *Street Fighter* games. Both of these women come out of complicated transnational and gendered circuits of production that render the tension between masculinity and femininity in action genres in rather unique terms. Croft's popularity as a figure of academic critique is no doubt due to the extensive fan following that she gained after her debut. See Deuber-Mankowsky, *Lara Croft*; Kennedy, "Lara Croft"; and Rehak, "Mapping the Bit Girl," for detailed accounts of her rise to prominence that break from the tradition of thinking about Croft in representational terms and offer multimodal analyses of her role as a gaming icon. Justine Cassell and Henry Jenkins write about her in *From Barbie to Mortal Kombat*, one

of the foundational texts in feminist game studies. Jansz and Martis propose "the Lara phenomenon," which is "the appearance of a competent female character in a dominant position" in gaming ("Lara Phenomenon," 141). See also Carr, "Playing with Lara"; Flanagan, "Mobile Identities"; Mikula, "Gender and Video Games"; and Schleiner, "Does Lara Croft Wear," for examples of the range of Lara Croft scholarship that exists.

Other early feminist game studies utilized social science approaches that sought to understand power through quantifiable data: industry employment statistics, consumer patterns, harassment discourse analysis, and more. These are useful to document practices and habits and to legitimize the lived experiences of minority communities in a world that discounts their personal reports.

3 See MacCallum-Stewart, "Take That, Bitches!," for an overview of feminist critiques of Croft's body.

4 Castration anxiety is a central organizing concept in psychoanalysis. Laura Mulvey's use of *male* in the "male gaze" is one legacy of the theory's emergence from the gender-essentialist paradigms of psychoanalysis and 1970s white feminism, and it is possibly the source of the slippage between the abstract gendered power dynamics that she writes about and the actual audience experience that many critics use to talk about the male gaze today.

5 In "Afterthoughts," Mulvey herself defended the essay as a provocation.

6 Malkowski and Russworm, *Gaming Representation*, 1.

7 Penley, "Feminism, Psychoanalysis, and Popular Culture."

8 hooks, "Oppositional Gaze"; Clover, *Men, Women, and Chain Saws*.

9 Mirzoeff, "Subject of Visual Culture," 18.

10 Boyle, "Not Waving . . . Agitating?"

11 tekanji, "FAQ"; TV Tropes, s.v. "male gaze"; Geek Feminism Wiki, s.v. "male gaze."

12 North, *Dinosaur Comics*, October 6, 2006.

13 Haraway, *Staying with the Trouble*, 12.

14 Atkins, "What Are We Looking At?," 134.

15 Chesher, "Neither Gaze nor Glance." In addition to the connotation of eyes glazing over, Chris Chesher draws on the "stickiness" of a glaze to think about the ways video games direct attention, much as James Ash does with the interface envelope.

16 I use the phrase *feminine bodies* instead of "women" or "female bodies" here to avoid any essentialist confusion about the bodies themselves rather than their cultural positioning as feminine in images. *Feminine bodies* is applicable to transgender, male, and cisgender femininities, and it acknowledges that even representations of female masculinities are often constrained within hegemonic understandings of the feminine body in mass media texts.

17 Such a tradition has been observed by many scholars, including Lev Manovich, who, following Janet Murray, identified navigable space as one of the primary forms of new media (*Language of New Media*, 245); Jesper Juul, who compared digital game states to the temporal data that is stored on a board game or a

physical playing field ("Introduction to Game Time," 133); and Henry Jenkins, who coined the term *narrative architecture* to account for the spatial qualities of narrative events in games ("Game Design as Narrative Architecture," 121).

18 See Gaboury, "Hidden Surface Problems," for more on how the visual rendering of virtual three-dimensional images makes them ontologically different from other visual forms.

19 Galloway, *Gaming*, 41.

20 Ibid., 69.

21 Clover, *Men, Women, and Chain Saws*, chap. 4.

22 Galloway, *Gaming*, 69.

23 Miller, "Anal Rope."

24 Ruberg, *Video Games*.

25 Chion, *Voice in Cinema*, 21.

26 Kubrick, "*Playboy* Interview."

27 O'Dell, "Daisy Bell."

28 The others, significantly, are robots or other mechanical devices that are extensions of GLaDOS's psyche, and all but one is voiced by actress Ellen McClain.

29 Valve Corporation, ApertureScience.com (website).

30 Nofz and Vendy, "When Computers Say It," 41.

31 Silverman, "Dis-embodying the Female Voice," 13.

32 Bowler, "Still Alive? She's Free."

33 Taylor, "When Seams Fall Apart."

34 Kocurek and deWinter, "Chell Game," 32.

35 This list could go on and include the Tuskegee syphilis experiment and the forced sterilization of incarcerated women up until the 1990s. See, for example, Washington, *Medical Apartheid*.

36 Murray, *On Video Games*, 89.

37 See, for example, Jeffords, "Battle of the Big Mamas"; and Bundtzen, "Monstrous Mothers."

38 Aarseth, "Genre Trouble."

39 Farr, "Bayonetta."

40 Huber, "Sexy Videogameland."

41 Alexander, "Bayonetta."

42 Higgin, "Making Men Uncomfortable."

43 Dahlen, "Her Sex Is A Weapon."

44 cárdenas, "Blah, Blah, Blah?"

45 Hashimoto, "Bayonetta Released in Japan."

46 FeministFrequency, "Bayonetta Subway Advertisements."

47 Randolph, "Q&A: Hideki Kamiya on Bayonetta."

48 Yoshimura, "Modeling Bayonetta."

49 Huber, "Sexy Videogameland."

50 During the cinematic components of a game, which are meant to be watched rather than played, there is more of a traditional relationship between creator and

visual scene. There are also certain genres of games, most notably the survival horror genre, that will use fixed camera positions in order to increase tension and restrict the player's sense of control over the game world.

51 Linda Williams is widely credited with the concept of the body genre, but she adopts the term that Carol J. Clover originally lays out in "Her Body, Himself." See Williams, "Film Bodies," 4.

52 Brathwaite, *Sex in Video Games*, 27.

53 Queer game designer Anna Anthropy used this rapid-fire single-button mechanic in her 2008 game *Mighty Jill-Off*, which was much more explicit about the masturbatory nature of the gameplay.

54 We can also compare this to clearly phallic masturbatory controller gestures such as in Grasshopper Manufacture's *No More Heroes* game, which requires Wii gamers to shake the rod-shaped Wii remote with one hand in order to charge the main character's lightsword.

55 Higgin, "Making Men Uncomfortable."

56 Clover, *Men, Women, and Chain Saws*, 226–27. One might compare this to other critiques of Mulvey's sadistic scopophilic gaze. For Gaylyn Studlar, for example, masochism is fundamental to cinematic experience and to male sexuality. Studlar, *In the Realm of Pleasure*.

57 Ibid., 228.

58 Alexander, "Bayonetta"; Chow, "Bayonetta"; Farr, "Bayonetta."

59 Shaw, "On Not Becoming Gamers."

60 Such advantages include being offered protection and help in the game, as well as receiving items as gifts from other players. Nicholas Yee's research was done in the context of cooperative online games like *EverQuest*, in which the advantageous behavior reported by these players can benefit the team as a whole. This should be placed in the context of the widely documented harassment that woman-identified gamers report when their gender is discovered by other players. The treatment described by Yee's man-identified gamers, moreover, exemplifies the type of infantilizing behavior that keeps woman-identified gamers out of the "boys' club." Yee, Daedalus Project.

61 Kennedy, "Lara Croft."

62 Historically, see, for example, Lorde, "Master's Tools"; Carby, "White Woman Listen!"; Hurtado, "Reflections on White Feminism"; Sandoval, "U.S. Third World Feminism"; and many more. This conversation continues in the present day. See, for example, #SolidarityIsForWhiteWomen, started by Mikki Kendall, and Ware, *Beyond the Pale*.

63 Murray, *On Video Games*.

64 Ibid., 132.

65 Ibid., 136.

66 It is worth noting that the original *Tomb Raider* had grisly death scenes for the heroine as well, including being lifted up and shaken around in the jaws of a Tyrannosaurus rex. There are numerous YouTube videos devoted to the numerous

death animations for the game. See, for example, GameOverContinue and Roli's Tomb Raider Channel.

67 See Adams, "Andromeda on the Rocks," on the spectacle of Lara Croft's death scenes and the gendered power dynamics of sacrificing women in *Tomb Raider*.

68 The earliest reference I can find to this is a 2012 blog post by user problemmachine on their eponymous blog, though others have credited critic Tobi Smethurst ("Playing Dead in Video Games") as well.

69 Williams, "Film Bodies," 4.

CHAPTER 4. DOES ANYONE REALLY IDENTIFY WITH FEMSHEP?

1 See Dutton, Consalvo, and Harper, "Digital Pitchforks and Virtual Torches."

2 BioWare's history with queer characters precedes *Mass Effect*, with both *Jade Empire* (2005) and *Neverwinter Nights: Kingmaker* (2005) offering same-sex romance options; however, *Mass Effect* received more attention for this.

3 Lavigne, "She's a Soldier."

4 Richard, "Playing as a Woman."

5 FeministFrequency, "Ms. Male Character."

6 See, for example, goku420bro, "High Horse"; Bourke, "Sleeps with Monsters"; Cobbett, "Ms. Effect."

7 Shaw, *Gaming at the Edge*; Yee, Daedalus Project.

8 See Waern, "I'm in Love," for more on the bleed effect and falling in love with fictional digital characters.

9 Notably, the series' most recent installation, *Mass Effect: Andromeda* (2017), left all hairstyles as gender neutral options, though the styles that "match" the selected gender were presented first on the slider bar.

10 Tasker, *Spectacular Bodies*.

11 Other common names for this character include ManShep and MShep. I will use FemShep and BroShep throughout this chapter in order to emphasize both gender differences as well as political affiliations: because FemShep is often an icon for feminist critiques of the games industry, BroShep stands in for the vast stable of bald white space marines who embody a particular kind of weaponized heteronormative masculinity common to game narratives.

12 Manovich, *Language of New Media*.

13 See Reed and Phillips, "Additive Race," for a discussion of how motion-capture animation engages postracial rhetorics of realism in digital games by using the bodies of people of color to lend authenticity to certain activities like sports or dance.

14 For example, user simongenius1's "Blonde Femshep Dress Wearing FAIL."

15 Lesbian Gamers, "Lesbian Uncanny Valley of Gaming."

16 See Shaw, "Lost Queer Potential of *Fable*," for more on *Fable*'s heteronormative structures of gender and sexuality.

17 They are in fact identical except for one: potential romantic interest Liara's scene for both FemShep and BroShep includes an extra few seconds that show off more of her body as well as her special psychic Asari lovemaking powers.

18 Later games introduced other women available for same-sex romance, but it wasn't until *Mass Effect 3* that FemShep could romance a woman other than Liara and have it matter in terms of gaining the "Paramour" achievement that marks a "real" romance in the game.

19 For a more thorough academic analysis of romance across the series, see Adams, "Renegade Sex." For more on interspecies sex in *Mass Effect*, see Zekany, "Horrible Interspecies Awkwardness Thing."

20 I make this claim tentatively based on the "masculine" behavior of FemShep and the "feminine" behavior of Liara rather than any other signifiers of butch and femme gender presentations that exist in queer communities. My Commander Shepard did mimic my own butch genderqueer stylings, but that obviously is not the case for most FemSheps.

21 Judith Butler addresses this difference between butch/femme and heterosexuality in *Gender Trouble*, but scholarly interest in the topic is prolific and has not waned. See, for example, Halberstam, *Female Masculinity*; and Rubin, "Of Catamites and Kings" for early work on female masculinities as they interact with and differ from other masculinities.

22 While the specific mechanics of Asari reproduction are beyond the scope of this analysis, it may clear up some confusion to note that cross-species children bear only the personality traits of their non-Asari parent. Physically, they remain "pure" Asari.

23 *Mass Effect* Wiki, s.v. "turian." As of this writing, I cannot confirm that BioWare representatives ever suggested this, but it is widely reported by fans and a common practice in the industry to leave out female character models and claim it was a matter of budget or time. In addition to Van Dyke's comments, a more recent furor over Ubisoft's comments about *Assassin's Creed Unity* sparked the #WomenAreTooHardToAnimate hashtag on Twitter in June 2014, in which fans and developers disputed precisely this claim.

24 Hanson, "*Mass Effect 3*."

25 Pralier et al., "*Mass Effect 3*," interview.

26 Quoted in Farokhmanesh, "Animating Women."

27 Quoted in Farokhmanesh, "Ubisoft Abandoned Women Assassins."

28 Farokhmanesh, "Animating Women."

29 The "gay button" was first proposed by Anna Anthropy in a news interview. See *San Francisco Examiner*, "At San Francisco Convention." It was later developed as critical vocabulary in Shaw, "Lost Queer Potential of *Fable*"; and Adams, "Renegade Sex."

30 Lauteria, "Ga(y)mer Theory."

31 Smee, "*Mass Effect 3* & Beyond." Notably, this distinction was made in response to a question about why there were no gay men for Commander Shepard to romance, particularly when *Dragon Age*, another BioWare property, had recently introduced men having sex with men as an option. Ray Muzyka's response was that Commander Shepard had a more defined personality than the protagonist

of *Dragon Age*, and thus certain things like sexuality were not up to the player. He likens *Mass Effect* to a third-person narrative, where the player is controlling from further away than the first-person *Dragon Age*, which leaves more up to the player's choices and imagination. Whether this is an actual description of their design process or an excuse made up after the fact is left for interpretation, though the explanation on its own demonstrates the uneasy relationship between game design companies and "progressive" politics.

32 See Shaw, *Gaming at the Edge*.

33 While Keeling largely theorizes these developments as separate but parallel, scholars like Tara McPherson and Jacob Gaboury understand the technological development of the mid-twentieth century as inextricable from, and consequently indebted to, the queer and racial politics at the time. McPherson, "U.S. Operating Systems"; Gaboury, "Queer History." Nick Dyer-Witheford and Greig de Peuter also make this argument about the games industry's relationship to the radical social politics of the 1960s in *Games of Empire*.

34 Keeling, "I = Another," 60–61.

35 Ibid., 57.

36 Shaw, "On Not Becoming Gamers."

37 "About," FemShep.com.

38 While it is possible and common for players to perform both Paragon and Renegade actions in the course of one playthrough, it is also common practice to identify one's Commander Shepard as either Paragon or Renegade. Hence Sage's gesture here is reaching out to a broader FemShep community.

39 Patterson, "Role-Playing the Multiculturalist Umpire," 219.

40 Zekany, "Horrible Interspecies Awkwardness Thing," 70. Not coincidentally, the color black also becomes the marker for radical alterity in this universe, from the Reapers, to the geth (a group of intelligent robots that fought their way out of slavery), to the rachni (an insectoid species that almost wiped out the galaxy in a previous conflict), to the Collectors (who were themselves enslaved by the Reapers and are now aiding them in their cause). All have black exoskeletons, in contrast to the rainbow array of colors in other sentient species.

41 Patterson, "Role-Playing the Multiculturalist Umpire," 222.

42 Ibid., 223.

43 Lorde, *Zami*, 226.

44 See Lavigne, "She's a Soldier," for an extended analysis of the *Mass Effect 3* Fem-Shep vote.

45 Puar, *Terrorist Assemblages*.

46 See Crenshaw, "Framing Affirmative Action," for a discussion of the public discourse about affirmative action, including the strategic shift to discussing white women rather than people of color as beneficiaries in order not to provoke racist opposition to these policies.

47 Ferguson, *Reorder of Things*, 62.

48 Coulthard, "Killing Bill," 173.

49 I am simplifying the conflict somewhat here. The original ending of *Mass Effect 3* not only subverted fan expectations of closure for some long-standing conflicts but also was a piece of storytelling that seemed inconsistent with gamer choices and the rest of the narrative universe. For example, the final assault force is said to have been completely wiped out, yet squad members that the gamer chose to accompany them for this mission can later be seen escaping Earth on the *Normandy*. Another contradiction is the destruction of all of the mass relays in the galaxy: as their society's primary form of transportation, this would effectively strand all citizens in their present locations and, as the key plot point in *Mass Effect 3*'s prologue demonstrated, result in a powerful explosion that could wipe out an entire star system; until the revised ending, it was unclear if either (or both) had occurred. These are only some of the complaints raised during the backlash.

50 The original post by El_Spiko, "I Filed an FTC Complaint," has disappeared with the shutdown of the BioWare Forum. See Good, "*Mass Effect 3* Fan," for documentation of the post.

51 Moore, "We Can Do Better." EA received the honor in 2013 as well, and its representatives' responses have been consistently sarcastic about the fact that a video game publisher can perform worse in this contest than the likes of AIG and Halliburton. The exchanges between EA, *The Consumerist*, and EA customers over this contest is worthy of its own study about entitlement culture, corporate bullying, and gaming.

52 Moriarty, "*Mass Effect 3*: Opinion Video."

53 Muzyka, "To *Mass Effect 3* Players."

54 "Retake Gaming," Facebook.

55 Hutchings, "Choosers or Losers?," 21.

56 Mahmood, *Politics of Piety*.

57 Gill and Donaghue, "As If Postfeminism."

58 Hutchings, "Choosers or Losers?," 25.

59 Chun, *Control and Freedom*.

60 Butler, *Gender Trouble*.

61 Green and Ellison, "Dispatch."

62 Keeling, "I = Another," 73.

CONCLUSION

1 Caillois, *Man, Play and Games*, 14.

2 Boluk and LeMieux, *Metagaming*, 226.

3 See Caillois, *Man, Play and Games*, chap. 4.

4 Ibid., 114.

5 Connolly, *Identity/Difference*; Honig, *Political Theory*; Mouffe, *Agonistics*. Each of these theorists has their own articulation of what agonistic politics means, though I find them all compatible enough in their insistence on the primacy of conflict to political life to read them together here. William E. Connolly and Bonnie

Honig work through Nietzschean formulations of agon, though Honig also draws from the work of Hannah Arendt. Chantal Mouffe distinguishes herself from the other two in her insistence on the ineradicability of antagonism from political life as well as her insistence on a structural critique of hegemony, which she finds missing from the work of the other two. I find her critique of Honig in particular to unfairly characterize the work of identity politics as having little to offer by way of strategy for political organizing. Nevertheless, I find Mouffe's account of the antagonist to be an important corrective to a theory of political relation that might otherwise encourage abuses of the kind we see with right-wing free speech absolutists who disingenuously claim space in the public square in the name of fairness and democracy.

6 Wark, *Gamer Theory*, 97.

7 Keeling, "I = Another."

8 See Fickle, *Race Card*, for an excellent examination of the Orientalist foundations embedded within the theories foundational to game studies, including the agon as theorized by Caillois. I regret that the publication of Fickle's book coincided with the copyediting process of this one; otherwise I would have engaged much more substantially with her critique.

9 Lorde, "Uses of Anger."

10 Caillois, *Man, Play and Games*, 46.

11 Ibid., 56.

12 Mouffe, *Agonistics*, 7.

13 See Raley, *Tactical Media*; and Raley, "Digital Humanities."

14 Honig, *Political Theory*, 16.

15 Honig, *Antigone, Interrupted*.

16 We are indebted to, among others, Wendy Chun, Cathy Davidson, Anna Everett, Alan Liu, Tara McPherson, Lisa Nakamura, and Rita Raley, some of our first senior mentors and amplifiers in the field. See Lothian and Phillips, "Can Digital Humanities Mean Critique?"; and Bailey et al., "Reflections on a Movement," for more on the history, politics, and troubles of #transformDH.

17 See NBC News, "How Gamers Are Facilitating Alt-Right"; Chess and Shaw, "Conspiracy of Fishes"; and Vossen, "On Cultural Inaccessibility."

18 This conflict was part of a longer pattern of behavior. Adrian Cheok publicly harassed other colleagues on Twitter and eventually lost support from publishers and institutions for the 2018 International Conference on Advances in Computer Entertainment Technology after inviting a prominent right-wing politician, who was not a computer scientist, to keynote the academic conference. See Whitehead et al., "Letter to FDG Community"; and Whitehead et al., "Second Letter to FDG Community," for the game studies response to his harassment of Gillian Smith.

19 See Tomlinson, *Feminism and Affect*.

20 See Kim, "Teaching Medieval Studies"; and Gallaher, "War on the Ivory Tower."

21 See CBC Radio, "Dangerous Game"; Condis, *Gaming Masculinity*; Green, *Devil's Bargain*; Nagle, *Kill All Normies*; and more.
22 Gallaher, "War on the Ivory Tower."
23 Quoted in Cross, "Press F to Revolt."
24 Haraway, *Staying with the Trouble*, 1.
25 Quinn, *Crash Override*, 7.

BIBLIOGRAPHY

A., Milli. 2010. "Rape Is Hilarious, Part 53 in an Ongoing Series." *Shakesville*, August 12. www.shakesville.com/.

Aarseth, Espen. 2001. "Computer Game Studies, Year One." *Game Studies* 1 (1). www.gamestudies.org/.

———. 2004. "Genre Trouble: Narrativism and the Art of Simulation." In *First Person: New Media as Story, Performance, and Game*, edited by Noah Wardrip-Fruin and Pat Harrigan, 45–55. Cambridge, MA: MIT Press.

———. 2012. "A Narrative Theory of Games." In *Proceedings of the International Conference on the Foundations of Digital Games*, 129–33. FDG 2012. New York: ACM. https://doi.org/10.1145/2282338.2282365.

"About." n.d. FemShep.com. Accessed June 24, 2018. www.femshep.com/.

Adams, Meghan Blythe. 2015. "Renegade Sex: Compulsory Sexuality and Charmed Magic Circles in the *Mass Effect* Series." *Loading . . .* 9 (14): 40–54.

———. 2017. "Andromeda on the Rocks: Retreading and Resisting Tropes of Female Sacrifice in *Tomb Raider*." In "Gender Issues in Video Games," special issue, *Kinephanos: Journal of Media Studies and Popular Culture* (July): 103–26.

Ahmed, Sara. 2010. *The Promise of Happiness*. Durham, NC: Duke University Press.

———. 2012. *On Being Included: Racism and Diversity in Institutional Life*. Durham, NC: Duke University Press.

———. 2017. *Living a Feminist Life*. Durham, NC: Duke University Press.

Aidoo, Ama Ata. 1994. *Our Sister Killjoy*. Harlow, UK: Longman.

Alexander, Leigh. 2010. "Bayonetta: Empowering or Exploitative?" *Gamepro*, January 6. www.gamepro.com/.

———. 2014. "'Gamers' Don't Have to Be Your Audience. 'Gamers' Are Over." Gamasutra, August 28. www.gamasutra.com/.

Anthropy, Anna. 2008. *Mighty Jill-Off*. PC.

Anzaldúa, Gloria, ed. 1990. *Making Face, Making Soul / Haciendo Caras: Creative and Critical Perspectives by Women of Color*. San Francisco: Aunt Lute Foundation.

apresvie. 2011. "Lupus Phallus—the Misunderstood Canid." *Postmortem Studios*, February 5. https://apresvie.livejournal.com/.

Ash, James. (2015) 2016. *The Interface Envelope: Gaming, Technology, Power*. Reprint, New York: Bloomsbury Academic.

Atkins, Barry. 2006. "What Are We Really Looking At? The Future-Orientation of Video Game Play." *Games and Culture* 1 (2): 127–40. https://doi.org/10.1177/1555412006286687.

Bailey, Moya, Anne Cong-Huyen, Alexis Lothian, and Amanda Phillips. 2016. "Reflections on a Movement: #transformDH, Growing Up." In *Debates in the Digital Humanities 2016*, edited by Matthew Gold and Lauren Klein, 71–80. University of Minnesota Press.

Beckmann-Wells, Patricia, and Scott Wells. 2013. *Face It: A Visual Reference for Multiethnic Facial Modeling*. Burlington, MA: Focal Press.

Bergstrom, Kelly, Stephanie Fisher, and Jennifer Jenson. 2016. "Disavowing 'That Guy': Identity Construction and Massively Multiplayer Online Game Players." *Convergence* 22 (3): 233–49. https://doi.org/10.1177/1354856514560314.

Bethesda Game Studios. *Fallout 3*. PlayStation 3, Xbox 360. Bethesda Softworks.

———. *Fallout 4*. PlayStation 4, Xbox One. Bethesda Softworks.

BioWare. 2005. *Jade Empire*. Xbox. Microsoft Game Studios.

———. 2005. *Neverwinter Nights: Kingmaker*. PC. Atari, Inc.

———. 2007. *Mass Effect*. Xbox 360. Microsoft Game Studios.

———. 2012. *Mass Effect 2*. Xbox 360. Electronic Arts, Incorporated.

———. 2012. *Mass Effect 3*. Xbox 360. Electronic Arts, Incorporated.

Blas, Zach. 2013. "Fag Face." Vimeo, January 21. https://vimeo.com/57882032.

Bogost, Ian. 2009. "Videogames Are a Mess." *Ian Bogost*, September 3. http://bogost.com/.

Boluk, Stephanie, and Patrick LeMieux. 2017. *Metagaming: Playing, Competing, Spectating, Cheating, Trading, Making, and Breaking Videogames*. Minneapolis: University of Minnesota Press.

Bourke, Liz. 2012. "Sleeps with Monsters: *Mass Effect* and the Normalisation of the Woman Hero." *Tor*, May 29. www.tor.com/.

Bowler, Steve. 2008. "Still Alive? She's Free." Game-ism, April 4. www.game-ism.com/.

Boyle, Karen. 2015. "Not Waving . . . Agitating? 'Visual Pleasure and Narrative Cinema,' the Second Wave, and Me." *Feminist Media Studies* 15 (5): 885–88. https://doi.org/10.1080/14680777.2015.1075273.

Braithwaite, Andrea. 2016. "It's about Ethics in Games Journalism? Gamergaters and Geek Masculinity." *Social Media + Society* 2 (4). https://doi.org/10.1177/2056305116672484.

Brathwaite, Brenda. 2007. *Sex in Video Games*. Hingham, MA: Charles River Media.

Brookey, Robert Alan. 2010. *Hollywood Gamers: Digital Convergence in the Film and Video Game Industries*. Bloomington: Indiana University Press.

Brown, Fraser. 2019. "Blizzard Explains Why It Took 15 Years to Add More Ethnicities to World of Warcraft." *PC Gamer*, Nov 3. http://www.pcgamer.com/.

Brown, Jeffrey A. 2011. *Dangerous Curves: Action Heroines, Gender, Fetishism, and Popular Culture*. Jackson: University Press of Mississippi.

Browne, Simone. 2015. *Dark Matters: On the Surveillance of Blackness*. Durham, NC: Duke University Press.

Buckley, Tim. 2005. "An Open Letter to Jack Thompson." *Ctrl+Alt+Del*, October 12. https://cad-comic.com/.

Bundtzen, Lynda K. 1987. "Monstrous Mothers: Medusa, Grendel, and Now Alien." *Film Quarterly* 40 (3): 11–17. https://doi.org/10.2307/1212458.

Butler, Judith. 1990. *Gender Trouble: Feminism and the Subversion of Identity*. New York: Routledge.

Caillois, Roger. (1961) 2001. *Man, Play and Games*. Translated by Meyer Barash. Reprint, Urbana: University of Illinois Press.

Calvert, Clay, and Robert D. Richards. 2004. "Precedent Be Damned—It's All about Good Politics & Sensational Soundbites: The Video Game Censorship Saga of 2005." *Texas Review of Entertainment & Sports Law* 6 (1): 79–155.

Carby, Hazel. 1982. "White Woman Listen! Black Feminism and the Boundaries of Sisterhood." In *The Empire Strikes Back: Race and Racism in Seventies Britain*, by Centre for Contemporary Cultural Studies, 212–35. London: Hutchinson.

cárdenas, micha. 2012. *The Transreal: Political Aesthetics of Crossing Realities*. Edited by Zach Blas and Wolfgang Schirmacher. New York: Atropos Press.

———. 2012. "Blah, Blah, Blah: Ke$ha Feminism?" *Journal of Popular Music Studies* 24 (2): 176–95. https://doi.org/10.1111/j.1533-1598.2012.01324.x.

Carr, Diane. 2002. "Playing with Lara." In *Screenplay: Cinema/Videogames/Interfaces*, edited by Tanya Krzywinska and Geoff King, 171–80. London: Wallflower Press.

Cassell, Justine, and Henry Jenkins, eds. 2000. *From Barbie to Mortal Kombat: Gender and Computer Games*. Cambridge, MA: MIT Press.

CBC Radio. 2016. "The Dangerous Game." *Ideas from the Trenches*, November 30. www.cbc.ca/.

Chesher, Chris. 2007. "Neither Gaze nor Glance, but Glaze: Relating to Console Game Screens." *Scan Journal* 4 (2). http://scan.net.au.

Chess, Shira. 2017. *Ready Player Two: Women Gamers and Designed Identity*. Minneapolis: University of Minnesota Press.

Chess, Shira, and Adrienne Shaw. 2015. "A Conspiracy of Fishes, or, How We Learned to Stop Worrying about #GamerGate and Embrace Hegemonic Masculinity." *Journal of Broadcasting & Electronic Media* 59 (1): 208–20. https://doi.org/10.1080/08838151.2014.999917.

———. 2016. "We Are All Fishes Now: DiGRA, Feminism, and GamerGate." *Transactions of the Digital Games Research Association* 2 (2). https://doi.org/10.26503/todigra.v2i2.39.

China Labor Watch. 2015. "Analyzing Labor Conditions of Pegatron and Foxconn: Apple's Low-Cost Reality." www.chinalaborwatch.org/.

Chion, Michel. 1999. *The Voice in Cinema*. Translated by Claudia Gorbman. New York: Columbia University Press.

Chow, Tiff. 2010. "Bayonetta—Sexuality as Decoration vs. Celebration." *Tiff*, January 12. http://tiffchow.typepad.com/.

Chun, Wendy Hui-Kyong. 2006. *Control and Freedom: Power and Paranoia in the Age of Fiber Optics*. Cambridge, MA: MIT Press.

Clover, Carol J. 1987. "Her Body, Himself: Gender in the Slasher Film." *Representations* 20 (Autumn): 187–228. https://doi.org/10.2307/2928507.

———. 1992. *Men, Women, and Chain Saws: Gender in the Modern Horror Film.* Princeton Classics edition. Princeton, NJ: Princeton University Press.

Cobbett, Richard. 2012. "Ms. Effect: The Rise of FemShep." Eurogamer, March 22. www.eurogamer.net/.

Condis, Megan. 2015. "No Homosexuals in Star Wars? BioWare, 'Gamer' Identity, and the Politics of Privilege in a Convergence Culture." *Convergence* 21 (2): 198–212. https://doi.org/10.1177/1354856514527205.

———. 2018. *Gaming Masculinity: Trolls, Fake Geeks, and the Gendered Battle for On-line Culture.* Iowa City: University of Iowa Press.

Connell, Noreen, and Cassandra Wilson, eds. 1974. *Rape: The First Sourcebook for Women by New York Radical Feminists.* New York: Plume Books.

Connolly, William E. 2002. *Identity/Difference: Democratic Negotiations of Political Paradox, Expanded Edition.* Expanded ed. Minneapolis: University of Minnesota Press.

Consalvo, Mia. 2009. *Cheating: Gaining Advantage in Videogames.* Cambridge, MA: MIT Press.

———. 2012. "Confronting Toxic Gamer Culture: A Challenge for Feminist Game Studies Scholars." *Ada: A Journal of Gender, New Media, and Technology*, no. 1. https://adanewmedia.org/.

Cooper, Jonathan. 2012. "Quantic Dream's 'Kay' Demo at GDC." *GAME ANIM*, March 8. www.gameanim.com/.

Cote, Amanda C. 2017. "'I Can Defend Myself': Women's Strategies for Coping with Harassment while Gaming Online." *Games and Culture* 12 (2): 136–55. https://doi.org/10.1177/1555412015587603.

———. 2018. "Writing 'Gamers': The Gendered Construction of Gamer Identity in *Nintendo Power* (1994–1999)." *Games and Culture* 13 (5): 479–503. https://doi.org/10.1177/1555412015624742.

Coulthard, Lisa. 2007. "Killing Bill: Rethinking Feminism and Film Violence." In *Interrogating Postfeminism: Gender and the Politics of Popular Culture*, edited by Yvonne Tasker and Diane Negra, 153–75. Durham, NC: Duke University Press.

Cowling, Mary. 1989. *The Artist as Anthropologist: The Representation of Type and Character in Victorian Art.* Cambridge: Cambridge University Press.

Crawford, Garry. 2011. *Video Gamers.* London: Routledge.

Crenshaw, Kimberlé. 1991. "Mapping the Margins: Intersectionality, Identity Politics, and Violence against Women of Color." *Stanford Law Review* 43 (6): 1241–99. https://doi.org/10.2307/1229039.

———. 2006. "Framing Affirmative Action." *Michigan Law Review First Impressions* 105 (4): 123–33.

Crogan, Patrick. 2011. *Gameplay Mode: War, Simulation, and Technoculture.* Minneapolis: University of Minnesota Press.

Cross, Katherine. 2016. "Press F to Revolt: On the Gamification of Online Activism." In *Diversifying Barbie and Mortal Kombat: Intersectional Perspectives and Inclusive Designs in Gaming*, edited by Yasmin B. Kafai, Gabriela T. Richard, and Brendesha M. Tynes, 23–34. Pittsburgh, PA: Carnegie Melon ETC Press.

———. 2017. "The Nightmare Is Over." In *Queer Game Studies*, edited by Bonnie Ruberg and Adrienne Shaw, 179–86. Minneapolis: University of Minnesota Press.

Crystal Dynamics. 2013. *Tomb Raider*. OS X, PC, PlayStation 3, PlayStation 4, Xbox 360, Xbox One. Square Enix.

CSPAN. 1993. *Video Game Violence*. www.c-span.org/.

Dahlen, Chris. 2010. "Her Sex Is a Weapon." *Edge: The Global Game Industry Network*, January 13. http://edge-online.com/.

Darwin, Charles. (1872) 1998. *The Expression of the Emotions in Man and Animals*. 3rd ed. Reprint, Oxford: Oxford University Press.

DePass, Tanya, ed. 2018. *Game Devs & Others: Tales from the Margins*. Boca Raton, FL: A K Peters/CRC Press.

Der Derian, James. 2001. *Virtuous War: Mapping the Military-Industrial-Media -Entertainment-Network*. Boulder, CO: Westview Press.

Deuber-Mankowsky, Astrid. 2005. *Lara Croft: Cyber Heroine*. Minneapolis: University of Minnesota Press.

DeVane, Ben, and Kurt Squire. 2008. "The Meaning of Race and Violence in *Grand Theft Auto: San Andreas*." *Games and Culture* 3 (3–4): 264–85. https://doi.org/10.1177/1555412008317308.

Dibbell, Julian. 1998. "A Rape in Cyberspace." In *My Tiny Life: Crime and Passion in a Virtual World*. New York: Henry Holt.

DMA Design. 1997. *Grand Theft Auto*. PlayStation. Take-Two Interactive.

———. 2001. *Grand Theft Auto III*. PlayStation 2, Xbox. Rockstar Games.

Đurić, Marija, Zoran Rakočević, and Danijela Đonića. 2005. "The Reliability of Sex Determination of Skeletons from Forensic Context in the Balkans." *Forensic Science International* 147 (2–3): 159–64. https://doi.org/10.1016/j.forsciint.2004.09.111.

Dutton, Nathan, Mia Consalvo, and Todd Harper. 2011. "Digital Pitchforks and Virtual Torches: Fan Responses to the *Mass Effect* News Debacle." *Convergence* 17 (3): 287–305. https://doi.org/10.1177/1354856511407802.

Dyer-Witheford, Nick. 2015. *Cyber-Proletariat: Global Labour in the Digital Vortex*. Toronto: Pluto Press.

Dyer-Witheford, Nick, and Greig de Peuter. 2009. *Games of Empire: Global Capitalism and Video Games*. Minneapolis: University of Minnesota Press.

El_Spiko. 2012. "I Filed an FTC Complaint." BioWare Forum, March 16. Accessed June 21, 2014. Site discontinued.

Entertainment Consumers Association. n.d. "About the ECA." www.theeca.com/.

Entertainment Software Association. 2019. "Essential Facts about the Computer and Video Game Industry." www.theesa.com/.

———. 2018. "US Video Game Industry Revenue Reaches $36 Billion in 2017." January 18. www.theesa.com/.

Erle, Sibylle. 2005. "Face to Face with Johann Caspar Lavater." *Literature Compass* 2 (1): 1–4. https://doi.org/10.1111/j.1741-4113.2005.00131.x.

Eskelinen, Markku. 2001. "The Gaming Situation." *Game Studies* 1 (1). www.gamestudies.org/.

Everett, Anna, and Craig Watkins. 2008. "The Power of Play: The Portrayal and Performance of Race." In *The Ecology of Games: Connecting Youth, Games, and Learning*, edited by Katie Salen Tekinbaş, 141–66. Cambridge, MA: MIT Press.

Farokhmanesh, Megan. 2014. "Animating Women Should Take 'Days,' Says *Assassin's Creed 3* Animation Director." Polygon, June 11. www.polygon.com/.

———. 2014. "Ubisoft Abandoned Women Assassins in Co-op Because of the Additional Work." Polygon, June 10. www.polygon.com/.

Farr, Denis. 2010. "Bayonetta: Dragging Angels to Hell." *Border House*, February 19. http://borderhouseblog.com/.

FeministFrequency. 2012. "Bayonetta Subway Advertisements in Japan." YouTube, June 4. https://youtu.be/17_bd03vGP0/.

———. 2013. "Ms. Male Character." YouTube, November 18. https://youtu.be/eYqYLfm1rWA.

Ferguson, Roderick. 2012. *The Reorder of Things: The University and Its Pedagogies of Minority Difference*. Minneapolis: University of Minnesota Press.

Fickle, Tara. 2019. *The Race Card: From Gaming Technologies to Model Minorities*. New York: New York University Press.

Filipovic, Jill. 2007. "Blogging While Female: How Internet Misogyny Parallels 'Real-World' Harassment." *Yale Journal of Law & Feminism* 19 (1): 295–303.

Flanagan, Mary. 1999. "Mobile Identities, Digital Stars, and Postcinematic Selves." *Wide Angle* 21 (1): 77–93.

Fraser, Nancy. 1999. "Social Justice in the Age of Identity Politics: Redistribution, Recognition, and Participation." In *Culture and Economy after the Cultural Turn*, 25–52. London: SAGE.

Gaboury, Jacob. 2013. "A Queer History of Computing." Rhizome, February 19. www.rhizome.org/.

———. 2015. "Hidden Surface Problems: On the Digital Image as Material Object." *Journal of Visual Culture* 14 (1): 40–60. https://doi.org/10.1177/1470412914562270.

Gabrys, Jennifer. 2011. *Digital Rubbish: A Natural History of Electronics*. Ann Arbor: University of Michigan Press.

Gallagher, Rob. 2018. "Minecrafting Masculinities: Gamer Dads, Queer Childhoods and Father-Son Gameplay in *A Boy Made of Blocks*." *Game Studies* 18 (2). www.gamestudies.org/.

Gallaher, Carolyn. 2018. "War on the Ivory Tower: Alt Right Attacks on University Professors." *Political Research Associates*, May 7. http://feature.politicalresearch.org/.

Galloway, Alexander R. 2006. *Gaming: Essays on Algorithmic Culture*. Minneapolis: University of Minnesota Press.

Garrelts, Nate, ed. 2006. *The Meaning and Culture of Grand Theft Auto: Critical Essays*. Jefferson, NC: McFarland.

GECK. 2008. "Race." Bethesda Softworks, November 24. http://geck.bethsoft.com/.

Geek Feminism Wiki. s.v. "male gaze." n.d. http://geekfeminism.wikia.com/.

Gill, Rosalind, and Ngaire Donaghue. 2013. "As If Postfeminism Had Come True: The Turn to Agency in Cultural Studies of 'Sexualisation.'" In *Gender, Agency, and Coercion*, 240–58. London: Palgrave Macmillan.

goku42obro. 2012. "High Horse: The Case for FemShep." Games Radar, March 10. www.gamesradar.com/.

Golding, Dan, and Leena van Deventer. 2016. *Game Changers*. New York: Simon and Schuster.

González, Jennifer. 2009. "The Face and the Public: Race, Secrecy, and Digital Art Practice." *Camera Obscura* 24 (1): 37–65.

Good, Owen. 2012. "*Mass Effect 3* Fan Complains to Feds over Game's Ending." Kotaku, March 18. https://kotaku.com/.

Graham, John. 1961. "Lavater's Physiognomy in England." *Journal of the History of Ideas* 22 (4): 561–72. https://doi.org/10.2307/2708032.

Grasshopper Manufacture. 2007. *No More Heroes*. Wii. Ubisoft.

Gray, Kishonna L. 2014. *Race, Gender, and Deviance in Xbox Live: Theoretical Perspectives from the Virtual Margins*. Edited by Victor E. Kappeler. Waltham, MA: Anderson.

———. 2015. "#CiteHerWork: Marginalizing Women in Academic and Journalistic Writing." KishonnaGray.com, December 28. www.kishonnagray.com/.

Gray, Kishonna L., Gerald Voorhees, and Emma Vossen, eds. 2018. *Feminism in Play*. Palgrave Games in Context. London: Palgrave Macmillan.

Gray, Richard T. 2004. *About Face: German Physiognomic Thought from Lavater to Auschwitz*. Kritik. Detroit: Wayne State University Press.

Green, Joshua. 2017. *Devil's Bargain: Steve Bannon, Donald Trump, and the Nationalist Uprising*. New York: Penguin Books.

Green, Kai M., and Treva Ellison. 2013. "Dispatch from the 'Very House of Difference': Anti-Black Racism and the Expansion of Sexual Citizenship—or—We Need to Do So Much Better at Loving Each Other." Feminist Wire, July 4. www.thefeministwire.com/.

Greenfield, Patricia M. 1984. *Mind and Media: The Effects of Television, Video Games, and Computers*. Cambridge, MA: Harvard University Press.

Grossman, Elizabeth. 2007. *High Tech Trash: Digital Devices, Hidden Toxics, and Human Health*. 2nd ed. Washington, DC: Shearwater.

Halberstam, Judith. 1991. "Automating Gender: Postmodern Feminism in the Age of the Intelligent Machine." *Feminist Studies* 17 (3): 439–60.

———. 1998. *Female Masculinity*. Durham, NC: Duke University Press.

Hampton, Rachelle. 2019. "The Black Feminists Who Saw the Alt-Right Threat Coming." Slate, April 23. www.slate.com/.

Hansen, Mark. 2006. *New Philosophy for New Media*. Cambridge, MA: MIT Press.

Haraway, Donna. 2016. *Staying with the Trouble: Making Kin in the Chthulucene*. Durham, NC: Duke University Press.

Harper, Todd, Meghan Blythe Adams, and Nicholas Taylor, eds. 2018. *Queerness in Play*. London: Palgrave Macmillan.

Harrell, D. Fox. 2013. *Phantasmal Media: An Approach to Imagination, Computation, and Expression*. Cambridge, MA: MIT Press.

Harrigan, Pat, and Noah Wardrip-Fruin. 2006. *First Person: New Media as Story, Performance, Game*. Cambridge, MA: MIT Press.

Harvey, Adam. n.d. "CV Dazzle: Camouflage from Face Detection." https://cvdazzle .com/.

Hashimoto Yusuke. 2009. "Bayonetta Released in Japan." *PlatinumGames Official Blog*, November 6. www.platinumgames.com/.

Heaven, Douglas. 2014. "ButtonMasher: Photorealism Takes Gaming Deeper." *New Scientist*, July 8. www.newscientist.com/.

Heineman, David S. 2014. "Public Memory and Gamer Identity: Retrogaming as Nostalgia." *Journal of Games Criticism* 1 (1): 1–24. www.gamescriticism.org/.

Hemmings, Clare. 2011. *Why Stories Matter: The Political Grammar of Feminist Theory*. Durham, NC: Duke University Press.

Herman, Dianne. 1984. "The Rape Culture." In *Women: A Feminist Perspective*, edited by Jo Freeman, 45–53. New York: McGraw-Hill.

Hernandez, Patricia. 2013. "*Penny Arcade* Artist: Pulling Dickwolves Merchandise 'Was a Mistake.'" Kotaku, September 3. https://kotaku.com/.

Herring, Susan. 1999. "The Rhetorical Dynamics of Gender Harassment On-Line." *Information Society* 15:151–67. https://doi.org/10.1080/019722499128466.

Herring, Susan, Kirk Job-Sluder, Rebecca Scheckler, and Sasha Barab. 2002. "Searching for Safety Online: Managing 'Trolling' in a Feminist Forum." *Information Society* 18:371–84. https://doi.org/10.1080/01972240290108186.

Higgin, Tanner. 2010. "Making Men Uncomfortable: What Bayonetta Should Learn from Gaga." Tanner Higgin (website), December 2. www.tannerhiggin.com/.

———. 2012. "*Fallout 3*'s Curious System of Race." Tanner Higgin (website), April 1. www.tannerhiggin.com/.

Hoelzl, Ingrid, and Rémi Marie. 2015. *Softimage: Towards a New Theory of the Digital Image*. Bristol, UK: Intellect Books.

Holkins, Jerry. 2010. "On the Matter of Dickwolves." *Penny Arcade*, August 13. www .penny-arcade.com/.

Holkins, Jerry, and Mike Krahulik. 2010. "Breaking It Down." *Penny Arcade*, August 13. www.penny-arcade.com/.

———. 2010. "The Sixth Slave." *Penny Arcade*, August 11. www.penny-arcade.com/.

Honig, Bonnie. 1993. *Political Theory and the Displacement of Politics*. Ithaca, NY: Cornell University Press.

———. 2013. *Antigone, Interrupted*. Cambridge: Cambridge University Press.

hooks, bell. 1996. "The Oppositional Gaze: Black Female Spectators." In *Movies and Mass Culture*, 247–67. New Brunswick, NJ: Rutgers University Press.

Horeck, Tanya. 2014. "#AskThicke: 'Blurred Lines,' Rape Culture, and the Feminist Hashtag Takeover." *Feminist Media Studies* 14 (6): 1105–7. https://doi.org/10.1080/14680777.2014.975450.

Huber, William. 2008. "Ludological Dynamics of *Fatal Frame 2*." Presented at the Software Studies Initiative, University of California at San Diego, June 19. http://lab .softwarestudies.com/.

———. 2010. "*Kingdom Hearts* Game Play Visualizations." Presented at the Software Studies Initiative, University of California at San Diego. http://lab.softwarestudies.com/.

———. 2010. "Sexy Videogameland: If You Run Out of Ammo, You Can Have Mine." Zang.org, January 13. https://zang.org/.

Humphreys, Sal. 2019. "On Being a Feminist in Games Studies." *Games and Culture* 14 (7–8): 825–42. https://doi.org/10.1177/1555412017737637.

Huntemann, Nina, ed. 2013. "Feminist Game Studies." Special issue, *Ada: A Journal of Gender, New Media, and Technology*, no. 2. https://adanewmedia.org/.

Hurtado, Aída. n.d. "Reflections on White Feminism: A Perspective from a Woman of Color." In *Social and Gender Boundaries in the United States*, 155–86. Lewiston, NY: Edwin Mellen Press.

Hutchings, Kimberly. 2013. "Choosers or Losers? Feminist Ethical and Political Agency in a Plural and Unequal World." In *Gender, Agency, and Coercion*, edited by Sumi Madhok, Anne Phillips, and Kalpana Wilson, 14–28. Palgrave Macmillan.

ImageMetrics. 2011. "Sculpting the Face—Webinar with Ryan Kingslien." YouTube, September 13. https://youtu.be/VEiBYgBmhHo/.

Ingebretsen, Robby. 2010. "40 Year Old 3D Computer Graphics (Pixar, 1972)." Vimeo, October 28. https://vimeo.com/16292363.

intplee. 2009. "A Good Looking Gal for *Fallout 3*." Game and Player Forums, May 31. Accessed July 23, 2014. Site discontinued.

Jansz, Jeroen and Raynel G. Martis. 2007. "The Lara Phenomenon: Powerful Female Characters in Video Games." *Sex Roles* 56:141–8.

Jeffords, Susan. 1987. "'The Battle of the Big Mamas': Feminism and the Alienation of Women." *Journal of American Culture* 10 (3): 73–84. https://doi.org/10.1111/j.1542 -734X.1987.1003_73.x.

Jenkins, Henry. 2004. "Game Design as Narrative Architecture." In *First Person: New Media as Story, Performance, and Game*, edited by Noah Wardrip-Fruin and Pat Harrigan, 118–31. Cambridge, MA: MIT Press.

———. 2006. *Fans, Bloggers, and Gamers: Media Consumers in a Digital Age*. New York: New York University Press.

Juul, Jesper. 2004. "Introduction to Game Time." In *First Person: New Media as Story, Performance, and Game*, edited by Noah Wardrip-Fruin and Pat Harrigan, 131–42. Cambridge, MA: MIT Press.

Kafai, Yasmin B., Brendesha M. Tynes, and Gabriela T. Richard. 2016. *Diversifying Barbie and Mortal Kombat: Intersectional Perspectives and Inclusive Designs in Gaming*. Pittsburgh, PA: Carnegie Mellon ETC Press.

Keeling, Kara. 2011. "I = Another: Digital Identity Politics." In *Strange Affinities: The Gender and Sexual Politics of Comparative Racialization*, edited by Grace Kyungwon Hong and Roderick A. Ferguson, 53–75. Durham, NC: Duke University Press.

Kendall, Mikki. 2015. "The Harassment Game." *Model View Culture*, February 23. https://modelviewculture.com/.

Kennedy, Helen W. 2002. "Lara Croft: Feminist Icon or Cyberbimbo? On the Limits of Textual Analysis." *Game Studies* 2 (2). www.gamestudies.org/.

Kenyota, Gregory. 2008. "Thinking of the Children: The Failure of Violent Video Game Laws." *Fordham Intellectual Property, Media and Entertainment Law Journal* 18 (3): 785–815.

Ketchum, Karyl E. 2009. "FaceGen and the Technovisual Politics of Embodied Surfaces." *WSQ: Women's Studies Quarterly* 37 (1): 183–99. https://doi.org/10.1353/wsq.0.0150.

Kim, Dorothy. 2017. "Teaching Medieval Studies in a Time of White Supremacy." *In the Middle*, August 28. www.inthemedievalmiddle.com/.

Kinder, Marsha. 1991. *Playing with Power in Movies, Television, and Video Games from Muppet Babies to Teenage Mutant Ninja Turtles*. Berkeley: University of California Press.

King, Geoff, and Tanya Krzywinska. 2006. *Tomb Raiders and Space Invaders: Video-game Forms and Contexts*. London: I. B. Tauris.

Kocurek, Carly A. 2015. *Coin-Operated Americans: Rebooting Boyhood at the Video Game Arcade*. Minneapolis: University of Minnesota Press.

Kocurek, Carly A., and Jennifer deWinter. 2015. "Chell Game: Representation, Identification, and Racial Ambiguity in *Portal* and *Portal 2*." In *The Cake Is a Lie: Polyperspektivische Betrachtungen Des Computerspiels Am Beispiel von Portal*, edited by Thomas Hensel, Britta Neitzel, and Rolf Nohr, 31–48. Münster: LIT.

Krahulik, Mike. 2003. "Child's Play." *Penny Arcade*, November 25. www.penny-arcade.com/.

———. 2003. "Star Wars." *Penny Arcade*, November 24. www.penny-arcade.com/.

———. 2010. "Tragedy Is When I Cut My Finger." *Penny Arcade*, August 13. www.penny-arcade.com/.

———. 2011. "Dickwolves." *Penny Arcade*, January 29. www.penny-arcade.com/.

———. 2011. "Okay That's Enough." *Penny Arcade*, February 2. www.penny-arcade.com/.

Kubrick, Stanley. (1968) 2001. "*Playboy* Interview: Stanley Kubrick." By Eric Nordern. *Playboy*, September. Reprinted in *Stanley Kubrick: Interviews*, edited by Gene Phillips, 47–74. Jackson: University Press of Mississippi.

LadyMilla. 2010. "Creating a Custom Race with a Custom Body Mesh and Textures without the Tranquility Lane Glitch." Fallout 3 Nexus Mods (forum), November 5. https://forums.nexusmods.com/.

Lamarre, Thomas. 2009. *The Anime Machine: A Media Theory of Animation*. Minneapolis: University of Minnesota Press.

Lambeth, William. n.d. "Interview with William Lambeth." Pixologic. Accessed November 18, 2019. www.pixologic.com/.

Laurel, Brenda. 1991. *Computers as Theatre*. Reading, MA: Addison-Wesley Pub.

Lauteria, Evan. 2012. "Ga(y)mer Theory: Queer Modding as Resistance." *Reconstruction* 12 (2). Accessed November 19, 2019. https://www.academia.edu/.

Lavater, Johann Caspar. 1789. *Essays on Physiognomy: For the Promotion of the Knowledge and Love of Mankind*. Translated by Thomas Holcroft. London: Printed for G. G. J. and J. Robinson.

Lavigne, Carlen. 2015. "'She's a Soldier, Not a Model': Feminism, FemShep and the *Mass Effect 3* Vote." *Journal of Gaming and Virtual Worlds* 2 (3): 317–29. https://doi .org/10.1386/jgvw.7.3.317_1.

Lazarus, Margaret, and Renner Wunderlich. 1975. *Rape Culture*. Cambridge, MA: Cambridge Documentary Films.

Lesbian Gamers. n.d. "The Lesbian Uncanny Valley of Gaming—What Is the Gay Uncanny Valley?" Lesbian Gamers. Accessed June 2014. https://lesbiangamers .com/.

Leonard, David J. 2006. "Not a Hater, Just Keepin' It Real: The Importance of Race- and Gender-Based Game Studies." *Games and Culture* 1 (1): 83–88. https://doi-org/ 10.1177%2F1555412005281910.

———. 2008. "Young, Black (& Brown) and Don't Give a Fuck: Virtual Gangstas in the Era of State Violence." *Cultural Studies <-> Critical Methodologies* 9 (2): 248–72. https://doi.org/10.1177/1532708608325938.

Levitine, George. 1954. "The Influence of Lavater and Girodet's *Expression Des Sentiments de L'Ame*." *Art Bulletin* 36 (1): 33–44. https://doi.org/10.2307/3047527.

Loftus, Geoffrey R., and Elizabeth F. Loftus. 1983. *Mind at Play: The Psychology of Video Games*. 3rd ed. New York: Basic Books.

Lorde, Audre. 1981. "The Uses of Anger: Women Responding to Racism." Presented at the National Women's Studies Association Conference, Storrs, Connecticut, June.

———. 1982. *Zami: A New Spelling of My Name—a Biomythography*. Trumansburg, NY: Crossing Press.

———. 1984. "The Master's Tools Will Never Dismantle the Master's House." In *Sister Outsider: Essays and Speeches*. Crossing Press Feminist Series. Trumansburg, NY: Crossing Press.

Lothian, Alexis, and Amanda Phillips. 2013. "Can Digital Humanities Mean Transformative Critique?" *Journal of E-Media Studies* 3 (1). https://doi.org/10.1349/PS1.1938 -6060.A.425/.

Lynch, Ashley. 2015. "A Final Word on #notyourshield." *Medium*, February 24. https:// medium.com/.

MacCallum-Stewart, Esther. 2014. "'Take That, Bitches!' Refiguring Lara Croft in Feminist Game Narratives." *Game Studies* 14 (2). www.gamestudies.org/.

Magnet, Shoshana Amielle. 2011. *When Biometrics Fail: Gender, Race, and the Technology of Identity*. Durham, NC: Duke University Press.

Mahmood, Saba. 2011. *Politics of Piety: The Islamic Revival and the Feminist Subject*. Reissue edition. Princeton, NJ: Princeton University Press.

Malkowski, Jennifer, and TreaAndrea M. Russworm, eds. 2017. *Gaming Representation: Race, Gender, and Sexuality in Video Games*. Bloomington: Indiana University Press.

Manovich, Lev. 2002. *The Language of New Media*. Cambridge, MA: MIT Press.

Mantilla, Karla. 2015. *Gendertrolling: How Misogyny Went Viral*. Santa Barbara, CA: Praeger.

Marcotte, Amanda. 2012. "Online Misogyny: Can't Ignore It, Can't Not Ignore It." *Slate*, June 13. www.slate.com/.

Massanari, Adrienne L., and Shira Chess. 2018. "Attack of the 50-Foot Social Justice Warrior: The Discursive Construction of SJW Memes as the Monstrous Feminine." *Feminist Media Studies* 18 (4): 525–42. https://doi.org/10.1080/14680777.2018.1447333.

Mass Effect Wiki. s.v. "turian." n.d. http://masseffect.wikia.com/.

Maxwell, Richard, ed. 2016. *The Routledge Companion to Labor and Media*. New York: Routledge.

Maxwell, Richard, and Toby Miller. 2012. *Greening the Media*. New York: Oxford University Press.

McEwan, Melissa. 2008. "*Fat Princess* Greatest Hits." *Shakesville*, July 25. www.shakesville.com/.

———. 2008. "*Fat Princess* Update." *Shakesville*, July 23. www.shakesville.com/.

———. 2008. "I Write Letters." *Shakesville*, July 21. www.shakesville.com/.

———. 2009. "I Get Letters." *Shakesville*, August 10. www.shakesville.com/.

———. 2010. "Commenting Policy." *Shakesville*, January 1. www.shakesville.com/.

———. 2010. "Survivors Are So Sensitive." *Shakesville*, August 13. www.shakesville.com/.

———. 2011. "My Point, Here It Is." *Shakesville*, February 4. www.shakesville.com/.

———. 2011. "*Penny Arcade* Open Thread." *Shakesville*, February 6. www.shakesville.com/.

———. 2011. "*Penny Arcade* Open Thread II." *Shakesville*, February 7. www.shakesville.com/.

McGonigal, Jane. 2011. *Reality Is Broken: Why Games Make Us Better and How They Can Change the World*. Penguin Books.

McKernan, Brian. 2013. "The Morality of Play: Video Game Coverage in the *New York Times* from 1980 to 2010." *Games and Culture* 8 (5): 307–29. https://doi.org/10.1177/1555412013493133.

———. 2015. "The Meaning of a Game: Stereotypes, Video Game Commentary and Color-Blind Racism." *American Journal of Cultural Sociology* 3 (2): 224–53. https://doi.org/10.1057/ajcs.2015.3.

McPherson, Tara. 2003. *Reconstructing Dixie: Race, Gender, and Nostalgia in the Imagined South*. Durham, NC: Duke University Press.

———. 2012. "U.S. Operating Systems at Mid-century: The Intertwining of Race and UNIX." In *Race after the Internet*, edited by Lisa Nakamura and Peter Chow-White, 21–37. New York: Routledge.

MCV Staff. 2011. "VIDEO: Black Kennedy Gets Develop's Vote." MCV, February 22. www.mcvuk.com/.

Mikula, Maja. 2003. "Gender and Video Games: The Political Valency of Lara Croft." *Continuum: Journal of Media and Cultural Studies* 17 (1): 79–87.

Miller, D. A. 1990. "Anal Rope." *Representations* (32): 114–33. https://doi.org/10.2307/2928797.

Miller, Patrick B. 1998. "The Anatomy of Scientific Racism: Racialist Responses to Black Athletic Achievement." *Journal of Sport History* 25 (1): 119–51.

Mirzoeff, Nicholas. 2002. "The Subject of Visual Culture." In *The Visual Culture Reader*, edited by Nicholas Mirzoeff, 2nd ed., 3–23. New York: Routledge.

Moberly, Kevin. "Pre-emptive Strikes: Ludology, Narratology, and Deterrence in Computer Game Studies." In *The Game Culture Reader*, edited by Jason Thompson and Marc Ouellette, 162–74. Newcastle: Cambridge Scholars.

Mongrel. 2006. "Colour Separation." *Mongrel*, August 22. Accessed September 18, 2012. https://mongrel.org.uk/. Site discontinued.

Moore, Peter. 2013. "We Can Do Better." Electronic Arts, May 4. www.ea.com/.

Moriarty, Colin. 2012. "*Mass Effect 3*: Opinion Video." IGN Entertainment, March 12. www.ign.com/.

Mouffe, Chantal. 2013. *Agonistics: Thinking the World Politically*. London: Verso.

Mulvey, Laura. 1975. "Visual Pleasure and Narrative Cinema." *Screen* 16 (3): 6–18. https://doi.org/10.1093/screen/16.3.6.

———. (1981) 1988. "Afterthoughts on 'Visual Pleasure and Narrative Cinema' Inspired by *Duel in the Sun*." *Framework* 15–17 (Summer): 12–15. Reprinted in *Feminism and Film Theory*, edited by Constance Penley, 69–79. New York: Routledge.

Murray, Janet. 2005. "The Last Word on Ludology v Narratology in Game Studies." Presented at the DiGRA, Vancouver, Canada, June 17. Posted online June 28, 2013, at http://inventingthemedium.com/.

———. (1997) 2017. *Hamlet on the Holodeck: The Future of Narrative in Cyberspace*. Updated edition. Cambridge, MA: MIT Press.

Murray, Soraya. 2017. *On Video Games: The Visual Politics of Race, Gender and Space*. London: I. B. Tauris.

Muzyka, Ray. 2012. "To *Mass Effect 3* Players, from Dr. Ray Muzyka, Co-founder of BioWare." *BioWare Blog*, March 21. http://blog.bioware.com/.

Nagle, Angela. 2017. *Kill All Normies: Online Culture Wars from 4Chan and Tumblr to Trump and the Alt-Right*. Winchester, UK: Zero Books.

Nakamura, Lisa. 2002. *Cybertypes: Race, Ethnicity, and Identity on the Internet*. New York: Routledge. https://doi.org/10.4324/9780203953365.

———. 2012. "Queer Female of Color: The Highest Difficulty Setting There Is? Gaming Rhetoric as Gender Capital." *Ada: A Journal of Gender, New Media, and Technology*, no. 1. https://adanewmedia.org/.

———. 2013. "'It's a N****r in Here! Kill the N****r!': User-Generated Media Campaigns against Racism, Sexism, and Homophobia in Digital Games." In *Media Studies Futures*, edited by Kelly Gates, 6:1–15. The International Encyclopedia of Media Studies. Hoboken, NJ: Wiley-Blackwell.

National Coalition Against Censorship. n.d. "A Timeline of Video Game Controversies." https://ncac.org/.

NBC News. 2017. "How Gamers Are Facilitating the Rise of the Alt-Right." https://youtu.be/uN1P6UA7pvM/.

Nguyen, Josef. 2016. "Performing as Video Game Players in Let's Plays." *Transformative Works and Cultures* 22 (September). https://doi.org/10.3983/twc.2016.0698.

Nofz, Michael P., and Phil Vendy. 2002. "When Computers Say It with Feeling: Communication and Synthetic Emotions in Kubrick's *2001: A Space Odyssey*." *Journal of Communication Inquiry* 26 (1): 26–45. https://doi.org/10.1177/0196859902026001003.

North, Ryan. 2006. *Dinosaur Comics*, October 6. www.qwantz.com/.

O'Dell, Cary. 2009. "'Daisy Bell (Bicycle Built for Two)' Max Mathews, John L. Kelly, Jr., and Carol Lochbaum (1961)." National Recording Preservation Board. http://www.loc.gov.

Parke, Frederic I. 1972. "Computer Generated Animation of Faces." In *Proceedings of the ACM Annual Conference—Volume 1*, 451–57. ACM 1972. New York: ACM. https://doi.org/10.1145/800193.569955.

Parke, Frederic, and Keith Waters. 1996. *Computer Facial Animation*. Wellesley, MA: A. K Peters.

Patterson, Christopher B. 2015. "Role-Playing the Multiculturalist Umpire: Loyalty and War in BioWare's *Mass Effect* Series." *Games and Culture* 10 (3): 207–28. https://doi.org/10.1177/1555412014551050.

Paul, Christopher A. 2018. *The Toxic Meritocracy of Video Games: Why Gaming Culture Is the Worst*. Minneapolis: University of Minnesota Press.

Pearl, Sharrona. 2010. *About Faces: Physiognomy in Nineteenth-Century Britain*. Cambridge, MA: Harvard University Press.

Penley, Constance. 1992. "Feminism, Psychoanalysis, and the Study of Popular Culture." In *Cultural Studies*, edited by Lawrence Grossberg, Cary Nelson, and Paula Treichle, 479–500. New York: Routledge.

Pettit, Emma. 2018. "Why Did a Small Conference in an Obscure Field Invite Steve Bannon to Give the Keynote?" *Chronicle of Higher Education*, October 31. www.chronicle.com/.

Phillips, Amanda. 2020. "Negg(at)ing the Game Studies Subject." *Feminist Media Histories* 6 (1): 12–36.

Phillips, Amanda, and Bonnie Ruberg, eds. 2018. "Queerness and Video Games: New Perspectives on LGBTQ Issues, Sexuality, Games, and Play." *Game Studies* 18 (2). www.gamestudies.org/.

Phillips, Whitney. 2015. *This Is Why We Can't Have Nice Things: Mapping the Relationship between Online Trolling and Mainstream Culture*. Cambridge, MA: MIT Press.

Platt, Stephen M., and Norman I. Badler. 1981. "Animating Facial Expressions." In *Proceedings of the 8th Annual Conference on Computer Graphics and Interactive Techniques*, 245–52. SIGGRAPH 1981. New York: ACM. https://doi.org/10.1145/800224.806812.

Porpentine. 2013. *How to Speak Atlantean*. PC. http://slimedaughter.com/.

Pralier, Rodrigue, Herbert Lowis, Rafael Grassetti, and Rion Swanson. n.d. "*Mass Effect 3*." Interview by Pixologic, Accessed November 18, 2019. http://pixologic.com/.

"Pratfall of *Penny Arcade*—a Timeline, The." 2011. *Debacle Timeline*, January 31. http://debacle-blog.tumblr.com/.

problemmachine. 2012. "The Passion of the Croft." *Problem Machine*, June 30. https://problemmachine.wordpress.com/.

Provenzo, Eugene. 1991. *Video Kids: Making Sense of Nintendo.* Cambridge, MA: Harvard University Press.

Puar, Jasbir K. (2007) 2017. *Terrorist Assemblages: Homonationalism in Queer Times.* Tenth anniversary expanded edition. Next Wave: New Directions in Women's Studies. Durham, NC: Duke University Press.

Pulido, Laura. 2000. "Rethinking Environmental Racism: White Privilege and Urban Development in Southern California." *Annals of the Association of American Geographers* 90 (1): 12–40.

Quantic Dream. 2010. *Heavy Rain.* PlayStation 3. Sony Computer Entertainment.

———. 2012. "Kara." Sony Computer Entertainment. Posted by sceablog on YouTube, March 7. https://youtu.be/j-pF56-ZYkY/.

———. 2012. "The Making of 'Kara.'" Sony Computer Entertainment. Posted by sceablog on YouTube, March 21. https://youtu.be/mSnFN8Ja58s/.

———. 2013. *Beyond: Two Souls.* PlayStation 3. Sony Computer Entertainment.

Quinn, Zoë. 2017. *Crash Override: How Gamergate (Nearly) Destroyed My Life, and How We Can Win the Fight Against Online Hate.* New York: PublicAffairs.

Raab, Josh. 2017. "How Video Game Makers Create Hyper-realistic Worlds." *Time*, May 10. http://time.com/.

Raley, Rita. 2009. *Tactical Media.* Minneapolis: University of Minnesota Press.

———. 2014. "Digital Humanities for the Next Five Minutes." *Differences* 25 (1): 26–45. https://doi.org/10.1215/10407391-2419991.

Ramsay, Randolph. 2009. "Q&A: Hideki Kamiya on Bayonetta." *GameSpot*, April 9. www.gamespot.com/.

Reddy, Chandan. 2011. *Freedom with Violence: Race, Sexuality, and the US State.* Durham, NC: Duke University Press.

Reed, Alison, and Amanda Phillips. 2013. "Additive Race: Colorblind Discourses of Realism in Performance Capture Technologies." *Digital Creativity* 24 (2): 130–44. https://doi.org/10.1080/14626268.2013.808965.

Rehak, Bob. 2003. "Mapping the Bit Girl: Lara Croft and New Media Fandom." *Information, Communication, and Society* 6 (4): 477–96.

Rentschler, Carrie A. 2014. "Rape Culture and the Feminist Politics of Social Media." *Girlhood Studies* 7 (1): 65–82. https://doi.org/10.3167/ghs.2014.070106.

"Retake Gaming." n.d. Facebook. Accessed June 10, 2018. www.facebook.com.

Richard, Gabriela T. 2012. "Playing as a Woman as a Woman as if a Man." *Loading . . .* 1 (3): 70–93.

Ruberg, Bonnie. 2019. *Video Games Have Always Been Queer.* New York: New York University Press.

Ruberg, Bonnie, and Adrienne Shaw, eds. 2017. *Queer Game Studies.* Minneapolis: University of Minnesota Press.

Rubin, Gayle. (1992) 2011. "Of Catamites and Kings: Reflections on Butch, Gender, and Boundaries." Reprinted in *Deviations: A Gayle Rubin Reader*, edited by Gayle Rubin, 241–53. Durham, NC: Duke University Press.

Russworm, TreaAndrea M. 2018. "A Call to Action for Video Game Studies in an Age of Reanimated White Supremacy." *Velvet Light Trap* 81 (1): 73–36.

Ryan, Marie-Laure. 2003. *Narrative as Virtual Reality: Immersion and Interactivity in Literature and Electronic Media*. Baltimore, MD: Johns Hopkins University Press.

Sage. 2011. "The Many Faces of FemShep." Posted by SageFic on YouTube, May 19. https://youtu.be/woMcQvKVrzk.

San Francisco Examiner. 2013. "At San Francisco Convention, Gay Gamers Are Diversifying the Industry." August 5. www.sfexaminer.com/.

Salen Tekinbaş, Katie, and Eric Zimmerman. 2003. *Rules of Play: Game Design Fundamentals*. Cambridge, MA: MIT Press.

Salter, Anastasia, and Bridget Blodgett. 2012. "Hypermasculinity & Dickwolves: The Contentious Role of Women in the New Gaming Public." *Journal of Broadcasting & Electronic Media* 56 (3): 401–16. https://doi.org/10.1080/08838151.2012.705199.

———. 2017. *Toxic Geek Masculinity: Sexism, Trolling, and Identity Policing*. London: Palgrave Macmillan.

Sandoval, Chela. 1991. "U.S. Third World Feminism: The Theory and Method of Oppositional Consciousness in the Postmodern World." *Genders* 10 (March): 1–24. https://doi.org/10.5555/gen.1991.10.1.

SCE Santa Monica Studio. 2005. *God of War*. PlayStation 2. Sony Interactive Entertainment.

Schleiner, Anne-Marie. 2001. "Does Lara Croft Wear Fake Polygons? Gender and Gender Role Subversion in Computer Adventure Games." *Leonardo* 34 (3): 221–26.

Shaw, Adrienne. 2010. "What Is Video Game Culture? Cultural Studies and Game Studies." *Games and Culture* 5 (4): 403–24. https://doi.org/10.1177/1555412009360414.

———. 2011. "Do You Identify as a Gamer? Gender, Race, Sexuality, and Gamer Identity." *New Media & Society* 14 (1): 28–44. https://doi.org/10.1177/1461444811410394.

———. 2013. "On Not Becoming Gamers: Moving beyond the Constructed Audience." *Ada: A Journal of Gender, New Media, and Technology*, no. 2. https://adanewmedia.org.

———. 2013. "The Lost Queer Potential of *Fable*—Culture Digitally." *Culture Digitally*, October 16. http://culturedigitally.org/.

———. 2015. *Gaming at the Edge: Sexuality and Gender at the Margins of Gamer Culture*. Minneapolis: University of Minnesota Press.

———. 2018. "Are We There Yet? The Politics and Practice of Intersectional Feminist Game Studies." *NYMG Feminist Games Studies Journal*, no. 1. www.nymgamer.com/.

Sihvonen, Tanja. 2011. *Players Unleashed!: Modding the Sims and the Culture of Gaming*. Amsterdam: Amsterdam University Press.

Silverman, Kaja. 1984. "Dis-embodying the Female Voice." In *Re-vision: Essays in Feminist Film Criticism*, edited by Mary Ann Doane, Patricia Mellencamp, and Linda Williams, 131–49. Los Angeles: American Film Institute.

Smee, Andrew. 2012. "*Mass Effect 3* & Beyond." *IGN*, May 9. www.ign.com/.

Smethurst, Tobi. 2015. "Playing Dead in Video Games: Trauma in *Limbo*." *Journal of Popular Culture* 48 (5): 817–35.

Stang, Sarah. 2017. "Big Daddies and Broken Men: Father-Daughter Relationships in Video Games." *Loading . . .* 10 (16). http://journals.sfu.ca/.

Stanton, Courtney. 2010. "Here Is a Shirt: Dickwolves Survivors Guild." *Here Is a Thing*, October 19.

———. 2011. "Here Is a Thought: Why I'm Not Speaking at PAX East 2011." *Here Is a Thing*, January 24.

———. 2011. "Here Is a Thought: Fuck This Noise." *Here Is a Thing*, January 30.

———. 2011. "Here Is a Project: Troll! Data! Analysis!" *Here Is a Thing*, February 8.

Stemmler, Joan K. 1993. "The Physiognomical Portraits of Johann Caspar Lavater." *Art Bulletin* 75 (1): 151–68. https://doi.org/10.2307/3045936.

Stuart, Keith. 2015. "Photorealism—the Future of Video Game Visuals." *Guardian*, February 12. www.theguardian.com/.

Studlar, Gaylyn. (1988) 1993. *In the Realm of Pleasure: Von Sternberg, Dietrich, and the Masochistic Aesthetic*. Reprint, New York: Columbia University Press.

StunningAnimation. 2008. "Image Metrics: How-To Video." YouTube, June 30. https://youtu.be/SwAV2fXoy6E/.

Suits, Bernard. 2005. *The Grasshopper: Games, Life and Utopia*. Peterborough, ON: Broadview Press.

Tasker, Yvonne. 1993. *Spectacular Bodies: Gender, Genre, and the Action Cinema*. New York: Routledge.

Tassi, Paul. 2016. "Can We Forgive Hillary Clinton for Her Past War on Video Games?" *Forbes*, February 6. Accessed June 21, 2018. www.forbes.com/.

Taylor, Laurie N. 2003. "When Seams Fall Apart: Video Game Space and the Player." *Game Studies* 3 (2). www.gamestudies.org/.

———. 2006. "From Stompin' Mushrooms to Bustin' Heads: *Grand Theft Auto III* as Paradigm Shift." In *The Meaning and Culture of* Grand Theft Auto: *Critical Essays*, edited by Nate Garrelts. Jefferson, NC: McFarland.

Taylor, Nicholas, and Gerald Voorhees, eds. 2018. *Masculinities in Play*. London: Palgrave Macmillan.

tekanji. 2007. "FAQ: What Is the 'Male Gaze'?" *Finally, a Feminism 101 Blog*, August 26. https://finallyfeminism101.wordpress.com/.

Thompson, Jack. n.d. "Transcripts." JackThomson.org. Accessed November 18, 2019. www.jackthompson.org/.

Tomlinson, Barbara. 2010. *Feminism and Affect at the Scene of Argument: Beyond the Trope of the Angry Feminist*. Philadelphia: Temple University Press.

Totillo, Stephen. 2010. "Why Modern Video Game Armies Lack Female Troops." Kotaku, March 3. https://kotaku.com/.

Truth, Sojourner. 1851. "Ain't I a Woman." Speech. Akron, Ohio, May 29.

TV Tropes. s.v. "male gaze." n.d. https://tvtropes.org/.

Valve Corporation. 2007. *Portal*. PC. Valve Corporation.

———. 2011. *Portal 2*. PC. Valve Corporation.

———. n.d. ApertureScience.com. Accessed June 13, 2008. http://aperturescience
.com/.

Vist, Elise. 2015. "Actually, It's About Aca-Fandom in Games Studies." *First Person Scholar*, May. www.firstpersonscholar.com/.

Voorhees, Gerald. 2013. "Criticism and Control: Gameplay in the Space of Possibility." In *Ctrl-Alt-Play: Essays on Control in Video Gaming*, edited by Matthew Wysocki. Jefferson, NC: McFarland.

Vossen, Emma. 2018. "On the Cultural Inaccessibility of Gaming: Invading, Creating, and Reclaiming the Cultural Clubhouse." PhD diss., University of Waterloo.

Waern, Annika. 2011. "'I'm in Love with Someone That Doesn't Exist!' Bleed in the Context of a Computer Game." *Journal of Gaming and Virtual Worlds* 3 (3): 239–57. https://doi.org/10.1386/jgvw.3.3.239_1.

Ware, Vron. 2015. *Beyond the Pale: White Women, Racism, and History*. New York: Verson Books.

Wark, McKenzie. 2007. *Gamer Theory*. Cambridge, MA: Harvard University Press.

Washington, Harriet A. 2008. *Medical Apartheid: The Dark History of Medical Experimentation on Black Americans from Colonial Times to the Present*. New York: Anchor.

Watts, Derek. 2011. "*Mass Effect 3*: Creating Garrus." Interview by Ben Hanson. *Game Informer*, April 22. www.gameinformer.com/.

Wernimont, Jacqueline. 2018. *Numbered Lives: Life and Death in Quantum Media*. Cambridge, MA: MIT Press.

Whitehead, Jim, R. Michael Young, Mia Consalvo, Drew Davidson, Mirjam Eladhari, Ian Horswill, Robin Hunicke, Andy Nealen, Jichen Zhu, Alessandro Canossa, Casper Harteveld, Miguel Sicart, and Julian Togelius. 2017. "Letter to the FDG Community." Society for the Advancement of the Science of Digital Games.

———. 2017. "Second Letter to the FDG Community." Society for the Advancement of the Science of Digital Games. 2017.

Wiegman, Robyn. 2012. *Object Lessons*. Next Wave. Durham, NC: Duke University Press.

Williams, Lance. 1990. "Performance-Driven Facial Animation." In *Proceedings of the 17th Annual Conference on Computer Graphics and Interactive Techniques*, 235–42. SIGGRAPH 1990. New York: ACM. https://doi.org/10.1145/97879.97906.

Williams, Linda. 1991. "Film Bodies: Gender, Genre, and Excess." *Film Quarterly* 44 (4): 2–13. https://doi.org/10.2307/1212758.

Wysocki, Matthew, and Evan W. Lauteria, eds. 2015. *Rated M for Mature: Sex and Sexuality in Video Games*. London: Bloomsbury Academic.

Yee, Nicholas. n.d. The Daedalus Project: The Psychology of MMORPGs. Accessed November 18, 2019. www.nickyee.com/.

Yiannopolous, Milo. 2015. "Who Said It: Anita Sarkeesian or Infamous Game Hater Jack Thompson?" Breitbart, April 25. www.breitbart.com/.

Yoshimura Kenichiro. 2009. "Modeling Bayonetta." *PlatinumGames Official Blog,* April 24. www.platinumgames.com/.

Zekany, Eva. 2016. "'A Horrible Interspecies Awkwardness Thing': (Non)Human Desire in the *Mass Effect* Universe." *Bulletin of Science, Technology & Society* 36 (1): 67–77. https://doi.org/10.1177/0270467615624565.

Zimmerman, Eric. 2006. "Narrative, Interactivity, Play, and Games: Four Naughty Concepts in Need of Discipline." In *First Person: New Media as Story, Performance, and Game,* edited by Noah Wardrip-Fruin and Pat Harrigan, 154–64. Cambridge, MA: MIT Press.

———. 2012. "Jerked Around by the Magic Circle—Clearing the Air Ten Years Later." Gamasutra, February 7. www.gamasutra.com/.

———. 2014. "Manifesto for a Ludic Century." In *The Gameful World,* edited by Steffan Walz and Sebastian Deterding, 19–22. Cambridge, MA: MIT Press.

INDEX

ABOUT THE AUTHOR

Amanda Phillips is Assistant Professor of English and Film and Media Studies at Georgetown University.

Lightning Source UK Ltd.
Milton Keynes UK
UKHW012012190521
384011UK00001B/27